I0754137

PLANE ANALYTIC GEOMETRY

WITH INTRODUCTORY CHAPTERS ON THE

DIFFERENTIAL CALCULUS

BY

MAXIME BÔCHER

PROFESSOR OF MATHEMATICS IN HARVARD UNIVERSITY

NEW YORK

HENRY HOLT AND COMPANY

8

Norwood Press
J. S. Cushing Co. — Berwick & Smith Co.
Norwood, Mass., U.S.A.

PREFACE

Analytic Geometry, if properly taught, is a difficult subject, and concentration on a few of its important principles is necessary if mastery is the aim. I have cut out, or put in small type (or in late chapters which may be easily omitted) what seems to me less essential. With very few exceptions I have used methods so straightforward that they can serve as models for the student in his own work. Neither the notation of determinants nor (except in Chapters XII, XIII) that of the calculus has been used, since a difficult new subject is only obscured by a notation which has not already become thoroughly familiar, and I am old-fashioned enough to believe in handling one difficulty at a time.

It need hardly be said that in teaching it may not be advisable to follow everywhere the order of the book, which is meant to serve not merely as a text-book from day to day but as a permanent book of reference. At Harvard, where most of the work here given is taken up in the Freshman class, a considerable part of Chapter X and the whole of Chapter XI are postponed till the Sophomore year, thus making room for Chapters XII and XIII. This introduction of a little calculus, not hashed fine but put squarely as a new subject, during the last six weeks of the Freshman year has been most successful. The parts of the calculus thus introduced are easier than the parts of analytic geometry they replace, and, to the average student, more interesting; and the student who has got somewhat beyond his depth has a chance for a new start. This book, however, is equally adapted to a course which includes no calculus if Chapters XII and XIII are omitted.

I have said that *if properly taught* analytic geometry is difficult. It is only by degrading it to a course in graphics (curve plotting, numerical problems, etc.) that a course in analytic geometry can be made easy to the average student. I have followed the Harvard tradition, inaugurated nearly forty years ago by Professor Byerly (whose courses are represented in a general way by the older editions of the text-books of Briggs and Ashton) that the one aim should be to put the student into possession of an instrument which he can himself use in proving new geometrical theorems or solving new problems. The specific geometric knowledge gained is of far less importance. In particular, if time requires, he may omit everything on conic sections except what is contained in Chapter IX. I have been at pains to collect a large number of problems for such a student.

The Exercises at the end of each section are largely numerical, and almost invariably of a very simple character. The more substantial problems, which give the better student his main chance of learning something worth while, will be found at the ends of the chapters.

The sources of the best problems in analytic geometry are, to a surprisingly large extent, the English text-books of sixty years ago by Salmon, Puckle, and Todhunter. These are now public property, and I have used them freely. Besides similar sources for calculus problems in Chapter XIII, I have, with the author's permission, made free use of the first chapters of Professor Byerly's *Differential Calculus* and of his *Problems in Differential Calculus* (both published by Ginn and Co.). I have followed Professor Byerly, and the further developments of the same idea in Professor Osgood's *Calculus*, in introducing a variety of applications of the calculus at a very early stage. The excellent collection of problems on Curve Tracing in L. S. Hulburt's *Calculus*

(Longmans, Green, & Co.) has been useful to me, and will prove valuable to the teacher who wishes to emphasize this subject even more than I have done here.

The most fundamental formulæ are printed in black type. These, at least, should be committed to memory by all students.

CONTENTS

INTRODUCTION

POSITIVE AND NEGATIVE SEGMENTS. PROJECTIONS

CHAPTER I

COÖRDINATES OF POINTS

CHAPTER II

THE LOCUS OF AN EQUATION

CHAPTER III

THE STRAIGHT LINE

CHAPTER IV

THE CIRCLE

CHAPTER V

POLAR COÖRDINATES

CHAPTER VI

SOME GENERAL METHODS

CHAPTER VII

TRANSFORMATION OF COÖRDINATES

CHAPTER VIII

PROBLEMS IN THE DETERMINATION OF LOCI

CHAPTER IX

THE CONIC SECTIONS — THEIR SHAPES AND THEIR STANDARD EQUATIONS

CHAPTER X

PROPERTIES OF CONIC SECTIONS

CHAPTER XI

THE GENERAL EQUATION OF THE SECOND DEGREE

CHAPTER XII

ELEMENTS OF THE DIFFERENTIAL CALCULUS. DIFFERENTIATION OF ALGEBRAIC FUNCTIONS

CHAPTER XIII

SIMPLE APPLICATIONS OF THE DIFFERENTIAL CALCULUS

ANALYTIC GEOMETRY

INTRODUCTION

POSITIVE AND NEGATIVE SEGMENTS. PROJECTIONS

1. Positive and Negative Segments on a Line. Analytic geometry is a method of applying in a systematic manner algebra to geometry. It was invented by René Descartes, and published in his Géométrie in 1637. One of its essential elements is the free use it makes of negative as well as positive quantities. We will consider in this section a simple case in which the advantage of the use of negative quantities in geometry becomes apparent.

Let AB, BC, etc. be segments on a straight line. Each of these segments we suppose to have a definite direction, and we indicate this direction by the order in which the ends are written. Thus if we write AB, we understand that the segment is taken as running from A to B, while if we wish to take the same segment in the opposite direction, we should write it BA.

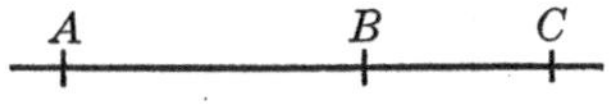

A B C

FIG. 1

By the side of the segments AB, BC, etc. we consider their numerical measures, which we will denote by $\overline{AB}$, $\overline{BC}$, etc. For this purpose we must first select a unit of length (centimeter, inch, etc.) and $\overline{AB}$ then indicates the number of times this unit is contained in AB. We will agree that segments measured in one direction (for instance to the right) shall have a positive numerical measure, those in the opposite direction, a negative measure. Thus if the points A, B, C lie as in Figure 1, $\overline{AB}$, $\overline{BC}$, $\overline{AC}$ are positive numbers, and

$\overline{BA}$, $\overline{CB}$, $\overline{CA}$ are negative numbers. In particular we note the general formula

(1) $$\overline{BA} = -\overline{AB}.$$

Now let A, B, C be *any* three points on a straight line. If these points lie as in Figure 1, the two numbers $\overline{AB}$ and $\overline{BC}$ are positive and their sum is evidently $\overline{AC}$:

(2) $$\overline{AB} + \overline{BC} = \overline{AC}.$$

Suppose, however, that these three points lie in the order indicated in Figure 2. Here $\overline{AB}$ is positive, $\overline{BC}$ negative. Consequently, when we add $\overline{BC}$ to $\overline{AB}$ we are really subtracting a positive quantity from $\overline{AB}$, and the result is the positive quantity $\overline{AC}$. Hence, in this case also, formula (2) is correct.

A C B

FIG. 2

The student should examine in a similar way all other possible figures and satisfy himself that in all cases formula (2) holds without change. We have thus proved the following result:

THEOREM 1. *If A, B, C are three points situated on a straight line in any order, formula* (2) *is always correct provided we regard segments measured in one direction as positive, those in the opposite direction as negative.*

This result shows clearly the advantage of the use of negative quantities in geometry, since in this way we get a single formula which applies to all cases.

The result just established may readily be extended to more than three points. If we have four points, A, B, C, D, on a straight line, then, no matter in what order these points may lie,

(3) $$\overline{AB} + \overline{BC} + \overline{CD} = \overline{AD}.$$

To prove this we notice that, by (2), the sum of the first two terms is $\overline{AC}$. If we now apply (2) with a change of letters to the three points A, C, D, we have

$$\overline{AC} + \overline{CD} = \overline{AD},$$

and this establishes our formula.

Similarly if we have five points on a line, A, B, C, D, E,

(4) $$\overline{AB} + \overline{BC} + \overline{CD} + \overline{DE} = \overline{AE},$$

a formula which is correct no matter in what order the five points lie. Etc.

Throughout this section we have carefully distinguished between the segment AB (a directed piece of a line) and the numerical measure, $\overline{AB}$, of this segment. In future, however, we shall use the notation AB indifferently for both purposes, since no real confusion is likely to result.

2. The Projection of a Broken Line. A very simple, and at the same time very useful, application of the principle of § 1 is the following. Let $PP_1P_2P_3P_4Q$ be a broken line, and let AB be an indefinite straight line. If from the points P, P_1, etc. we drop perpendiculars on AB meeting it in M, M_1, M_2, M_3, M_4, N, these points are called the *projections* of P, P_1, etc. on AB. The projections of the segments PP_1, P_1P_2, etc. on AB are the segments MM_1, M_1M_2, etc. If we select one direction on AB as the positive direction, and consider, as in § 1, the various segments on it as positive or negative as the case may be, we have by formulæ (3), (4), etc. of § 1,

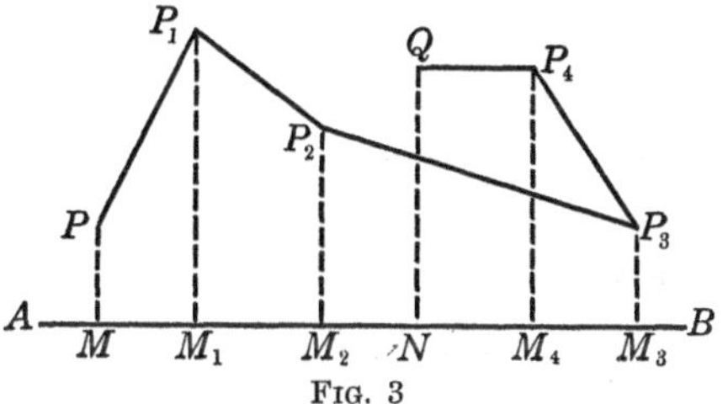

FIG. 3

$$MM_1 + M_1M_2 + M_2M_3 + M_3M_4 + M_4N = MN.$$

But MN is the projection of the segment PQ on AB. Consequently *the projection of a segment, PQ, on a line, AB, is equal to the algebraic sum of the projections of the segments PP_1, P_1P_2, etc. of any broken line connecting P and Q.*

CHAPTER I

COÖRDINATES OF POINTS

3. Rectangular Coördinates. A second essential element of analytic geometry is the systematic use of *coördinates*, that is, numbers which determine the position of a point in the plane. We consider in this section the simplest, and by far the most important, system of coördinates.*

We start from two indefinite straight lines at right angles to each other which we call the *coördinate axes*. Their point of intersection, O, is called the *origin*. One direction on each axis is taken as the positive direction, not only for the axes themselves but for all lines parallel to them. Let us denote these positive directions as OX and OY respectively. If these directions are so chosen that a rotation through a *positive* right angle carries the direction OX into the direction OY, we say that we have a right-handed system, otherwise a left-handed system. In this book we shall always suppose, unless the contrary is explicitly stated, that the coördinate systems are right-handed. If we take counterclockwise rotation as positive, we may therefore take the direction OX as extending to the right, OY as extending upward, and this is the position in which we shall most commonly draw our axes. The line OX is called the axis of x (or the axis of abscissas), OY is called the axis of y (or the axis of ordinates). It should be noticed that for a line parallel to neither axis no convention of sign has been made. Segments on such lines will usually be regarded as essentially positive, as is done in elementary plane geometry.

* These rectangular coördinates, together with the oblique system of § 9, are called Cartesian coördinates from the latinized form (Cartesius) of Descartes' name.

Now let P be any point in the plane, and consider the segment OP. The lengths of the projections of OP on the x and y axes respectively we call the x and y coördinates of P and denote them by x and y:

$$x = OM, \; y = ON.$$

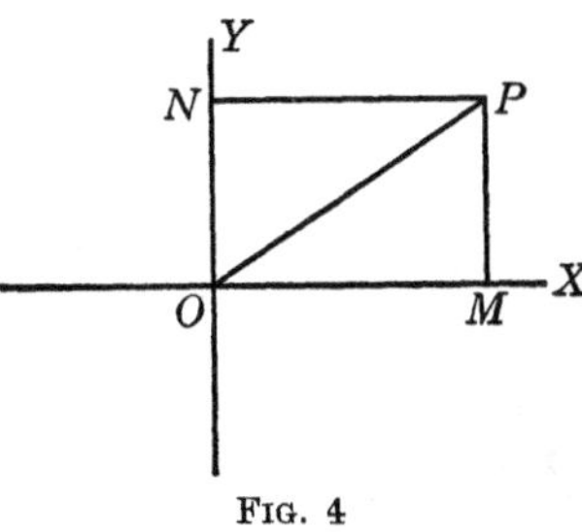

Fig. 4

In place of the terms: x coördinate and y coördinate, the words *abscissa* and *ordinate* are sometimes used. It should be noticed that x and y may be either positive or negative; for instance, in Figure 4 they are both positive, in Figure 5 x is negative, y is positive.

In practice one of the two projecting lines may be dispensed with, and, of course, the line OP need not be drawn. It is often convenient to draw only the perpendicular MP, and to write

$$x = OM, \; y = MP.$$

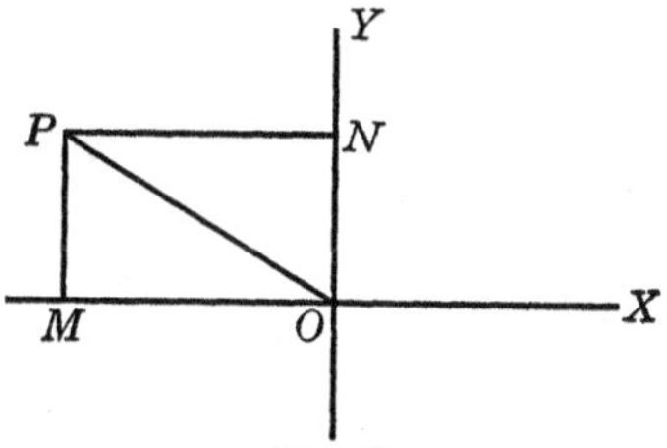

Fig. 5

When a point, P, is given we can, then, by simple measurement, determine the values of its coördinates. Conversely, it is a simple matter to construct, or *plot*, the point when its coördinates are given. For instance, to plot the point for which $x = 2$, $y = -3$, or as we say for brevity, the point $(2, -3)$, we start from the origin and lay off a distance OM two units long and running to the right along the axis of x. From M we lay off a segment three units long, parallel to the axis of y, and downward (since y is to be negative). The point, P, thus reached is the point $(2, -3)$. The labor of this process of plotting may be considerably lightened by using *squared paper*, that is, paper ruled into small squares of equal size by means of two sets of parallel lines. If one line of each set is taken as a coördinate axis, and the unit of length is taken either as one side of a square or as some multiple of this length, points may be plotted by counting off squares and estimating fractions.

If, in particular, a point lies on the axis of x, its y coördinate is zero; if it lies on the axis of y, its x coördinate is zero. The origin is the point (0, 0).

If we wish to deal with several points at once, it is often convenient to denote them as* P_1, P_2, P_3, or, perhaps as† P', P'', P'''. Their coördinates will then ordinarily be called $(x_1, y_1), (x_2, y_2), (x_3, y_3)$, or $(x', y'), (x'', y''), (x''', y''')$.

EXERCISES

Plot the points (2, 5), (7, 3), (9, − 2), (− 3, − 5), (− 5, 4), $(3\frac{1}{2}, 2\frac{2}{3})$, (5.2, − 9.3), $(\frac{1}{2}, -\frac{1}{2})$, (7, 4.25).

4. Projections of a Segment on the Axes. Let P_1, P_2 be any two points in the plane, and call their coördinates $(x_1, y_1), (x_2, y_2)$. If we project the segments of the broken line P_1OP_2 on the axis of x, we have, by § 2,

Proj. of P_1P_2
= Proj. of P_1O + Proj. of OP_2
= Proj. of OP_2 − Proj. of OP_1.

But these projections are, by definition, precisely x_2 and x_1. Hence

(1) Projection on x-axis of $P_1P_2 = x_2 - x_1$.

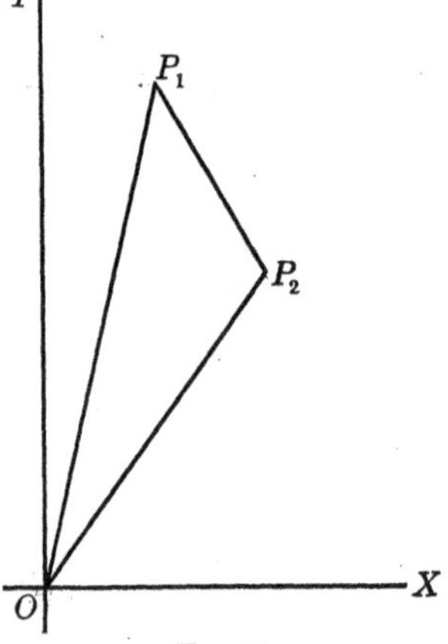

Fig. 6

Similarly, by projecting the broken line P_1OP_2 on the axis of y,

(2) Projection on y-axis of $P_1P_2 = y_2 - y_1$.

Formula (1) may also be used if, instead of the projection

* Read P-one, P-two, P-three.
† Read P-prime, P-second, P-third.

of P_1P_2 on the axis of x, we want its projection on some line parallel to this axis, since these two projections are evidently equal. Similarly formula (2) may be used to find the projection of P_1P_2 on any line parallel to the axis of y.

5. Distance Between Two Points. Given two points P_1, P_2 with coördinates (x_1, y_1) and (x_2, y_2). Through P_1 draw a line parallel to the x-axis and through P_2 a line parallel to the y-axis, and let Q be the point where these lines meet. Then P_1Q is the projection of P_1P_2 on the axis of x, and QP_2 its projection on the axis of y, and consequently, by § 4,

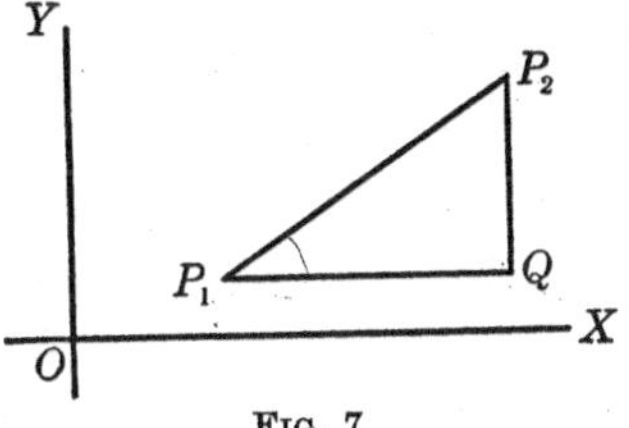

FIG. 7

$$(1) \qquad \begin{aligned} P_1Q &= x_2 - x_1, \\ QP_2 &= y_2 - y_1. \end{aligned}$$

But P_1Q and QP_2 are the two sides of a right triangle of which P_1P_2 is the hypotenuse. Hence

$$(2) \qquad \boldsymbol{P_1P_2 = \sqrt{(x_2 - x_1)^2 + (y_2 - y_1)^2}}.$$

This is the formula which we shall constantly have to use to find the distance between two given points. It should be noticed that the reasoning by which we have established this formula is entirely general and applies not merely to the figure we have drawn but to any position whatever of the points P_1P_2. It is true that the formulæ (1) give, in some cases, negative values for the sides of the triangle P_1QP_2, but since it is merely the squares of these sides we use, this will make no difference.

EXERCISES

1. Find the distances between the following pairs of points:

(2, 3) (9, 1); (3, −7) (−5, −2); (−2, −3) (−4, 0).

Express the results in decimals correct to three significant figures.

2. Find the lengths of the sides of the triangle whose vertices are the points (4, 6), (– 1, – 6), (2, – 2).

3. Find the distances from the origin to the vertices of the triangle of Exercise 2.

6. Slope of Line Through Two Points. Besides the length of the segment P_1P_2, we must also consider its direction. This direction may be determined by means of the angle between P_1P_2 and the axis of x. We will call this angle θ, and we will suppose it measured *from* the positive direction of the axis of x *to* the direction P_1P_2. That is, θ is the angle through which the direction OX must be turned in order to bring it parallel to, *and in the same direction as*, P_1P_2. Instead of this angle, θ, which may be called the *inclination* of P_1P_2, it is usually more convenient to use its tangent

$$\lambda = \tan \theta.$$

This quantity, λ, is called the *slope* of P_1P_2. From Figure 7 we see at once that

$$\lambda = \frac{QP_2}{P_1Q},$$

a formula which, from the definition of the tangent of an angle in the second, third, or fourth quadrant, is seen to be correct in all cases. If we replace P_1Q and QP_2 by their values from (1), § 5, we find

$$\lambda = \frac{y_2 - y_1}{x_2 - x_1}. \tag{1}$$

From this formula, or, if we prefer, from the definition of $\tan \theta$, it is evident that the slopes of P_1P_2 and of P_2P_1 are the same. We may, therefore, speak of λ as the slope of the indefinite straight line through P_1 and P_2 without regard to direction.

Finally we note that the slope of a straight line is positive or negative according as the smallest angle through which the axis of x can be revolved to make it parallel to this line is positive or negative.

EXERCISES

1. Find the slopes of the lines mentioned in Exercise 1, § 5.

2. Find the inclinations of the sides of the triangle of Exercise 2, § 5, and hence find the angles of this triangle.

7. The Mid-Point of a Segment. If P, with coördinates (x, y), is the middle point of the segment P_1P_2, the two segments P_1P and PP_2 are equal both in magnitude and in direction, and consequently their projections, M_1M and MM_2, on the axis of x are equal. By § 4 these projections have the values $x - x_1$ and $x_2 - x$ respectively. Hence

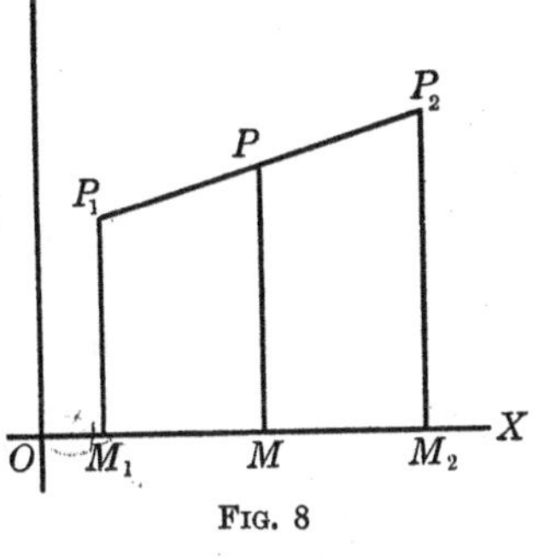

Fig. 8

$$x - x_1 = x_2 - x,$$

or, solving for x,

$$x = \frac{x_1 + x_2}{2}. \tag{1}$$

Similarly, by projecting P_1, P, P_2 on the axis of y, we find

$$y = \frac{y_1 + y_2}{2}. \tag{2}$$

By means of (1) and (2) we can find the coördinates of the point halfway between any two given points.

EXERCISES

1. Find the coördinates of the middle points of the three segments of Exercise 1, § 5.

2. Find the coördinates of the middle points of the sides of the triangle of Exercise 2, § 5.

3. A quadrilateral has its vertices at the points (2, 1),

(7, 1), (9, 3), (4, 3). Show that the middle points of its diagonals coincide.

8. Division of a Segment in Any Ratio. Let us try to find the coördinates of the point, P, which divides the segment P_1P_2 internally in the ratio $m_1 : m_2$,

$$\frac{P_1P}{PP_2} = \frac{m_1}{m_2}.$$

The projections of the segments P_1P and PP_2 are evidently in the same ratio as these segments. That is,

$$\frac{x - x_1}{x_2 - x} = \frac{m_1}{m_2}.$$

Solving this equation for x, we find

(1) $$x = \frac{m_2x_1 + m_1x_2}{m_2 + m_1}.$$

Similarly, by considering the projections on the axis of y, we find

(2) $$y = \frac{m_2y_1 + m_1y_2}{m_2 + m_1}.$$

These formulæ reduce, as they should, to the formulæ of the preceding section when $m_1 = m_2$.

In applying (1) and (2), we must remember that m_1 and m_2 need not be the exact lengths P_1P and PP_2, but may be any quantities proportional to these lengths. Furthermore we must always take m_1 proportional to P_1P, *i.e.* to that one of the two segments nearest P_1, and m_2 to that one nearest P_2.

We leave it for the student to show, by a method similar to that used above, that if P divides the segment P_1P_2 *externally* in the ratio $m_1 : m_2$, we have the formulæ*

(3) $$x = \frac{m_2x_1 - m_1x_2}{m_2 - m_1}, \qquad y = \frac{m_2y_1 - m_1y_2}{m_2 - m_1}.$$

*These formulæ may be included as a special case under (1) and (2) if we agree to regard external division as division in a negative ratio.

EXERCISES

1. Find the coördinates of the two points which divide the segment $(-2, 3)$, $(5, 7)$ internally in the ratio $2:3$, and indicate which of these points is nearer to the first end of the segment.

2. Find the coördinates of the two points of trisection of the segment of Exercise 1. Plot the segment and these two points.

3. A triangle has its vertices at the points $(3, 7)$, $(5, -3)$, $(1, 1)$. Find the coördinates of the points two thirds of the way from each vertex to the middle point of the opposite side, and show that these three points all coincide.

4. The sides of the triangle of Exercise 3 which meet at the point $(1, 1)$ are extended away from this point to three times their original length. Find the coördinates of the points thus reached, and find the coördinates of the point halfway between them. Show that this last point is the same as the one obtained by extending to three times its original length the line joining the vertex $(1, 1)$ with the middle point of the opposite side.

9. Oblique Coördinates. Occasionally it is convenient to use a system of coördinates in which the axes are not perpendicular to each other. We speak of the x-axis and the y-axis, and, as before, we call their point of intersection, O, the origin. We also make a convention, as above, concerning the sign of segments on the coördinate axes or parallel to them. The angle from the positive half of the axis of x to the positive half of the axis of y we call ω.*

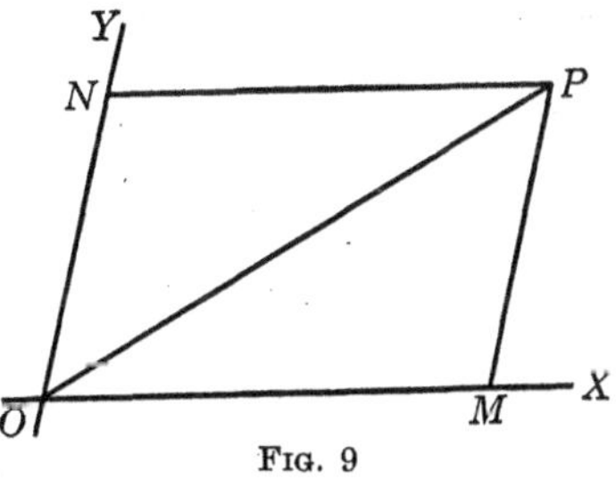

FIG. 9

* We do not assume that ω is necessarily positive. If $\omega = +90°$, we have ordinary rectangular coördinates. If $\omega = -90°$, we have the left-handed rectangular system mentioned in § 3.

In connection with oblique coördinates we use not ordinary (or orthogonal) projections made by perpendicular lines, but oblique projections made by lines parallel to the coördinate axes. Thus the oblique projections of the points A and B (see Figure 10) on the axis of x are the points M and R, and the projection of the segment AB is the segment MR. Similarly the projection of the segment AB on the axis of y is the segment NS. The theorem of § 2 is readily seen to hold for oblique as well as for orthogonal projections.

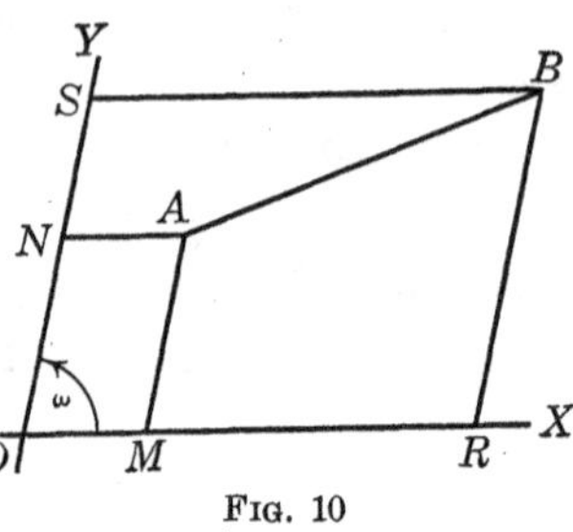

FIG. 10

We define the oblique coördinates of a point P as the projections of the segment OP on the axes of x and y:

$$OM = x, \; ON = y, \text{ (see Figure 9).}$$

It is now clear, as in § 4, that if P_1 and P_2 are any two points, the oblique projections of the segment P_1P_2 on the axes of x and y respectively (or on lines parallel to them) are $x_2 - x_1$ and $y_2 - y_1$.

The work and formulæ of §§ 7, 8 apply without change to oblique coördinates since no use was made in those sections of the fact that we were dealing with rectangular projections.

On the other hand, §§ 5, 6 depended essentially on the fact that the triangle P_1QP_2 was a right triangle. These sections, therefore, require modification.

In the triangle P_1QP_2, Figure 11, the angle Q is $180° - \omega$. Consequently, by the law of cosines,

$$\overline{P_1P_2}^2 = \overline{P_1Q}^2 + \overline{QP_2}^2 + 2\,\overline{P_1Q} \cdot \overline{QP_2} \cos \omega.$$

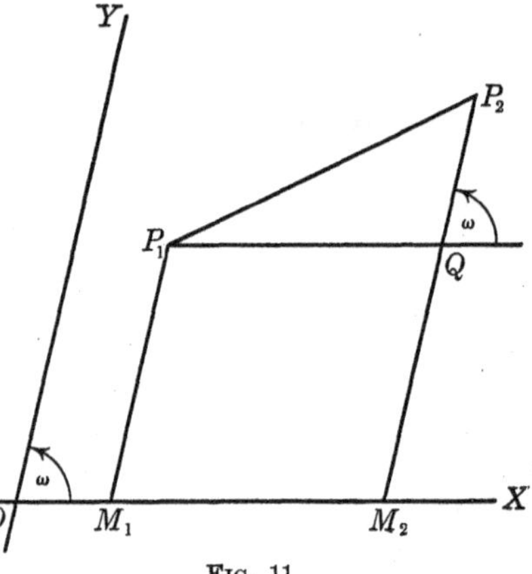

FIG. 11

Hence

(1) $$P_1P_2 = \sqrt{(x_2 - x_1)^2 + (y_2 - y_1)^2 + 2(x_2 - x_1)(y_2 - y_1) \cos \omega}.$$

The student may satisfy himself that this formula holds in all cases by drawing other figures.

The formula just obtained is more complicated than the formula for the distance between two points in rectangular coördinates, to which it reduces when $\omega = 90°$. It will be found that in problems in which it is necessary to express the length of a segment which is not parallel to one of the coördinate axes it is almost invariably preferable to use rectangular coördinates.

In the same way the slope of the line P_1P_2 is no longer given by formula (1), § 6 when the coördinate axes are oblique, and consequently, in problems involving the slopes of lines, rectangular coördinates are almost always preferable.

Even when we use oblique coördinates it will be desirable to define a quantity λ by means of the equation

$$\lambda = \frac{y_2 - y_1}{x_2 - x_1}. \tag{2}$$

We will call λ the *direction-ratio* of the line P_1P_2. It should be noticed that this direction-ratio will serve just as well to determine the direction of a line as its slope.

EXERCISES

1. Plot the triangle whose vertices are the points (2, 3), (5, 7), (4, − 2) in the three systems of coördinates in which $\omega = 60°, 90°, 120°$ respectively.

2. Find the lengths and the direction-ratios of the sides of the three triangles of Exercise 1.

3. Find the coördinates of the middle points of the sides of the triangles of Exercise 1.

4. If $\omega = 45°$, plot the lines through the point (2, 1) whose direction-ratios are $\frac{2}{3}$ and $-\frac{3}{2}$. Find the slopes of these lines.

10. Applications of Analytic Geometry to the Proofs of Geometric Theorems. Analytic geometry gives us, as we shall repeatedly find in subsequent chapters, a powerful method for treating all kinds of geometrical questions. We give a few elementary illustrations of this fact in this section.

Example 1. To prove that the diagonals of a rectangle are equal.

Let $ABCD$ be any rectangle. In order to apply the methods of analytic geometry, we must first of all select our coördinate axes. Any pair of perpendicular lines may be taken for this purpose, but the work will be simplified if we take two lines which have a simple connection with the figure. In the present case we will take as our axes two adjacent sides, AB and AD, of the rectangle. Let us call the length AB, a, the length AD, b. Then the coördinates of the four vertices of the rectangle are

A	$(0, 0)$
B	$(a, 0)$
C	(a, b)
D	$(0, b)$

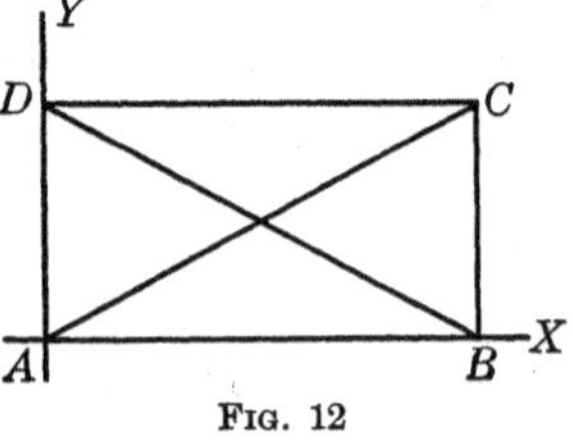

Fig. 12

Consequently, by formula (2), § 5, the lengths of the diagonals are

$$AC = \sqrt{(a-0)^2 + (b-0)^2} = \sqrt{a^2 + b^2},$$

$$BD = \sqrt{(a-0)^2 + (0-b)^2} = \sqrt{a^2 + b^2}.$$

Hence the diagonals are equal, as was to be proved.

Example 2. To prove that the diagonals of a parallelogram bisect each other.

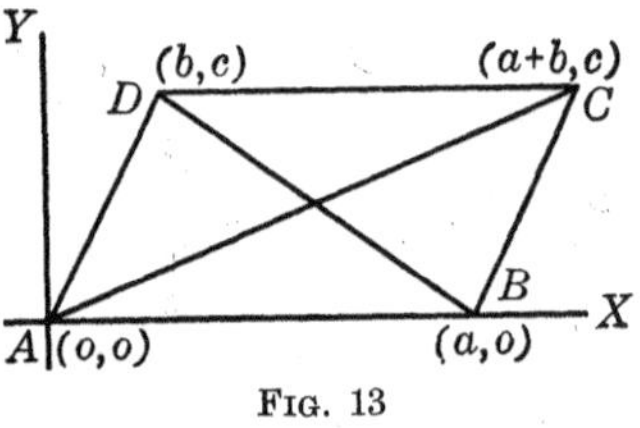

Fig. 13

Let $ABCD$ be the parallelogram. We take the point A as origin and the side AB as the axis of x. The coördinates of A and B are then $(0, 0)$ and $(a, 0)$ respectively. Let us call the coördinates of D (b, c) so that c is the altitude of the parallelogram and b the distance D lies to the right of A. Since C lies as far to the right of B as D lies to the right of A, the coördinates of C will be $(a + b, c)$.

The coördinates of the middle point of AC will then, by formulæ (1) and (2), §7, be

$$\left(\frac{a+b}{2}, \frac{c}{2}\right),$$

and the coördinates of the middle point of BD are exactly the same, as we see by using the same formulæ. Consequently, since this point is the middle point of both diagonals, it must be their point of intersection, and the theorem is proved.

It would have been a little simpler to have used oblique coördinates in this problem, taking two adjacent sides of the parallelogram as coördinate axes.

Example 3. To prove that the lines joining the vertices of a triangle to the middle points of the opposite sides meet in a point and trisect each other.

Let us take one side, AB, of the triangle as axis of x and the perpendicular dropped from the opposite vertex, C, as axis of y. The coördinates will be taken as indicated in the figure.* The middle points of the sides AB, BC, CA are then

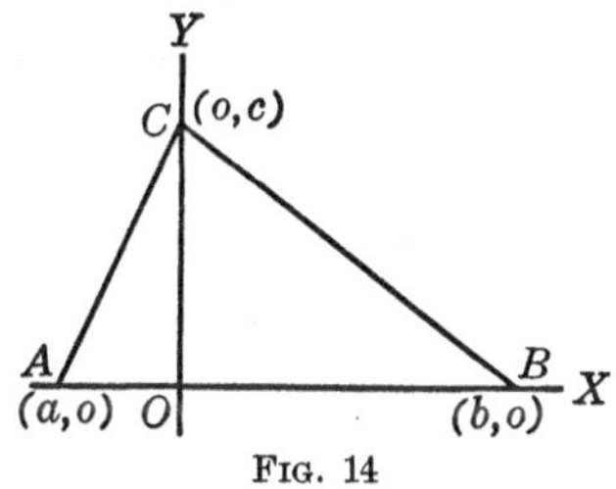

FIG. 14

$$\left(\frac{a+b}{2}, 0\right), \left(\frac{b}{2}, \frac{c}{2}\right), \left(\frac{a}{2}, \frac{c}{2}\right).$$

We now apply formula (1), § 8, and find as the x-coördinate of the point two thirds of the way from A to the middle point of BC

* If the triangle is shaped as in the figure, a is a negative quantity. It should be noticed that the demonstration about to be given applies equally well to the case where a is positive, *i.e.* where A or B is obtuse. It is one of the great advantages of analytic geometry that separate proofs need not be given for different forms of the figure.

$$x = \frac{1 \cdot a + 2 \cdot \frac{b}{2}}{1+2} = \frac{a+b}{3}.$$

Similarly, by (2), § 8, the y-coördinate of this point is

$$y = \frac{1 \cdot 0 + 2 \cdot \frac{c}{2}}{1+2} = \frac{c}{3}.$$

In the same way we find as the point two thirds of the way from B to the middle point of CA

$$x = \frac{1 \cdot b + 2 \cdot \frac{a}{2}}{1+2} = \frac{a+b}{3},$$

$$y = \frac{1 \cdot 0 + 2 \cdot \frac{c}{2}}{1+2} = \frac{c}{3}.$$

Finally, as the point two thirds of the way from C to the middle point of AB

$$x = \frac{1 \cdot 0 + 2 \cdot \frac{a+b}{2}}{1+2} = \frac{a+b}{3},$$

$$y = \frac{1 \cdot c + 2 \cdot 0}{1+2} = \frac{c}{3}.$$

Hence, since the point

$$\left(\frac{a+b}{3}, \frac{c}{3}\right)$$

is a point of trisection of each of the lines joining the vertices to the middle points of the opposite sides, these lines all pass through this point and trisect each other.

Here too the use of oblique coördinates would slightly simplify the algebraic work if we took two sides of the triangle as coördinate axes.

PROBLEMS TO CHAPTER I

1. Prove that the line joining the vertex of any right-angled triangle to the middle point of the hypotenuse is equal to half the hypotenuse.

2. Prove that the line joining the middle points of two sides of a triangle is equal to half the third side.

3. In any quadrilateral the lines joining the middle points of the opposite sides and the line joining the middle points of the diagonals meet in a point and bisect each other.

4. M is the middle point of the side AB of the parallelogram $ABCD$. Prove that the line MC and the diagonal BD trisect each other.

5. Prove that the lines which join the middle points of adjacent sides of any quadrilateral form a parallelogram.

[SUGGESTION. Show that the slopes (or the direction-ratios) of opposite sides are equal.]

6. Prove that the sum of the squares of the sides of any quadrilateral is equal to the sum of the squares of the diagonals plus four times the square of the distance between the middle points of the diagonals.

7. Prove that if the lines joining two vertices of a triangle to the middle points of the opposite sides are equal, the triangle is isosceles.

8. Prove that the distance between the middle points of the non-parallel sides of a trapezoid is equal to half the sum of the parallel sides.

9. If P is any point in the plane of a rectangle, prove that the sum of the squares of the distances from P to two opposite vertices of the rectangle is equal to the sum of the squares of the distances from P to the other two vertices.

10. Prove that if the diagonals of a parallelogram are equal, the figure is a rectangle.

The following problems illustrate the advantage in increased symmetry which may sometimes be secured by taking coördinate axes having no relation to the figure.

11. By the *barycenter* (or center of gravity) of three points is meant the point two thirds of the distance from any one of these points to the point halfway between the other two. See Example 3, § 10. Show that the barycenter of the points (x_1, y_1), (x_2, y_2), (x_3, y_3) is

$$(\tfrac{1}{3}(x_1 + x_2 + x_3), \tfrac{1}{3}(y_1 + y_2 + y_3)).$$

12. By the barycenter of four points is understood the point halfway between the middle points of two opposite sides of the quadrilateral formed by the points. See Problem 3 above. Show that the barycenter of the points (x_1, y_1), (x_2, y_2), (x_3, y_3), (x_4, y_4) is

$$(\tfrac{1}{4}(x_1 + x_2 + x_3 + x_4), \tfrac{1}{4}(y_1 + y_2 + y_3 + y_4)).$$

13. By means of the results of Problems 11 and 12, show that the barycenter of four points divides in the ratio 3 : 1 the line joining any one of them to the barycenter of the other three.

14. If Q_1 is the barycenter of $P_2P_3P_4$, Q_2 of $P_1P_3P_4$, Q_3 of $P_1P_2P_4$, and Q_4 of $P_1P_2P_3$, prove that $Q_1Q_2Q_3Q_4$ have the same barycenter as $P_1P_2P_3P_4$.

15. Given five points P_1, P_2, P_3, P_4, P_5 with coördinates (x_1, y_1), $\cdots$ (x_5, y_5). Show that the point four fifths of the way from P_1 to the barycenter of P_2, P_3, P_4, P_5 is $(\tfrac{1}{5}(x_1 + x_2 + x_3 + x_4 + x_5), \tfrac{1}{5}(y_1 + y_2 + y_3 + y_4 + y_5))$. This point, Q, is called the barycenter of the five points P_1, P_2, P_3, P_4, P_5. Prove that we reach the same point, Q, if we start from P_2, or any of the other points, instead of P_1.

16. Prove that the barycenter of five points lies three fifths of the distance from the point halfway between any two of them and the barycenter of the other three.

CHAPTER II

THE LOCUS OF AN EQUATION

11. First Illustrations. The position of the point (x, y) is completely determined if the values of both x and y are given. Suppose we give the value of only one coördinate, for instance

(1) $$x = c.$$

This equation tells us that the point is situated c units to the right* of the axis of y, but gives us no information as to how far it is from the axis of x. In fact, if the point (x, y) moves along the line parallel to the axis of y and lying c units to its right, the equation (1) will always be fulfilled, and hence we speak of this line as being the *locus* of the equation (1), and, conversely, we call (1) the *equation* of the line in question.

Similarly, the equation

(2) $$y = c$$

has as its locus the straight line parallel to the axis of x and lying c units above it.

Again, suppose we have the equation

(3) $$x = y.$$

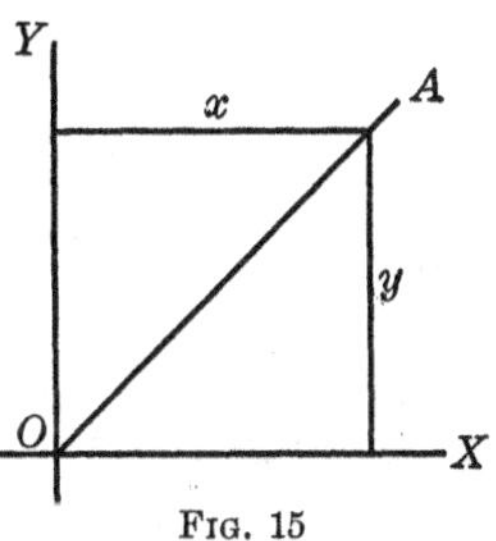

FIG. 15

A point (x, y) for which this equation is true lies just as far above the axis of x as it lies to the right of the axis of y; or else just as far below the axis of x as it lies to the left of the axis of y. In either case it lies on that bisector, OA, of the angle between the coördinate axes which passes through the first and third quadrants. Conversely, if the point (x, y) moves along this

* If c is a negative quantity, this, of course, means that the point is to the left of the axis of y.

line, its two coördinates will always be equal, and (3) is fulfilled. Consequently equation (3) has as its locus the indefinite straight line OA.

The other bisector of the angle between the coördinate axes, lying in the second and fourth quadrants, is seen in the same way to have as its equation

(4) $$x = -y.$$

As a last example we take the circle of radius c whose center is at the origin. Let P be the moving point (x, y) which describes this circle.* The distance from P to the origin is, by formula (2), § 5, $\sqrt{x^2+y^2}$. Hence, for any position of P on the circle,

$$\sqrt{x^2+y^2} = c,$$

and therefore

(5) $$x^2 + y^2 = c^2.$$

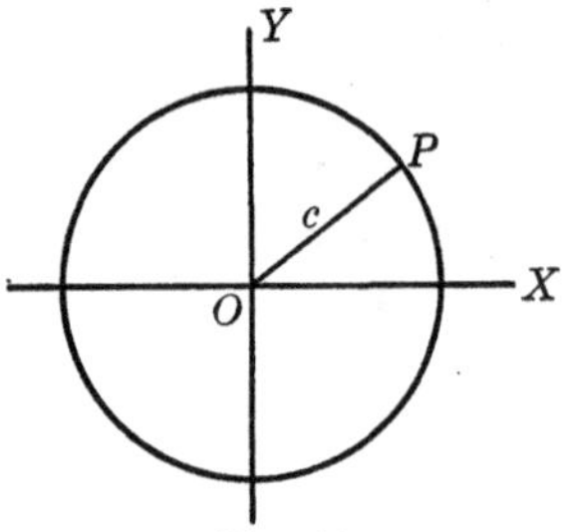

FIG. 16

Conversely, if (x, y) satisfies this equation, its distance from the origin is c, that is, it lies on the circle. Consequently, the circle has (5) as its equation.

These examples illustrate the general fact that if a curve (under which generic term we shall in future always include the straight line as a special case) is regarded as the locus of a moving point, P, the coördinates (x, y) of this point will satisfy a certain equation as long as P lies on the curve, but will not satisfy it if P moves off the curve. This equation is called the equation of the curve.

Conversely, if an equation in x, y is given, it determines a definite locus. This will become more evident in the next section.

It is essential to understand that the quantities x and y which occur in the equations of curves are *variables*.

* By a circle we understand throughout this book the curved line, not the part of the plane bounded by this line.

12. Curve Plotting. We will explain in this section how, when a numerical equation in x and y is given, its locus can be drawn or *plotted*.

Example 1. As a first illustration we take the equation

$$(1) \qquad y^2 = 4x.$$

This equation does not determine the value of either x or y, but if either one of these quantities is given, the other is determined by it. Thus

$$\begin{array}{ll} \text{if } x = 0, & y = 0, \\ \text{if } x = 1, & y = \pm 2, \\ \text{if } x = 2, & y = \pm 2\sqrt{2} = \pm 2.83, \\ \text{if } x = 3, & y = \pm 2\sqrt{3} = \pm 3.46, \\ \text{if } x = 4, & y = \pm 4, \\ \text{if } x = 5, & y = \pm 2\sqrt{5} = \pm 4.47, \\ \text{if } x = 6, & y = \pm 2\sqrt{6} = \pm 4.90, \\ \text{if } x = 7, & y = \pm 2\sqrt{7} = \pm 5.29, \\ \text{if } x = 8, & y = \pm 2\sqrt{8} = \pm 5.66, \\ \text{if } x = 9, & y = \pm 6. \end{array}$$

We have thus found nineteen points on the curve, and these are plotted in Figure 17. For negative values of x, y is imaginary. That is, the curve does not extend to the left of the axis of y. We can now draw the curve free-hand, or with the help of a French Curve, through the successive points we have found. The only place where we are thus left in any doubt as to the shape

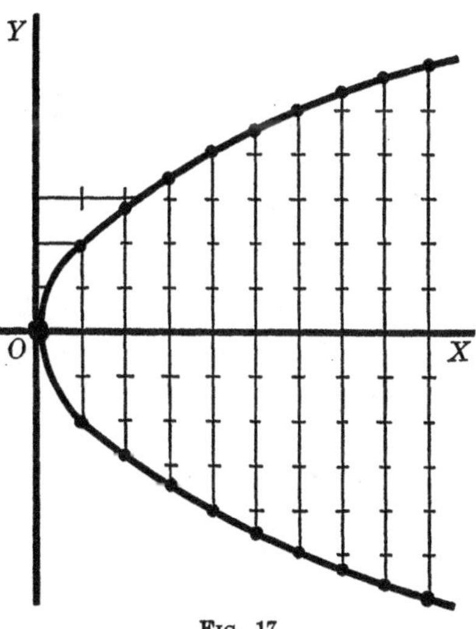

Fig. 17

of the curve is near the origin, where the gap between successive points is rather large. This gap we can fill in to any extent we please. For instance, we find

$$\text{if } x = 0.5, \quad y = \pm 2\sqrt{0.5} = \pm 1.41,$$
$$\text{if } x = 0.2, \quad y = \pm 2\sqrt{0.2} = \pm 0.89,$$
$$\text{if } x = 0.1, \quad y = \pm 2\sqrt{0.1} = \pm 0.63.$$

By means of these points, we can easily draw the curve as indicated in the figure. The curve does not, of course, stop when $x = 9$ but goes on indefinitely to the right both above and below the axis of x.

An alternative way of plotting this curve is to assign arbitrarily the values of y instead of those of x. Thus

$$\text{if } y = 0, \quad x = 0,$$
$$\text{if } y = 1, \quad x = 0.25,$$
$$\text{if } y = 2, \quad x = 1.00,$$
$$\text{if } y = 3, \quad x = 2.25,$$

etc. The points we get in this way are, in the main, wholly different from those we got before; but they serve equally well to determine the curve. One of these two methods will often be much simpler than the other, though in this case there is not much to choose between them.

Example 2. As a second illustration we take the equation

$$(2) \qquad (x^2 - 1)^2 y - x^3 = 0.$$

If, here, we assign a definite value to y, we shall have an equation of the fourth degree for determining x, and such equations cannot be solved by elementary algebra. If we assign the value of x, y is determined by an equation of the first degree. Instead of substituting in (2) in succession various values for x and solving each time the resulting equation for y, it will be better to solve the equation (2) once for all for y, thus:

$$(3) \qquad y = \frac{x^3}{(x^2 - 1)^2}.$$

We substitute here in succession various values for x. One of the first values we should naturally try would be $x = 1$. The second member of (3) then takes the form $\frac{1}{0}$, which is meaningless since it is impossible to divide by zero.* Consequently there is no point on this curve for which $x = 1$. It is, however, customary to write $\frac{1}{0} = \infty$, and there is no objection to this if we understand that it is merely a short way of expressing the fact that if we divide 1 not by 0 but by a very small quantity (say 0.01) we get a large result (100), and that if we then allow the denominator to become smaller and approach zero as a limit, the value of the fraction increases beyond all limits. With this understanding, we may make the following table:

$$
\begin{array}{ll}
\text{if } x = 0, & y = 0, \\
\text{if } x = \frac{1}{2}, & y = \frac{2}{9} = 0.22, \\
\text{if } x = \frac{3}{4}, & y = \frac{108}{49} = 2.20, \\
\text{if } x = 1, & y = \infty, \\
\text{if } x = \frac{3}{2}, & y = \frac{54}{25} = 2.16, \\
\text{if } x = 2, & y = \frac{8}{9} = 0.89, \\
\text{if } x = 3, & y = \frac{27}{64} = 0.42, \\
\text{if } x = 4, & y = \frac{64}{225} = 0.28, \\
\text{if } x = 5, & y = \frac{125}{576} = 0.22, \\
\text{if } x = 10, & y = \frac{1000}{9801} = 0.10.
\end{array}
$$

This table enables us to plot the curve so far as it lies to the right of the axis of y. It will be noticed that the curve rises indefinitely as x approaches the value $+1$ from either side. The line $x = +1$ is what is called an *asymptote* of the curve, that is a line which the curve approaches indefinitely but never reaches.

* When we perform the division indicated by the equation $\frac{a}{b} = c$, we have to determine the quantity c which when multiplied by b gives a. The division $\frac{1}{0}$ requires us to determine a quantity which when multiplied by 0 gives 1; an impossibility. On the other hand $\frac{0}{1} = 0$, since $0 \times 1 = 0$.

Beyond this point, $+1$, the curve falls off and comes nearer and nearer to the axis of x, approaching it as its limit but never reaching it. The axis of x is therefore another asymptote of the curve.

Finally, if we give to x a negative value, we find for the second member of (3) the value with its sign reversed that we should have got if we had taken for x the corresponding positive value. We thus obtain the part of the curve to the left of the axis of y, as drawn in Figure 18. There are in all three asymptotes, the lines $x = \pm 1$ and the axis of x.

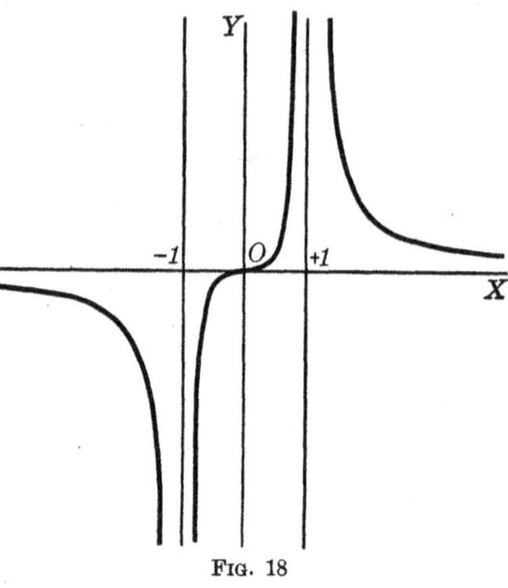

FIG. 18

We see also that the locus consists of three separate pieces, and we might be inclined to say that the locus of the equation is not one curve but three. It is, however, customary in such a case to say that we have a single curve consisting of three *branches*.

Example 3. Consider finally the equation

(4) $$x^2 + y^2 + 1 = 0.$$

If we try to plot the locus of this equation as we plotted the loci of (1) and (2), we find that whatever value we give to x, y is always imaginary. Consequently there are no points in the plane whose coördinates satisfy (4). This is a case of an equation which has no locus.

Other cases of this sort sometimes occur, and still other equations occasionally present themselves which have only one or more points as their loci. In the great majority of cases, however, we shall find that the equations that present themselves in practice have as their loci true curves (under which term, as has already been said, straight lines are included).

EXERCISES

Plot the following curves:

1. $2x = 3y$.	**3.** $x^2 = 4y$.	**5.** $xy = 1$.
2. $3x + 2y = 12$.	**4.** $y = x^3$.	**6.** $4x^2 + 9y^2 = 36$.

13. Test that a Point Lie on a Curve. As has been said, the equation of a curve is an equation connecting the coördinates (x, y) of a variable point which is of such a sort that when this point lies on the curve the equation is satisfied, while when it does not lie on the curve the equation is not satisfied. If, then, we wish to determine whether a given point does or does not lie on a given curve whose equation is known, we *substitute the coördinates of the given point in place of the variables (x, y) in the equation of the curve and see whether the equation is satisfied or not.*

For instance, to determine whether the point $(3\frac{1}{2}, 4)$ lies on the curve $y^2 = 4x$, we substitute in this equation the values $x = 3\frac{1}{2}$, $y = 4$. The first member becomes 16, the second 14. The equation is not satisfied; and the point does not lie on the curve.

If, in particular, we want to determine whether a given curve passes through the origin, we have merely to let $x = 0$ and $y = 0$ in the equation of the curve and see whether the resulting equation is true. If the equation of the curve is an algebraic equation cleared of fractions and cleared of radicals (and hence containing no fractional or negative exponents), all the terms which contain x or y reduce to zero when we let $x = y = 0$. Consequently the locus of such an equation passes through the origin when (and only when) the equation contains no constant term (*i.e.* no term independent of x and y). Thus the two curves (1) and (2) in § 12 are seen to pass through the origin, as we found was the case in plotting them. On the other hand, the curves of Exercises 2, 5, 6, § 12 do not pass through the origin since they have constant terms.

EXERCISES

1. Do the points $(-1, 2)$, $(0, 3)$ lie on the curves

$$y^2 + 4x = 0,\ x - y + 3 = 0,\ 9x^2 + 5y^2 = 45,\ y^3 = x^4?$$

2. Which of the curves of Exercise 1 pass through the origin?

14. Intercepts. If a curve meets the axis of x in a point A, the distance OA, which may be either positive or negative, is called the *intercept* of this curve on the axis of x. Similarly the distance OB from the origin to a point B where the curve meets the axis of y is called an intercept on the axis of y. A curve may have several intercepts on either or both axes, as is illustrated by the circle of radius c whose center is at the origin. This circle has two intercepts, $\pm c$, on each axis.

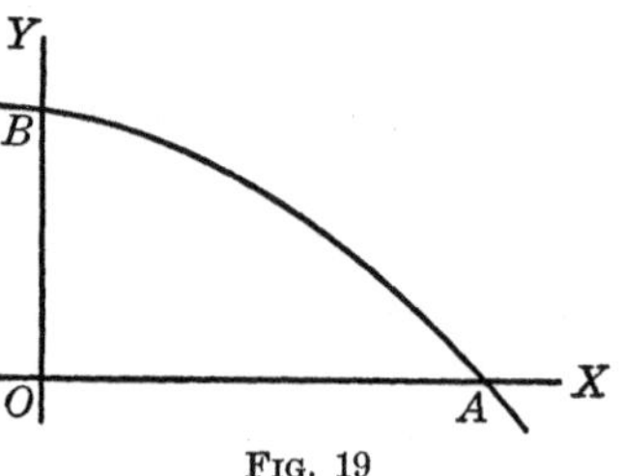

FIG. 19

If the equation of a curve is given, we can find the intercepts as follows:

The intercept OB on the axis of y is simply the y-coördinate of the point B. This point on the curve may be obtained, exactly as when we are plotting the curve, by letting $x = 0$ in the equation of the curve and solving the resulting equation for y. Similarly, OA is the x-coördinate of the point A and may be found by letting $y = 0$ in the equation of the curve and solving the resulting equation for x.

Suppose, for instance, we want the intercepts of the curve

$$3x - 5y - 15 = 0.$$

Letting $x = 0$, we find $y = -3$, so that the intercept on the axis of y is -3. Letting $y = 0$, we find as the intercept on the axis of x the value $+5$.

If the curve has two or more intercepts, they will all be given by this method.

EXERCISES

1. Find the intercepts of the curves of the Exercises in § 12.

2. Find the intercepts of the curves in Exercise 1, § 13.

15. Points of Intersection of Two Curves. It frequently happens that in a single problem we have to deal with two or more curves given by their equations. Suppose, for instance, we had the two curves

$$(1) \qquad y^2 = 4x,$$

$$(2) \qquad x^2 + y^2 = 16$$

(see equation (1), § 12 and equation (5), § 11). It must be clearly understood that the letters x and y do not mean the same thing in these two equations. In (1) they represent the coördinates of a moving point which traces out the first curve; in (2), the coördinates of a moving point which traces out the second curve. At the points of intersection of these two curves, and only there, can these two points coincide. Consequently, these points, and no other points in the plane, have coördinates which satisfy both (1) and (2). Thus we see that the coördinates of the points of intersection of (1) and (2) will be found if we solve (1) and (2) as simultaneous algebraic equations.

This can be done by substituting in (2) the value of y^2 from (1), which gives

$$x^2 + 4x = 16.$$

This quadratic equation has the two roots

$$x = 2[\pm\sqrt{5} - 1].$$

Substituting these values in (1), we find as the equation for determining y

$$y^2 = 8[\pm\sqrt{5} - 1].$$

The lower sign gives us a negative value for y^2, and hence an imaginary value for y. Consequently, this value is impossible, and we have only two points of intersection

$$(2[\sqrt{5} - 1],\ \pm 2\sqrt{2[\sqrt{5} - 1]});$$

or, reduced to decimals,

$$(2.47,\ \pm 3.14).$$

The accuracy of this result may readily be tested by means of Figure 17 if we remember that (2) is the circle of radius 4 described about the origin as center.

The method here illustrated is readily seen to be entirely general. *To find the points of intersection of two curves we need merely to solve their equations as simultaneous equations.*

EXERCISES

Find the coördinates of the points of intersection of the curves given in

1. Exercises 1 and 2, § 12.

2. Exercises 1 and 3, § 12.

3. Exercises 1 and 4, § 12.

4. Exercises 1 and 5, § 12.

5. Exercises 1 and 6, § 12.

6. Exercises 2 and 3, § 12.

7. Exercises 2 and 5, § 12.

8. Exercises 2 and 6, § 12.

9. Exercises 3 and 4, § 12.

10. Exercises 3 and 5, § 12.

11. Exercises 3 and 6, § 12.

12. Exercises 4 and 5, § 12.

13. Exercises 5 and 6, § 12.

16. Oblique Coördinates. Everything of importance said in this chapter holds for oblique coördinates as well as for rectangular. It should be noticed, however, that a particular equation has a different locus in oblique coördinates from what it had in rectangular coördinates. Thus, the equation (5), § 11, no longer represents a circle if the axes are oblique. What was said about equations (1), (2), (3), (4) of § 11 remains true here without change, except that the c units the line (2) lies above the axis of x must now be measured, not vertically, but in a direction parallel to the axis of y.

EXERCISES

1. Plot the curve

$$x^2 + y^2 = 25$$

first when the angle between the axes is 60°, secondly when it is 120°.

2. Plot the curve

$$y^2 = 4x$$

if the angle between the axes is 45°.

3. Plot the curve

$$xy = 1$$

if the angle between the axes is 30°. If this angle is 150°.

4. Find the intercepts of the curve of Exercise 1. Does it make any difference whether the angle between the axes is 60° or 120°?

5. Show that the answers to Exercise 1, § 13 and to Exercises 1–2, § 14 are the same for oblique as for rectangular coördinates.

PROBLEMS TO CHAPTER II

Plot the following curves, noting in each case the values of the intercepts, and also any asymptotes you can find:

1. $x^2 - y^2 = 9$.

2. $x^3 - 5x - y = 0$.

3. $x^2y - y + 1 = 0$.

4. $x^4 + y^4 = 1$.

5. $x^{10} + y^{10} = 1$.

6. $x^2 - 2xy + y^2 - 2x - 2y + 1 = 0$.

7. $x^3 - y^2 - x = 0$.

8. $y^2 = x^3$.

9. $x^3 - x^2 - y^2 = 0$.

10. $x^3 + x^2 - y^2 = 0$.

11. $y = 2^x$.

12. $y = \log x$.

13. $x^2y - 2y - 1 = 0$.

14. $xy - 2x + y = 3$.

15. $x^2 + 4y^2 = 0$. *Ans.* A single point.

16. $3x^2 + 5y^2 + 1 = 0$. *Ans.* No locus. Why?

CHAPTER III

THE STRAIGHT LINE

17. Equation in Terms of Point and Slope. We have seen in Chapter II how to plot a curve when its equation is given. The converse problem is: given a curve, to find its equation. We now consider the simplest case of this problem, namely that in which the given curve is a straight line.

In this section we suppose the slope, λ, of the line to be known and also a point (x_1, y_1) through which it passes.

Let (x, y) be the moving point which traces out the line For every position of this point the slope of the line connecting it with (x_1, y_1) is, by hypothesis, λ. Consequently, by formula (1), § 6,

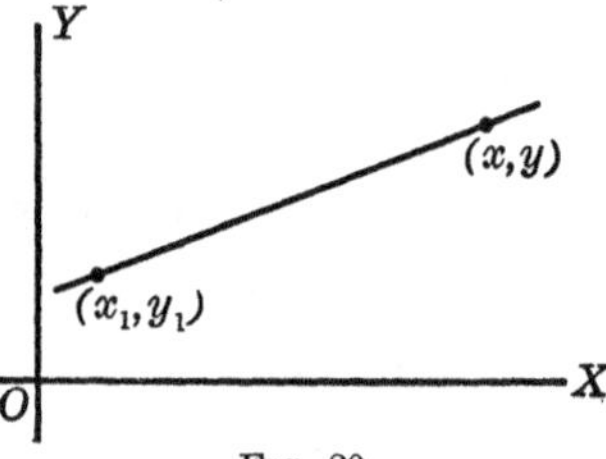

Fig. 20

(1) $$\lambda = \frac{y - y_1}{x - x_1}.$$

Moreover (1) is not only an equation which is true just as long as (x, y) remains on the given line, but it ceases to be true when (x, y) is not on the line. This, however, is what we mean when we say that (1) is the equation of the line.

By clearing (1) of fractions, we find

(2) $$y - y_1 = \lambda(x - x_1),$$

and this is the standard form of the equation of a line in terms of its slope and of the coördinates of a point through which it passes.

An important special case is obtained by letting $x_1 = 0$, $y_1 = b$. Equation (2) then becomes

(3) $$y = \lambda x + b,$$

and this is the standard form of the equation of a line in terms of its slope, λ, and its intercept, b, on the axis of y.

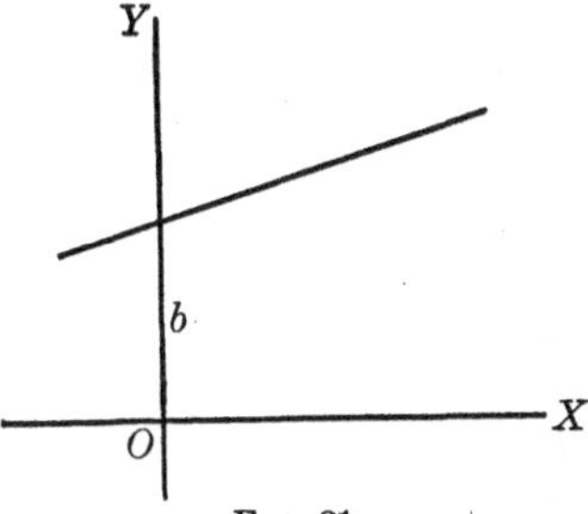

FIG. 21

The axis of y, and lines parallel to it, are the only lines whose equations cannot be written in the forms (2) and (3) of this section, their slopes being infinite. The equation of the line parallel to the axis of y and passing through the point (x_1, y_1) is obviously, see § 11, formula (1),

(4) $$x = x_1.$$

In the analogous case of the line through (x_1, y_1) parallel to the axis of x the equation is

(5) $$y = y_1.$$

EXERCISES

Find the equation of the line

1. Through the point (3, 5) and with the slope 2.

2. Through the point $(-1, -3)$ and making an angle of 45° with the axis of x.

3. Through the point $(-1, -3)$ and making an angle of 135° with the axis of x.

4. Whose intercept on the axis of y is 5 and slope -3.

5. Whose intercept on the axis of y is -3 and which makes an angle of 60° with the axis of x.

6. Whose intercept on the axis of x is 2 and slope $\frac{1}{2}$.

18. Line Through Two Points. A second way in which a line may be determined is by giving two points, (x_1, y_1) and (x_2, y_2), through which it is to pass. The slope is not here given but may be computed by formula (1), § 6. Putting this value into (2), § 17, we find as the desired equation of the line

$$y - y_1 = \frac{y_2 - y_1}{x_2 - x_1}(x - x_1). \tag{1}$$

This is the standard form of the equation of a line in terms of two points. Unless the line is parallel to the axis of y, its equation can always be written in this form.

An important special case is that in which the two intercepts, a and b, of the line on the axes of x and y are given. Here the points where the line cuts the coördinate axes are $(a, 0)$ $(0, b)$. We may, then, let $x_1 = a$, $y_1 = 0$, $x_2 = 0$, $y_2 = b$ in (1), and we find as the desired equation

$$y = \frac{b}{-a}(x - a),$$

or, after dividing by b and transposing,

$$\frac{x}{a} + \frac{y}{b} = 1, \tag{2}$$

and this is the standard form of the equation of a line in terms of its intercepts.

EXERCISES

Find the equation of the line

1. Through the points (3, 2) and (5, 7).
2. Through the points (2, − 5) and (− 3, 7).
3. With intercepts 5 and 2.
4. With intercepts 3 and − 1.
5. Through the points (3, 5) and (3, 7). *Ans.* $x = 3$.

[In problems like this no formula should be used since the line is obviously parallel to the axis of y.]

6. Through the points $(-2, -1)$ and $(-2, 4)$.

7. Through the points $(2, 3)$ and $(-2, 3)$.

19. The General Equation of the First Degree. We have now found various forms of equation for straight lines, namely (2), (3), (4), (5) in § 17 and (1), (2) in § 18. All of these forms, it will be noticed, are of the first degree in the variables (x, y). Consequently, since the equation of every line can be written in at least one of these forms, we see that *the equation of every straight line is of the first degree.* We will now prove the converse of this, namely, that *every equation of the first degree in (x, y) repesents a straight line.*

If in an equation in (x, y) we collect all the terms in x into a single term, also all the terms in y, and, finally, all the constant terms, the equation may be written

$$(1) \qquad Ax + By + C = 0.$$

This is what is called the *general* equation of the first degree in (x, y) since, by assigning to the constants A, B, C suitable values, (1) may be made to reduce to any particular equation of the first degree we please.

In order to prove that (1) always represents a straight line, we will try to throw it into a form more closely resembling one of our standard forms. For this purpose we select equation (3), § 17. To reduce (1) to this form, we first transpose everything except the y-term to the second member, and then divide by B:

$$y = -\frac{A}{B}x - \frac{C}{B}.$$

This is, however, precisely the equation we obtain if we use formula (3), § 17 to find the equation of the line for which

$$(2) \qquad \lambda = -\frac{A}{B}, \quad b = -\frac{C}{B}.$$

Thus we have not merely proved that (1) always represents a straight line but we have found exactly what line it represents, namely that one for which λ and b have the values given by (2).* To these formulæ (2) we may add the value of the intercept, a, on the axis of x, obtained by letting $y = 0$ in equation (1), as in § 14. We thus find

$$a = -\frac{C}{A}. \tag{3}$$

There is one case to which the above proof that (1) always represents a straight line does not apply, namely that in which the coefficient B in equation (1) is zero, since we could not here divide by B. In this case, (1) may be written

$$x = -\frac{C}{A}.$$

It therefore represents a line perpendicular to the axis of x.

EXERCISES

Find the intercepts and slopes of the lines represented by the following equations:

1. $2x + 3y + 5 = 0$.
2. $3x - 5y - 1 = 0$.
3. $2x + y = 0$.
4. $5x + 7 = 0$.
5. $2y - 3 = 0$.
6. $x - y + 3 = 0$.
7. Find the intercepts and slope of the line through the points (5, 7) and (4, -2).

20. Parallel and Perpendicular Lines. Angle Between Two Lines. Suppose we have two lines which make with the axis of x angles θ_1 and θ_2 respectively, these being the angles through

* The first of formulæ (2) is very important. Instead of learning it by heart, it is better to become so familiar with the method of deducing it that this method can be applied at a moment's notice to any special case which may arise. Thus, to find the slope of $3x + 2y - 7 = 0$. Transpose and divide by 2: $y = -\frac{3}{2}x + \frac{7}{2}$. Hence $\lambda = -\frac{3}{2}$.

which the axis of x must be revolved to take the directions of the lines in question.* The slopes of these lines are then

$$\lambda_1 = \tan\theta_1, \qquad \lambda_2 = \tan\theta_2.$$

It is clear that these lines will be parallel when, and only when,

(1) $$\lambda_2 = \lambda_1.$$

If the lines are perpendicular, we may suppose that

$$\theta_2 = \theta_1 + 90°.$$

Hence

$$\lambda_2 = \tan(\theta_1 + 90°) = -\operatorname{ctn}\theta_1 = -\frac{1}{\tan\theta_1} = -\frac{1}{\lambda_1}.$$

Conversely, if this formula is satisfied, the lines are evidently perpendicular.

Hence two lines are perpendicular when and only when

(2) $$\lambda_2 = -\frac{1}{\lambda_1}.$$

The formulæ (1) and (2) are the tests for parallelism and perpendicularity which are of constant use.

Without assuming that the lines are either parallel or perpendicular, let us determine the angle, ϕ, between them. We will suppose that ϕ is the angle *from* the first line *to* the second, that is, the angle through which the first line must be turned to take the direction of the second.* We may then suppose that

$$\phi = \theta_2 - \theta_1.$$

Consequently

$$\tan\phi = \tan(\theta_2 - \theta_1) = \frac{\tan\theta_2 - \tan\theta_1}{1 + \tan\theta_1 \tan\theta_2}.$$

We thus have the formula

(3) $$\tan\phi = \frac{\lambda_2 - \lambda_1}{1 + \lambda_1\lambda_2},$$

where ϕ is the angle from the line with slope λ_1 to the line with slope λ_2.

* An infinite number of choices for these angles are possible, the values differing by 180°. Since only the tangents of the angles are used, it makes no difference which values we take.

EXERCISES

Are the following pairs of lines parallel or are they perpendicular?

1. $3x - y + 2 = 0,\quad 6x - 2y - 1 = 0.$
2. $x + y + 1 = 0,\quad x - y - 1 = 0.$
3. $2x + 3y + 5 = 0,\ 2x + 3y - 1 = 0.$
4. $2x + 3y + 5 = 0,\ 3x - 2y + 1 = 0.$
5. $5x + 2y - 3 = 0,\ 2x + 5y + 3 = 0.$
6. $x + 2y = 0,\quad x - 2y = 0.$

7. Find the angle in degrees and fractions of a degree between the lines

(*a*) $2x - y = 0,\ x + y = 0.$

(*b*) $x + 2y + 3 = 0,\ 2x + y - 4 = 0.$

Check your result in each case by drawing a careful figure and measuring the angle.

8. Prove that the two lines

$$A_1x + B_1y + C_1 = 0,$$
$$A_2x + B_2y + C_2 = 0$$

are parallel when, and only when,

$$A_1B_2 - A_2B_1 = 0.$$

9. Prove that the two lines of Exercise 8 are perpendicular to each other when and only when,

$$A_1A_2 + B_1B_2 = 0.$$

10. Prove that, if ϕ is the angle from the first line of Exercise 8 to the second,

$$\tan\phi = \frac{A_1B_2 - A_2B_1}{A_1A_2 + B_1B_2}.$$

21. Line Through Given Point Parallel or Perpendicular to Given Line. The formulæ we have obtained enable us to solve at once the problem here suggested.

Suppose, for instance, we wish to find the equation of the line through the point (2, 3) parallel to the line

$$(1) \qquad 7x - y + 8 = 0.$$

The slope of this line is 7. Consequently we have to find the line with slope 7 through the point (2, 3), and this, by (2), § 17, is

$$y - 3 = 7(x - 2),$$

or

$$7x - y - 11 = 0.$$

If, on the other hand, we wanted the line through (2, 3) perpendicular to (1), we should say that, since the slope of (1) is 7, the slope of the desired line, by (2), § 20, is $-\frac{1}{7}$. Hence the line is

$$y - 3 = -\tfrac{1}{7}(x - 2),$$

or

$$x + 7y - 23 = 0.$$

This method is always available except when the given line is parallel to one of the coördinate axes, in which case the other line is also parallel to one or the other of the coördinate axes, and the problem is so simple that it should be solved by inspection without reference to any formula.

EXERCISES

1. Find the equations of the lines through the point (5, − 3) parallel and perpendicular to the line

$$3x + y - 5 = 0.$$

2. Find the equations of the lines through the origin parallel and perpendicular to the line

$$2x - y + 3 = 0.$$

3. Find the equations of the altitudes of the triangle whose vertices are at the points (0, 0), (3, 0), (2, 2).

4. Prove that the equations of the lines through the point (x_1, y_1) parallel and perpendicular to the line

$$Ax + By + C = 0$$

are respectively

$$Ax + By = Ax_1 + By_1,$$
$$Bx - Ay = Bx_1 - Ay_1.$$

22. Distance from a Point to a Line. Let us find the distance from the point P_1, with coördinates (x_1, y_1), to the line

(1) $$Ax + By + C = 0.$$

For this purpose we drop a perpendicular from P_1 on (1), and call its foot (x_2, y_2), or P_2. Since the slope of (1) is $-\frac{A}{B}$, the slope of P_1P_2 is $\frac{B}{A}$. That is,

$$\frac{y_2 - y_1}{x_2 - x_1} = \frac{B}{A},$$

or

$$\frac{x_2 - x_1}{A} = \frac{y_2 - y_1}{B}.$$

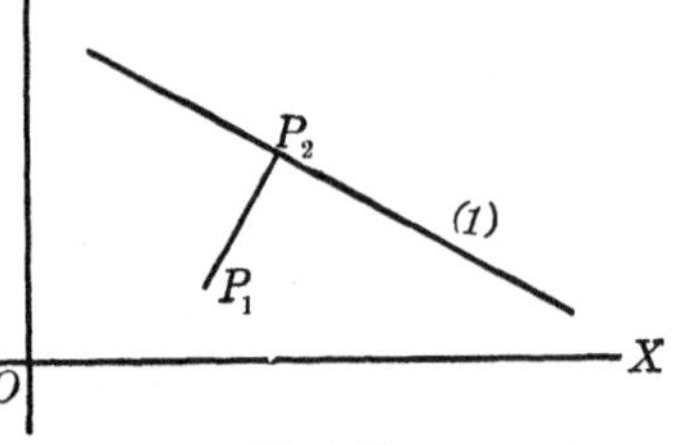

FIG. 22

Call the value of these two equal fractions h. Then

(2) $$x_2 - x_1 = Ah,$$
(3) $$y_2 - y_1 = Bh.$$

Hence, letting $\delta = P_1P_2$ be the distance desired,

$$\delta^2 = (x_2 - x_1)^2 + (y_2 - y_1)^2 = (A^2 + B^2)h^2.$$

It remains, then, merely to find for h an expression which does not involve the unknown quantities (x_2, y_2). For this purpose, multiply (2) by A, (3) by B and add:

$$Ax_2 + By_2 - Ax_1 - By_1 = (A^2 + B^2)h.$$

Since (x_2, y_2) lies on (1), we have

$$Ax_2 + By_2 = -C,$$

which, substituted in the preceding equation, gives

$$h = -\frac{Ax_1 + By_1 + C}{A^2 + B^2}.$$

Using this value for h in the expression for δ^2, we find as the final formula for the distance from a point to a line

$$\delta = \pm\frac{Ax_1 + By_1 + C}{\sqrt{A^2 + B^2}}. \tag{4}$$

For most purposes it is desirable to regard δ as essentially positive, the line P_1P_2 not being, in general, parallel to either coördinate axis. If this is the understanding, we must choose the sign in (4) so as to make the value of δ positive.

We have established formula (4) on the assumption that neither A nor B is zero, since in the course of our work we divided by both of these quantities. The reader may readily verify, however, that formulæ (2) and (3) hold even if one of the quantities A or B is zero. It follows that formula (4) is valid in all cases. In practice, however, we should never use this formula to find the distance from a point to a line parallel to one of the coördinate axes since, in this case, the distance in question may be read off at once from the figure.

While, as has just been said, it is usually desirable to regard the distance from a point to a line as being essentially positive, there are some cases in which it is convenient to distinguish, here too, between positive and negative distances. This may be done in various ways.

Suppose, first, that the line is not parallel to the axis of x. It then divides the plane into a right-hand half and a left-hand half. Let us agree that if the point lies to the right of the line, the distance shall be called positive, if to the left, negative. The question then is: how must the sign in formula (4) be determined?

Through (x_1, y_1) draw a line parallel to the axis of x and call the point where it meets the line (1) (x_2, y_1). Then

$$Ax_2 + By_1 + C = 0.$$

Consequently

$$Ax_1 + By_1 + C = (Ax_1 + By_1 + C) - (Ax_2 + By_1 + C) = A(x_1 - x_2).$$

This shows that if (x_1, y_1) lies to the right of (1), the numerator in (4) has the same sign as A, otherwise the opposite sign. Hence, *if we agree that the distance between a point and a line shall be positive when the point lies to the right of the line, negative when it lies to the left, the doubtful sign in* (4) *must be taken as positive when A is positive, negative when A is negative.*

It must be remembered that what has just been said does not apply to lines parallel to the axis of x, that is, to lines for which $A = 0$. For such lines we should naturally agree that the distance is positive if the point lies above the line, negative if it lies below. If we do this, however, a very slight change in the position of the line may suddenly change the distance of a point from it from a large positive to a large negative value. This makes the above convention (or any other one which could be made) not very satisfactory.

What is of real importance here is that the numerator in (4) is positive for all points (x_1, y_1) on one side of the line (1), negative for all points on the other side.

EXERCISES

1. Find the distance from the point (3, 2) to the line $4x - y + 2 = 0$.

2. Find the distance from the point $(-1, 3)$ to the line $4x - y = 0$.

3. How far is the origin from the line $x + y - 3 = 0$?

4. Find the lengths of the three altitudes of the triangle whose vertices are $(1, 2)$, $(-1, 2)$, $(-2, -3)$.

5. How far is the point (3, 1) from the line whose intercepts are $a = 3$, $b = 1$?

23. The Area of a Triangle. Let us find the area of the triangle whose vertices are (x_1, y_1), (x_2, y_2), (x_3, y_3), or, for brevity, P_1, P_2, P_3. The equation of P_1P_2 is given by (1), § 18, which, when cleared of fractions, becomes

(1) $$(y_1 - y_2)x + (x_2 - x_1)y + x_1y_2 - x_2y_1 = 0.$$

The distance, P_3Q, from P_3 to this line is, by (4), § 22,

(2) $$\frac{(y_1 - y_2)x_3 + (x_2 - x_1)y_3 + x_1y_2 - x_2y_1}{\pm\sqrt{(y_1 - y_2)^2 + (x_2 - x_1)^2}}.$$

But the area, Δ, of the triangle is $\frac{1}{2} P_1P_2 \cdot P_3Q$, which, when we use for P_1P_2 its value (2), § 5, reduces to

(3) $\Delta = \pm \frac{1}{2} [(y_1 - y_2)x_3 + (y_2 - y_3)x_1 + (y_3 - y_1)x_2].$

For most purposes we regard areas as essentially positive. The sign in (3) is then to be so determined as to make Δ positive.

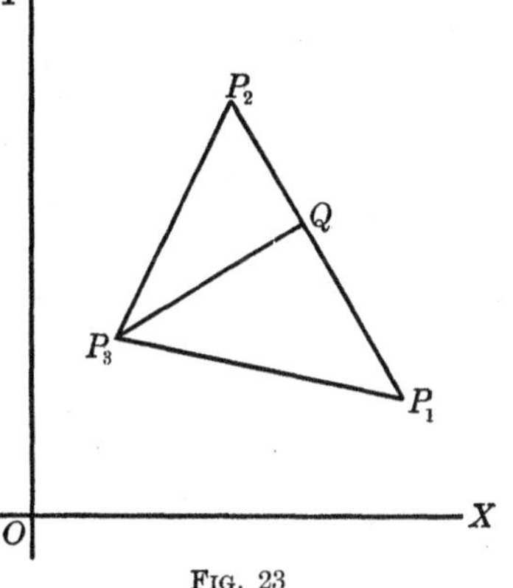

FIG. 23

Sometimes, however, it is desirable to distinguish between positive and negative areas. For this purpose, note the sense in which the perimeter of the triangle is described as we go from P_1 to P_2, from there to P_3 and then back to P_1. If this sense of description is in the positive direction of rotation (counter-clockwise), that is, if as we go around the triangle in this way we leave the interior of the triangle to the left, we regard the area of $P_1P_2P_3$ as positive, in the opposite case, as negative.

With this definition, it may be shown that formula (3) will be correct if the double sign is omitted, that is, if the plus sign is used.

To prove this, let us first assume that the line P_1P_2 is not parallel to the axis of x, and that, as in Figure 23, $y_2 > y_1$. If, as in the figure, P_3 lies to the left of the line P_1P_2, the plus sign must be used in the denominator of (2) in order to make the value of (2) positive, since the coefficient of x in (1) is negative and P_3 lies to the left of the line (1); see the closing paragraphs of § 22. Consequently, if we use the plus sign in (3), Δ will be positive; and this is as it should be since, as we see from the figure, the area $P_1P_2P_3$ is positive in this case. On the other hand, if, P_1, P_2 being situated as before, P_3 lies to the right of P_1P_2, the plus sign in (2) makes the value of (2) negative, as we see from § 22. Consequently, the plus sign in (3) will make Δ negative, and this is again as it should be. Finally if P_1P_2 are reversed in position, so that $y_1 > y_2$, the coefficient of x in (1) is positive. Hence, if we take the positive sign in (3), Δ is positive if P_3 lies to the right of P_1P_2, negative if it lies to the left. This, again, is seen by a figure to be in accordance with the definition of positive and negative areas given above.

We leave it for the reader to show that the plus sign in (3) gives the proper sign for Δ in the cases in which the line P_1P_2 is parallel to the axis of x.

EXERCISES

Find the areas of the triangles whose vertices are

1. $(3, 1)$, $(2, 4)$, $(0, 0)$.
2. $(-5, 1)$, $(-1, 3)$, $(1, -2)$.
3. $(1.5, 2.3)$, $(2, 3.5)$, $(3, -1)$.
4. Find the area of the triangle whose sides are the lines

$$3x + 5y - 2 = 0, \quad 2x - y + 3 = 0, \quad x - y - 1 = 0.$$

5. Find the area of the quadrilateral whose vertices are

$$(2, 3), (4, 5), (7, 6), (6, -3).$$

[SUGGESTION. Divide the quadrilateral into triangles.]

24. Two Equations of the First Degree with the Same Locus. If one equation of the first degree can be obtained from another by multiplication by a constant, the two equations obviously represent the same line, since if the coördinates of a point satisfy one equation, they also satisfy the other. We wish, in the present section, to prove the converse of this, namely:

If two equations of the first degree,

$$A_1x + B_1y + C_1 = 0, \tag{1}$$

$$A_2x + B_2y + C_2 = 0, \tag{2}$$

represent the same line, either one can be obtained from the other by multiplication by a constant.

Suppose, first, that neither B_1 nor B_2 is zero. Then (1) and (2) can be written in the forms

$$y = -\frac{A_1}{B_1}x - \frac{C_1}{B_1}, \tag{1'}$$

$$y = -\frac{A_2}{B_2}x - \frac{C_2}{B_2}. \tag{2'}$$

Since, by hypothesis, these two equations represent the same line, the slope of this line may be computed either from (1′) or from (2′). Hence

$$\frac{A_1}{B_1} = \frac{A_2}{B_2}. \tag{3}$$

In the same way, by computing the intercept on the axis of y, first from (1′) and then from (2′), we find

$$\frac{C_1}{B_1}=\frac{C_2}{B_2}. \tag{4}$$

Now multiply (1) by $\frac{B_2}{B_1}$. This gives

$$B_2\frac{A_1}{B_1}x+B_2y+B_2\frac{C_1}{B_1}=0.$$

If the fractions which occur here are replaced by their values from (3) and (4), this last equation becomes identical with (2). Thus our statement is established.

We leave it for the reader to show that it is still true if B_1 or B_2 is zero.

25. Hesse's Normal Form. Besides the four standard forms for the equation of a straight line given in §§ 17, 18 there is a fifth form which is sometimes useful and which is known as Hesse's Normal Form, having been used systematically by the German geometer Hesse.*

Let us drop a perpendicular, OQ, on the given line, from the origin. Let p be the length of this perpendicular, and let α be the angle it makes with the axis of x. We wish to find the equation of the line in terms of p and α. For this purpose, let P be any position of the moving point (x, y) which traces out this line; and draw the coördinates $OM = x$, $MP = y$. The projection of the broken line OMP on the indefinite line OQ is p. The projections of the parts, OM and MP, are, by trigonometry, respectively $x \cos \alpha$ and $y \sin \alpha$. Consequently, by § 2,

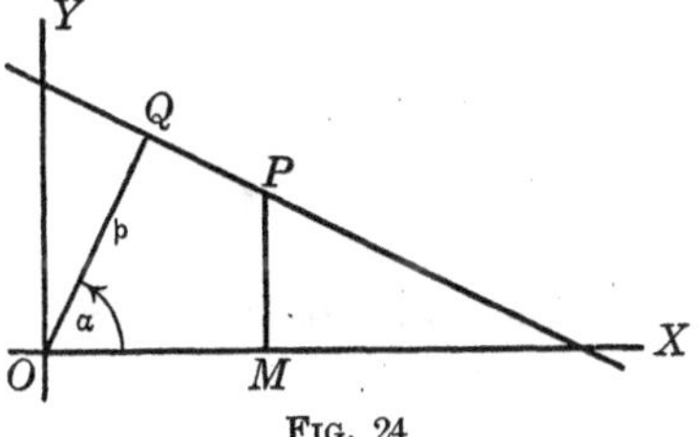

FIG. 24

$$x \cos \alpha + y \sin \alpha = p. \tag{1}$$

On the other hand, if P does not lie on the line AB, the projection of OMP on OQ will not be equal to p, and therefore (1) will not be satisfied. Hence (1) is the equation of the line in the desired form.

* 1811–1874. The word "normal" is here used in the sense of "standard." It has nothing to do, as some American text-books have implied, with the normal to a curve or line (see § 38).

The quantity p may be taken as positive, in which case α is the angle through which the positive half of the axis of x must be turned to coincide with OQ. If we prefer, we may, however, take p as negative, in which case α is the angle through which the positive half of the axis of x must be turned to coincide with the portion of OQ extended beyond O.

26. Reduction to Hesse's Normal Form. Suppose we have given the line

(1) $$Ax + By + C = 0.$$

Let the equation of this line in Hesse's normal form be

(2) $$x \cos \alpha + y \sin \alpha - p = 0.$$

Since, by hypothesis, (1) and (2) represent the same line, it must be possible, as we see from § 24, to obtain (2) by multiplying (1) by a suitable constant, R. We have, then,

$$RA = \cos \alpha, \quad RB = \sin \alpha, \quad RC = -p.$$

Squaring and adding the first two of these equations, we find

$$R^2(A^2 + B^2) = 1,$$

or

$$R = \frac{\pm 1}{\sqrt{A^2 + B^2}}.$$

The equation (1) *can be reduced to Hesse's Normal Form by being divided by* $\pm\sqrt{A^2 + B^2}$.

We have, then,

(3) $$\cos \alpha = \frac{\pm A}{\sqrt{A^2 + B^2}}, \quad \sin \alpha = \frac{\pm B}{\sqrt{A^2 + B^2}}, \quad p = \frac{\mp C}{\sqrt{A^2 + B^2}}.$$

We may take either the upper or the lower sign here, one giving a positive and the other a negative value for p. See the last paragraph of § 25.

EXERCISES

Reduce the following equations to Hesse's Normal Form, and find in each case the numerical values of p and α:

1. $3x + 4y - 5 = 0$.

2. $x + y - 7 = 0$.

3. $2x - y + 4 = 0$.

4. The line through the points $(2, 3)$, $(-1, 5)$.

5. The line through the point $(-3, 1)$ with slope 2.

6. The line whose intercepts are 5 and -2.

7. $3x = 2y$. **8.** $2x = 5$. **9.** $5y + 2 = 0$.

27. The Straight Line in Oblique Coördinates. If we use oblique coördinates, and understand by λ not the slope but the direction-ratio, as explained in § 9, it will be seen that the work of §§ 17, 18 requires no change, and that the four standard forms there given for the equation of a straight line remain valid in oblique coördinates. Similarly, § 19 requires no modification except replacing the word *slope* by *direction-ratio.*

On the other hand, the greater part of § 20 is no longer valid since it depends essentially on the fact that $\lambda = \tan\theta$. It may be readily seen, however, that the results here obtained concerning parallel (but not those concerning perpendicular) lines are still true in the case of oblique coördinates. Similarly § 21, *so far as it refers to parallel lines,* requires no change.

Of the remainder of this chapter only § 24 applies without change to oblique coördinates. All the other formulæ and results given require change, and for the most part the modified results are so unimportant (since it will almost always be better to use rectangular coördinates when questions of distances or angles are to be involved) that it would be a waste of time for us to deduce them here. The only exception is in the case of the area of a triangle, § 23, where the modification necessary is very slight. We give the result, reserving the proof to a later chapter (§ 46):

$$\Delta = \pm\frac{\sin\omega}{2}[(y_1 - y_2)x_3 + (y_2 - y_3)x_1 + (y_3 - y_1)x_2].$$

What has been said concerning the latter part of this chapter applies to most of the later sections of this book. We shall therefore refer to oblique coördinates in future only in the comparatively few cases where their use is of some importance.

28. Illustrative Applications. We take up in this section the proofs of a few simple geometrical theorems by the method of analytic geometry.

Example 1. To prove that the lines joining the vertices of a triangle to the middle points of the opposite sides meet in a point.

This is a *part* of the theorem we proved in § 10, Example 3. We were there asked in addition to prove that these lines trisect each other. If we had not known this additional fact, the method of proof there used could not possibly have occurred to us. We should then proceed as follows:

We take the coördinate axes and the coördinates as in § 10 (see Figure 25). The equations of the lines joining the vertices to the middle points of the opposite sides are, by (1), § 18,*

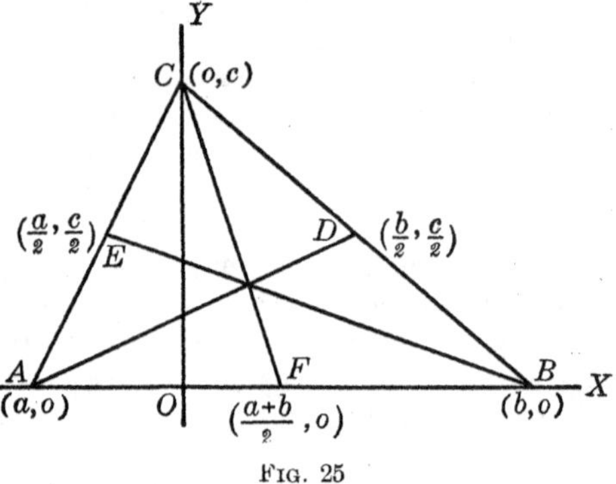

FIG. 25

$$AD \qquad y - 0 = \frac{\frac{c}{2} - 0}{\frac{b}{2} - a}(x - a),$$

$$BE \qquad y - 0 = \frac{\frac{c}{2} - 0}{\frac{a}{2} - b}(x - b),$$

$$CF \qquad y - c = \frac{0 - c}{\frac{a+b}{2} - 0}(x - 0).$$

These equations reduce to the forms

$$AD \qquad cx + (2a - b)y - ac = 0,$$

$$BE \qquad cx + (2b - a)y - bc = 0,$$

$$CF \qquad 2cx + (a + b)y - (a + b)c = 0.$$

The point of intersection of AD and BE is obtained by solving the first two of these equations as simultaneous.

* For the line CF, equation (2), § 18 may be used instead.

This gives the point

$$\left(\frac{a+b}{3}, \frac{c}{3}\right).$$

Our theorem will be proved if we can show that the line CF passes through this point. For this purpose we substitute in the equation of CF the values $x = \frac{1}{3}(a+b)$, $y = \frac{1}{3}c$; and since the equation is then seen to be satisfied, the theorem is proved.

In the course of this proof we have again determined the coördinates of the point of intersection of these lines.

Example 2. Prove that the diagonals of a square are perpendicular to each other.

Taking two adjacent sides of the square as coördinate axes, and calling the length of a side a, the coördinates of the vertices are $(0, 0)$, $(a, 0)$, (a, a), $(0, a)$. The slopes of the two diagonals are therefore

$$\lambda_1 = \frac{a-0}{a-0} = 1,\ \lambda_2 = \frac{a-0}{0-a} = -1.$$

Consequently $\lambda_2 = -\frac{1}{\lambda_1}$, and the lines are perpendicular by § 20, formula (2).

Example 3. To prove that the diagonals of a rhombus are perpendicular to each other.

We take the coördinate axes and the notation as indicated in Figure 26. The slopes of the diagonals are

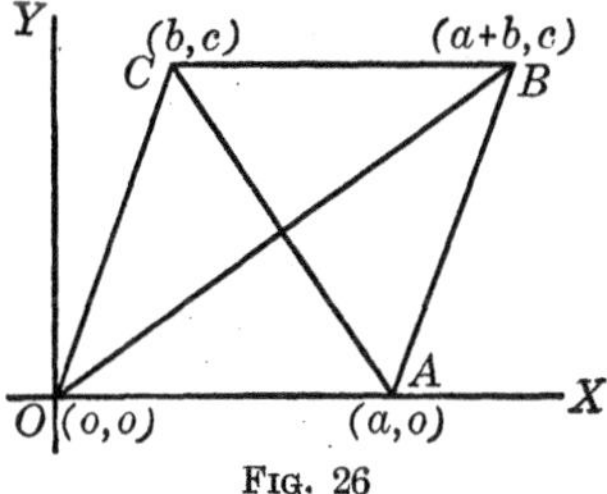

FIG. 26

$$\lambda_1 = \frac{c}{a+b},\ \lambda_2 = \frac{c}{b-a}.$$

We wish to prove that one of these quantities is the negative of the reciprocal of the other; or, what amounts to the same thing, that their product

$$(1) \qquad \lambda_1\lambda_2 = \frac{c^2}{b^2 - a^2}$$

has the value -1. This does not, at first, seem to be the case, but we still have to make use of the fact that the figure is a rhombus, not merely a parallelogram, which is all our algebraic notation has implied.

Since the length of one side, OA, is a, the same must be true of each of the other sides. By (2), § 5, $OC = \sqrt{b^2 + c^2}$. Hence $a^2 = b^2 + c^2$, and, this value being substituted in (1), reduces the value of $\lambda_1\lambda_2$ to -1.

PROBLEMS TO CHAPTER III

1. Prove that the three altitudes of a triangle meet in a point. Show that, using the same coördinates and notation as in Example 1, § 28, the coördinates of this point are

$$\left(0, -\frac{ab}{c}\right).$$

2. Prove that the perpendicular bisectors of the sides of a triangle meet in a point. Show that, using the same coördinates and notation as in Problem 1, the coördinates of this point are

$$\left(\frac{a+b}{2}, \frac{ab+c^2}{2c}\right).$$

3. Prove that in any triangle the point of intersection of the lines joining the vertices to the middle points of the opposite sides, the point of intersection of the perpendicular bisectors of the sides, and the point of intersection of the altitudes lie on a line; and that the first is one third of the way from the second towards the third.

4. Prove that in a trapezoid the diagonals and the line joining the middle points of the parallel sides meet in a point.

5. Prove that the non-parallel sides of a trapezoid and the line joining the middle points of the parallel sides meet in a point.

6. Prove that any line parallel to the line

$$Ax + By + C = 0$$

may be written in the form

$$Ax + By + C' = 0.$$

7. Prove that when two parallel lines are given by equations in the form of Problem 6, the distance between them is

$$\pm\frac{C - C'}{\sqrt{A^2 + B^2}}.$$

8. If we agree that, for lines not passing through the origin, the distance from a point to a line shall be taken as positive when the point lies on the same side of the line as the origin, negative when it lies on the opposite side, show that in formula (4), § 22 the doubtful sign must be taken as positive when C is positive, negative when C is negative.

9. What condition must be satisfied in order that the three points (x_1, y_1), (x_2, y_2), (x_3, y_3) should lie on a straight line? Obtain the answer to this question first by using the equation of the line connecting two of the points and expressing the fact that the third shall lie upon it; secondly by expressing the fact that the area of the triangle which has the three points as vertices shall be zero. Show that these two methods lead to the same result.

10. If the equations of the sides of a triangle are

$$A_1x + B_1y + C_1 = 0,$$
$$A_2x + B_2y + C_2 = 0,$$
$$A_3x + B_3y + C_3 = 0,$$

prove that the area of the triangle is

$$\pm\frac{[A_1(B_2C_3 - B_3C_2) + A_2(B_3C_1 - B_1C_3) + A_3(B_1C_2 - B_2C_1)]^2}{2\,(A_1B_2 - A_2B_1)(A_2B_3 - A_3B_2)(A_3B_1 - A_1B_3)}.$$

11. The vertices of a quadrilateral are the points

$$(x_1, y_1),\ (x_2, y_2),\ (x_3, y_3),\ (x_4, y_4).$$

Prove that its area is

$$\pm \tfrac{1}{2}\left[(x_2 - x_4)(y_3 - y_1) - (y_2 - y_4)(x_3 - x_1)\right].$$

12. Internal division being regarded as positive, external division as negative, prove that the ratio in which the line

$$Ax + By + C = 0$$

divides the segment (x_1, y_1), (x_2, y_2) is

$$-\frac{Ax_1 + By_1 + C}{Ax_2 + By_2 + C}.$$

[SUGGESTION. By remembering that the ratio of the segments of a line is equal to the ratio of their projections on either axis, this formula may readily be established for oblique as well as for rectangular coördinates.]

13. [Theorem of Menelaos.] A straight line cuts the sides P_2P_3, P_3P_1, P_1P_2 of a triangle in the points Q_1, Q_2, Q_3, respectively. Segments which lie wholly on the sides *extended* being taken as negative, those which lie partly or wholly on the sides themselves as positive, prove that

$$\overline{Q_1P_2} \cdot \overline{Q_2P_3} \cdot \overline{Q_3P_1} = -\overline{Q_1P_3} \cdot \overline{Q_2P_1} \cdot \overline{Q_3P_2}.$$

[SUGGESTION. Use the result of Problem 12.]

14. [Theorem of Ceva.] A point, R, is joined with the vertices, P_1, P_2, P_3, of a triangle and the joining lines meet the opposite sides in Q_1, Q_2, Q_3, respectively. With the same convention of sign as in Problem 13, prove that

$$\overline{Q_1P_2} \cdot \overline{Q_2P_3} \cdot \overline{Q_3P_1} = \overline{Q_1P_3} \cdot \overline{Q_2P_1} \cdot \overline{Q_3P_2}.$$

15. If two opposite sides of a quadrilateral meet in the point M and the other pair of opposite sides in N, prove that the middle point of MN and the middle points of the diagonals of the quadrilateral lie on a straight line.

[SUGGESTION. Use oblique coördinates.]

16. By regarding the bisectors of the angles between two lines as the locus of the points equidistant from the two lines, prove that the equations of the bisectors of the angles between the lines

$$A_1x + B_1y + C_1 = 0,$$
$$A_2x + B_2y + C_2 = 0$$

are

$$\frac{A_1x + B_1y + C_1}{\sqrt{A_1^2 + B_1^2}} = \pm \frac{A_2x + B_2y + C_2}{\sqrt{A_2^2 + B_2^2}}.$$

17. By means of the formula of Problem 16, prove that the bisectors of the angles between two intersecting lines are perpendicular to each other.

18. Prove that the bisectors of the angles of a triangle meet in a point; and also that the external bisectors of two angles and the internal bisector of the third meet in a point.

19. A line (1) has slope λ. The tangent of the angle *from* the line (1) *to* the line (2) is μ. Prove that the slope of (2) is $\frac{\lambda + \mu}{1 - \lambda\mu}$.

Hence find the equations of the line which passes through the point (2, 3) and makes with the line $5x + y - 3 = 0$ an angle of 110°.

CHAPTER IV

THE CIRCLE

29. Equation in Terms of Center and Radius. In § 11, formula (5), we found the equation of the circle having its center at the origin and given radius. If we call this radius ρ, the equation of this circle is

$$x^2+y^2=\rho^2. \tag{1}$$

More generally, suppose we want the equation of the circle whose center is at the point C with coördinates (α, β), and whose radius is ρ. The distance CP is $\sqrt{(x-\alpha)^2+(y-\beta)^2}$, and, consequently, the equation of the circle is

$$(x-\alpha)^2+(y-\beta)^2=\rho^2, \tag{2}$$

a formula which, of course, reduces to (1) when $\alpha=\beta=0$.

EXERCISES

Find the equations of the following circles and reduce them to their simplest forms:

1. Center at (2, 0), radius 2. *Ans.* $x^2+y^2=4x$.

2. Center at (3, 4), radius 5. *Ans.* $x^2+y^2-6x-8y=0$.

3. Center at (0, 3), radius 3.

4. Center at $(-2, 5)$, radius 6.

5. Center at $(-1, 0)$, radius 2.

6. Center at (0, 0), radius 4.

7. Center at $(1, \frac{1}{2})$, radius $1\frac{1}{2}$.

8. Center at $(-\frac{2}{3}, \frac{1}{2})$, radius 3.

30. The Expanded Form of the Equation of the Circle. If equation (2), § 29 is expanded, it takes the form

$$(1)\qquad \boldsymbol{x^2 + y^2 + ax + by + c = 0.}$$

The equation of every circle can therefore be written in this form (1). We wish now to examine whether the converse is also true, that is, whether every equation of the form (1) represents a circle.

Let us arrange the terms of (1) as follows:

$$x^2 + ax \quad + y^2 + by \quad = -c.$$

We complete the square in the first group of two terms by adding $\frac{1}{4}a^2$, and in the second group by adding $\frac{1}{4}b^2$. These two quantities must, of course, also be added on the right-hand side. The equation then becomes

$$x^2 + ax + \left(\frac{a}{2}\right)^2 + y^2 + by + \left(\frac{b}{2}\right)^2 = -c + \frac{a^2}{4} + \frac{b^2}{4}$$

or

$$(2)\qquad \left(x + \frac{a}{2}\right)^2 + \left(y + \frac{b}{2}\right)^2 = \frac{a^2 + b^2 - 4c}{4}.$$

This reduces to equation (2), § 29 if we let

$$\alpha = -\frac{a}{2},\quad \beta = -\frac{b}{2},\quad \rho = \frac{1}{2}\sqrt{a^2 + b^2 - 4c}.$$

Hence, if $a^2 + b^2 - 4c$ is positive, equation (1) represents a circle whose center is $\left(-\frac{a}{2}, -\frac{b}{2}\right)$ and whose radius is

$$\tfrac{1}{2}\sqrt{a^2 + b^2 - 4c}.$$

If $a^2 + b^2 - 4c$ is negative, equation (2) has no locus, since its left-hand side is not negative for any values of (x, y) and, hence, can never be equal to its right-hand side.

Finally, if $a^2 + b^2 - 4c = 0$, equation (2) can be fulfilled only when *both* squares on the left are zero, since these squares cannot add up to zero in any other way. That is, the point $x = -\frac{a}{2}$, $y = -\frac{b}{2}$ is the only point of the locus in this case. This may be regarded as the limit of a circle as the radius approaches zero, and thus we may say that the locus in this case is a null circle, or circle of zero radius, instead of saying, what amounts to the same thing, that the locus is a point.

If we agree to speak of the case in which $a^2 + b^2 - 4c$ is negative as an *imaginary circle*, understanding thereby merely that the equation has no locus, we may summarize by saying:

The equation (1) *represents a circle which is real, null, or imaginary according as* $a^2 + b^2 - 4c$ *is positive, zero, or negative.*

More generally, we may consider an equation of the form

$$(3) \qquad Ax^2 + Ay^2 + Dx + Ey + F = 0.$$

If $A = 0$, this, of course, represents a straight line. Otherwise, we may divide by A and thus reduce (3) to the form (1).

It should be noticed that, if A is not zero, (3) is an equation of the second degree in (x, y), but not the *general* equation of the second degree; for in (3) the coefficients of the x^2 and y^2 terms are the same, and there is no xy term. The general equation is

$$(4) \qquad Ax^2 + Bxy + Cy^2 + Dx + Ey + F = 0.$$

This general equation of the second degree represents a circle, real, null, or imaginary when $B = 0$ and $A = C$. In other cases it represents, in general, a more complicated locus, as we shall see later.

EXERCISES

Determine what the following equations represent. In doing this the *method* of this section (completing the square) should be used, not the formulæ found.

1. $x^2 + y^2 + 4x - 2y + 1 = 0$.

Ans. Circle, radius 2, center $(-2, 1)$.

2. $x^2 + y^2 + 6x - 4y + 13 = 0.$

Ans. The point $(-3, 2)$.

3. $x^2 + y^2 + 2x + 2y + 6 = 0.$ *Ans.* No locus.

4. $x^2 + y^2 - 2x + 6y + 9 = 0.$

5. $x^2 + y^2 + 4x + 4y + 8 = 0.$

6. $4x^2 + 4y^2 - 4x + 12y + 9 = 0.$

7. $x^2 + y^2 - 2x + 4y + 2 = 0.$

8. $x^2 + y^2 + 4x - 8y + 21 = 0.$

31. The Tangent to the Circle. Let us consider the circle with center at the origin and radius ρ:

(1) $x^2 + y^2 = \rho^2,$

and let P_1, with coördinates (x_1, y_1), be any fixed point on this circle.

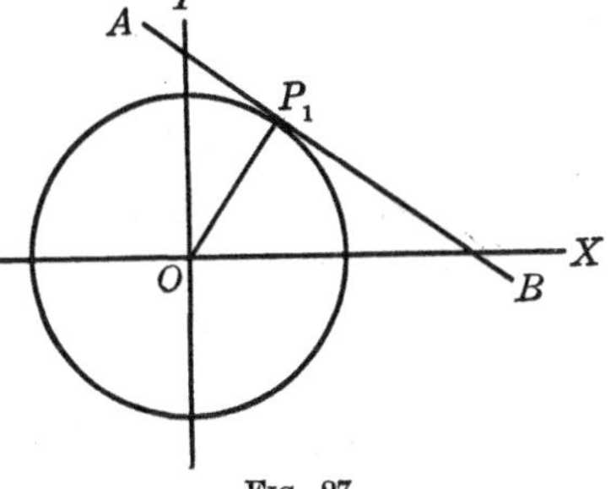

FIG. 27

Since P_1 lies on the circle, its coördinates satisfy (1), and we have *

(2) $x_1^2 + y_1^2 = \rho^2.$

Let us now find the equation of the tangent, AB, at P_1. This line, as we know from elementary geometry, is perpendicular to the radius OP_1. The slope of OP_1, by (1), § 6, is $\frac{y_1}{x_1}$. Consequently, the slope of AB, by (2), § 20, is $-\frac{x_1}{y_1}$. The equation of AB, by (2), § 17, is

$$y - y_1 = -\frac{x_1}{y_1}(x - x_1),$$

or, simplified,

$$x_1x + y_1y = x_1^2 + y_1^2.$$

* It should be clearly understood that (2) is *not* the equation of the circle. The equation of a curve always contains the *variable* coördinates (x, y) of the point which traces out the curve, while equation (2) contains nothing but constants.

This is the desired equation of the tangent. It can be still further simplified by replacing $x_1^2 + y_1^2$ by its value from (2). We thus get

(3) $$x_1x + y_1y = \rho^2$$

as the standard form of the equation of the tangent to (1) at (x_1, y_1).

Precisely the method here used can be employed to find the tangent at the point (x_1, y_1) to the circle with center at (α, β) and radius ρ (equation (2), § 29). We give merely the result, leaving the details of the work to the reader:

(4) $$(x_1 - \alpha)(x - \alpha) + (y_1 - \beta)(y - \beta) = \rho^2.$$

Finally, suppose the equation of the circle is given in the form

$$x^2 + y^2 + ax + by + c = 0.$$

This reduces to the case just considered, as we saw in § 30, if we let

$$\alpha = -\frac{a}{2},\quad \beta = -\frac{b}{2},\quad \rho = \tfrac{1}{2}\sqrt{a^2 + b^2 - 4c}.$$

Consequently, by (4), the equation of the tangent at (x_1, y_1) is

$$\left(x_1 + \frac{a}{2}\right)\left(x + \frac{a}{2}\right) + \left(y_1 + \frac{b}{2}\right)\left(y + \frac{b}{2}\right) = \frac{a^2 + b^2 - 4c}{4},$$

or, simplified,

(5) $$x_1x + y_1y + \frac{a}{2}(x + x_1) + \frac{b}{2}(y + y_1) + c = 0.$$

These equations, (3), (4), (5), are the standard forms of the equation of the tangent to a circle. Of them, (3) may be regarded as a special case of either (4) or (5).

EXERCISES

Find the equations of the tangents to the following circles at the points indicated :

1. $x^2 + y^2 = 25$, at (3, 4); at (4, − 3); at (0, 5).

2. $x^2 + y^2 = 2x$; at (1, 1); at (0, 0); at a point whose abscissa is $1\frac{1}{2}$.

3. The circle whose center is (5, 3) and radius 13, at the point (10, 15).

32. Tangents to a Circle from a Point Outside. In § 31 we assumed that (x_1, y_1) was a point on the circle, and it is only in that case that the formulæ we have obtained are valid.

Suppose, now, that (x_1, y_1) is a point outside of the circle, and that we wish to find the equation of the tangent drawn from this point. In the first place, we see geometrically that there are two answers, and this must, of course show itself in the algebraic solution of the problem. We explain the method to be used by means of a numerical example.

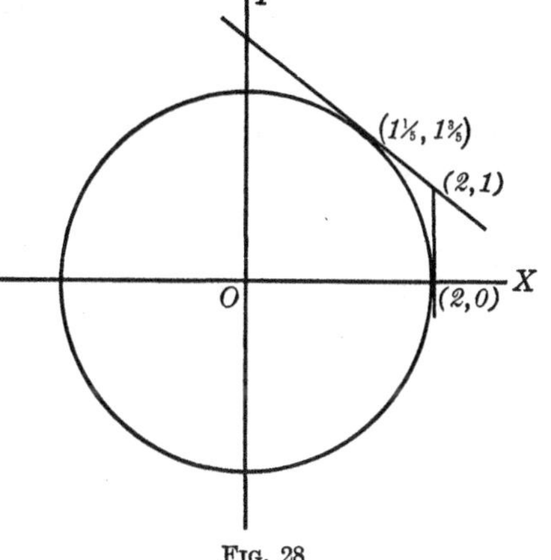

Fig. 28

Let us find the equations of the tangents to the circle

(1) $$x^2 + y^2 = 4$$

from the point (2, 1).

Let (x_1, y_1) be the point of contact of *one* of the tangents drawn from this point. Then the equation of this tangent is, by (3), § 31,

(2) $$x_1x + y_1y = 4.$$

Here x_1 and y_1 are unknown constants which are to be determined by means of the following two facts: *first*, that, by hypothesis, (2) passes through (2, 1) and that, consequently, $x = 2$, $y = 1$ satisfies (2)

(3) $$2x_1 + y_1 = 4,$$

and *secondly*, that, by hypothesis, (x_1, y_1) is on the circle (1), and hence

(4) $$x_1^2 + y_1^2 = 4.$$

In (3) and (4) we have two equations * for determining the two unknowns (x_1, y_1). If we eliminate y_1 between (3) and (4) by substituting its value from (3) in (4), we find for x, the equation

$$5\,x_1^2 - 16\,x_1 + 12 = 0.$$

Hence $$x_1 = 2 \text{ or } 1\tfrac{1}{5}.$$

Substituting these values in (3), we find

$$y_1 = 0 \text{ or } 1\tfrac{3}{5}.$$

Consequently, there are two points (x_1, y_1), namely the points (2, 0) and $(1\frac{1}{5}, 1\frac{3}{5})$, and these are the points of contact of the two tangents drawn from (2, 1) to the circle (1).

These points being found, the equations of the tangents can be immediately written down by means of (2), viz.

$$x = 2, \text{ and } 3\,x + 4\,y = 10.$$

This illustration is typical except in one respect: the work of solving the simultaneous equations like (3), (4) will usually lead to incommensurable values for x_1 and y_1, so that these quantities must be expressed by means of radicals or, if we prefer, approximately by means of decimals. If the point from which the tangents are to be drawn lies within the circle, the problem has no answer, and this fact will show itself by the values for (x_1, y_1) coming out imaginary.

It is not necessary that the circle have its center at the origin. If its equation is given in either of the forms (2), § 29 or (1), § 30, the method will apply without change

* We again remind the reader that (3) and (4) are *not* the equations of lines or curves, since they involve no variables. They are simply equations for determining unknown constants of exactly the kind with which we are familiar from elementary algebra.

provided we use the correct form for the tangent as given in § 31.

It would, of course, be possible to work out general formulæ for the equations of tangents drawn to a circle from a point outside; but these formulæ would be so complicated and so seldom used that it is better to work out every case which presents itself by the method just explained, which is known as the method of undetermined constants.

EXERCISES

Find the equations of the tangents drawn to the following circles:

1. $x^2 + y^2 = 25$, from the point (1, 7).

Ans. $4x + 3y = 25, \quad -3x + 4y = 25$.

2. $x^2 + y^2 = 169$, from the point (17, 7).

3. $x^2 + y^2 = 13$, from the point (5, 1).

4. $x^2 + y^2 = 25$, from the point (6, 0).

5. $x^2 + y^2 + 4x - 6y = 0$, from the point (3, 2).

6. $(x - 4)^2 + (y - 5)^2 = 25$, from the point (3, − 2).

7. $x^2 + y^2 - 10x - 24y = 0$, from the point (− 5, 2); from the point (− 3, 2).

33. Circle Through Three Points. What was said at the close of the last section applies also to the problem to be considered here. The general formula would be too complicated to be of much value,* but the method of undetermined constants, which we illustrate by a numerical example, can always be easily applied.

Let us find the equation of the circle which passes through the three points (5, 10), (6, 9), (− 2, 3). We know that the equation of the circle through these points can be written in the form

$$x^2 + y^2 + ax + by + c = 0. \tag{1}$$

* Unless we use the notation of determinants.

If we only knew the values of the constants a, b, c, we should have solved our problem. These three unknowns * we determine by making use of the fact that (1) is, by hypothesis, to pass through each of the three given points. Substituting in (1) in succession the coördinates of the three points, we find

$$\begin{aligned} &125 + 5a + 10b + c = 0, \\ (2)\qquad &117 + 6a + 9b + c = 0, \\ &13 - 2a + 3b + c = 0. \end{aligned}$$

If we solve this system of equations, we find

$$a = -4,\ b = -12,\ c = 15.$$

Consequently, the desired circle is

$$x^2 + y^2 - 4x - 12y + 15 = 0,$$

an equation which, by completing the square as in § 30, may be reduced to the form

$$(x-2)^2 + (y-6)^2 = 25,$$

and, hence, represents the circle whose center is at (2, 6) and whose radius is 5.

This method will always be applicable unless the three given points lie on a straight line, in which case the problem evidently has no solution. This will show itself when we try to solve the equations like (2), which will then be found to be inconsistent.

EXERCISES

Find the equations of the circles through the following sets of points :

1. (3, 5), (3, – 1), (4, 0). *Ans.* $x^2+y^2-2x-4y-8=0$.
2. (3, 4), (5, 2), (1, – 2).
3. (5, 7), (3, 2), (1, 3).

* Notice that a, b, c are unknowns of exactly the sort we are constantly determining in elementary algebra, while x and y are *variables* which it would be quite impossible to determine since they have no fixed values but vary as (x, y) moves around the curve.

4. Find the equation of the circle circumscribed about the triangle formed by the coördinate axes and the line $x + 2y = 2$.

5. Find the equation of the circle circumscribed about the triangle formed by the lines $x = y$, $2x - y = 2$, $2x + 3y - 3 = 0$.

6. Find the equation of the circle circumscribed about the triangle whose vertices are $(a, 0)$, $(b, 0)$, $(0, c)$. Check your answer by showing that the center of this circle is the point determined in Problem 2 at the close of Chapter III.

PROBLEMS TO CHAPTER IV

1. Prove by analytic geometry that every angle inscribed in a semicircle is a right angle.

[SUGGESTION. Take the coördinate axes so that the origin falls at the center of the circle and the two ends of the semicircle fall on the axis of x.]

2. Prove that if a perpendicular is dropped from a point on a circle to a diameter, the length of this perpendicular is a mean proportional between the segments it cuts off on the diameter.

3. Prove that the middle point of an arc of a circle is at the same distance from the chord of this arc as from the tangent drawn at one end of the arc.

4. Prove that the line

$$y = \lambda x + b$$

is tangent to the circle

$$x^2 + y^2 = \rho^2$$

when and only when

$$b^2 = \rho^2(1 + \lambda^2).$$

5. Prove that the line

$$\frac{x}{a} + \frac{y}{b} = 1$$

is tangent to the circle

$$x^2 + y^2 = \rho^2$$

when and only when

$$\frac{1}{a^2} + \frac{1}{b^2} = \frac{1}{\rho^2}.$$

6. Let O and P be the points where the line $y = \lambda x$ cuts the circle $x^2 + y^2 = 2\,ax$. On OP as diameter a second circle is described. Find its equation.

7. CM is a radius of a circle whose center is C. On CM as diameter a second circle is drawn. Prove that any chord of the first circle through M is bisected by the second circle.

[SUGGESTION. Take M as origin and CM as axis of x. The equation of the chord may then be written $y = \lambda x$.]

8. Two circles are tangent to each other at M and two straight lines through M meet the first circle in A, B, the second in A', B'. Prove that the lines AB and $A'B'$ are parallel. Show that your work covers both the case in which the circles are tangent internally and that in which they are tangent externally.

9. At the ends of a chord of a circle tangents are drawn. Prove that the distance from any point, P, of the circle to the chord is a mean proportional between the distances from P to the tangents.

10. Show that the equation of the circle through the middle points of the sides of the triangle whose vertices are $(a, 0)$, $(b, 0)$, $(0, c)$ is

$$x^2 + y^2 - \frac{a+b}{2}x + \frac{ab - c^2}{2\,c}y = 0.$$

11. Hence prove that in every triangle the circle through the middle points of the sides passes through the feet of the perpendiculars dropped from the vertices on the opposite sides, and also through the points halfway between the vertices and the point of intersection of the altitudes. This circle is called the Nine Point Circle of the triangle.

12. A chord is drawn through a point, P, on a diameter, AB, of a circle, and its extremities are joined to one end, A, of the diameter. These joining lines meet the diameter perpendicular to AB in Q and R. Prove that, as the chord revolves about P, the product of the distances from the center of the circle to Q and R is constant, and has the value $\rho^2 PB/PA$, where ρ is the radius of the circle.

13. If the equations

$$x^2 + y^2 + a_1 x + b_1 y + c_1 = 0,$$
$$x^2 + y^2 + a_2 x + b_2 y + c_2 = 0$$

represent intersecting circles, show that they intersect at right angles when and only when

$$a_1 a_2 + b_1 b_2 = 2\, c_1 + 2\, c_2.$$

[SUGGESTION. Notice that, if the circles intersect at right angles, the triangle whose vertices are the centers of the circles and one of their points of intersection is a right triangle.]

Show that two real non-intersecting circles never satisfy this condition.

14. By using the result of Problem 13, find the equation of the circle which passes through the points (8, 9) (1, 2) and cuts the circle $x^2 + y^2 = 25$ at right angles.

15. Find under what conditions the circle

$$x^2 + y^2 + ax + by + c = 0$$

cuts the line

$$Ax + By + C = 0$$

at right angles.

Hence find the equation of the circle which cuts both the circle

$$x^2 + y^2 = 10$$

and the line

$$2x + y = 2$$

at right angles, and also passes through the point (3, 0).

16. Is there any circle which cuts at right angles the three circles

$$x^2 + y^2 = 4,$$
$$x^2 + y^2 = 4x,$$
$$x^2 + y^2 = 6y?$$

If so, find its equation, and draw an accurate figure.

CHAPTER V

POLAR COÖRDINATES

34. Definition of Polar Coördinates. Let us take a point, O, as origin or *pole*, and a straight line, OA, — the *initial line*, — running out to infinity in one direction from O. Any point, P, in the plane may be determined by its distance, r, from O and by the angle, ϕ, which the line OP makes with the initial line; that is, the angle through which OA must be revolved in order to come into the position OP. This angle, in Figure 29, may be taken as a positive acute angle; but it may also, if we prefer, be increased or decreased by any multiple of 360°.

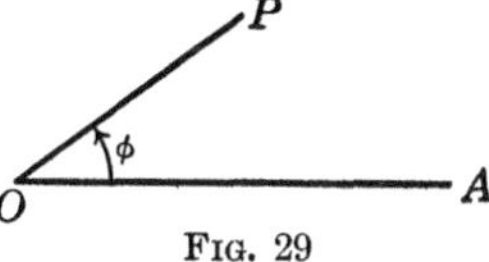

FIG. 29

We may also allow the coördinate r to be negative. Thus if, in Figure 30, P is the point $r = 5$, $\phi = 45°$, — or, as we will say for brevity,* the point (5, 45°), — the point (– 5, 45°) will be P', it being agreed that when r is negative this distance must be laid off, not along the terminal side of the angle ϕ, but along this side produced backward. According to this understanding, the point P of Figure 30 may also be designated as (– 5, 225°) and P' as (+ 5, 225°).

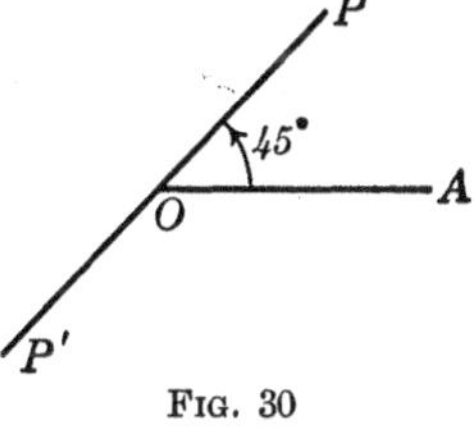

FIG. 30

It will be seen that in polar coördinates each point has an infinite number of sets of coördinates. Conversely, however, and this is the important thing, when the values of r and ϕ

* The degree mark (°) makes it impossible to mistake this notation for coördinates in a Cartesian system.

are given, the point is uniquely determined, since all we have to do is to lay off the angle ϕ with a protractor starting from OA, and on its terminal side lay off the length r starting from O and measuring along the terminal side itself if r is positive, along this side extended backward if r is negative.

This work of plotting can be considerably simplified by the use of what is called Polar Coördinate Paper, on which lines radiating from O are ruled at intervals of 5° or 10°, and also circles with centers at O and whose radii are successive multiples of the radius of the smallest one. See, for example, Figure 31.

EXERCISES

Plot the following points:

1. $(3, 30°)$.
2. $(5, 120°)$.
3. $(-10, 80°)$.
4. $(8, -20°)$.
5. $(-5, -145°)$.
6. $(5, 17°)$.
7. $(7.3, 63°)$.
8. $(-4.9, 111°)$.
9. $(\frac{7}{3}, 180°)$.
10. $(12, 0°)$.

11. Indicate in each of the Exercises 1–10 two other pairs of coördinates which determine the same point; showing, in particular, how the sign of r can be changed.

35. Plotting of Curves in Polar Coördinates. We have seen that when we use Cartesian coördinates an equation in x and y represents a curve.

Similarly, if we have an equation between the polar coördinates (r, ϕ) of a variable point, this point will be restricted to a certain locus, which may be plotted very much as in the case of Cartesian coördinates. The following example will make this clear.

Let us plot the curve

$$r^2 = 144 \cos 2\phi. \tag{1}$$

This equation may be written

$$(2) \qquad r = \pm 12\sqrt{\cos 2\phi}.$$

We now assign to ϕ in succession the values 0°, 10°, 20°, etc. and compute the corresponding values of r by means of a table of cosines. Unless our figure is drawn on a very large scale, it will be sufficient to get our results correct to two significant figures, since this is as accurately as we can use them in plotting. We find

$\phi = 0°$,	$r = \pm 12.0$,	$\phi = 30°$,	$r = \pm 8.5$,
$\phi = 10°$,	$r = \pm 11.6$,	$\phi = 40°$,	$r = \pm 5.0$,
$\phi = 20°$,	$r = \pm 10.5$,	$\phi = 45°$,	$r = 0$.

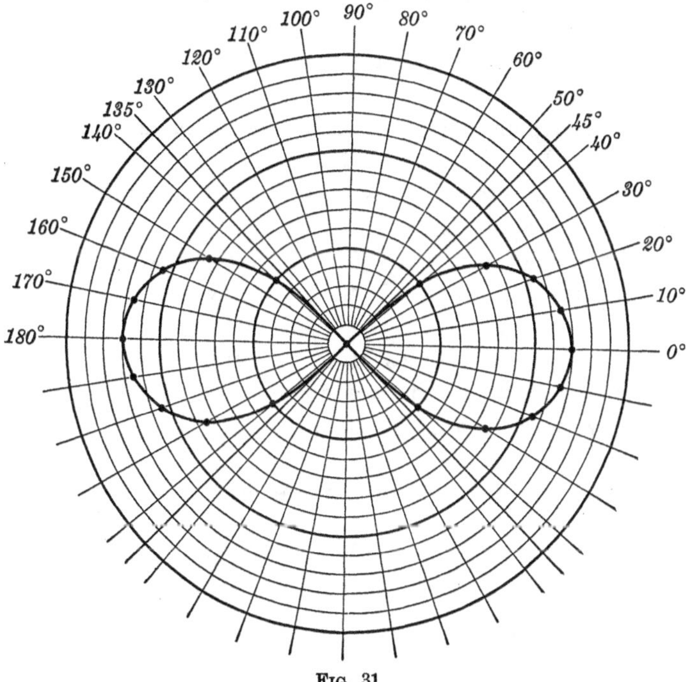

Fig. 31

When ϕ is greater than 45°, 2ϕ is greater than 90° and, consequently, its cosine is negative. The value of r in (2) thus becomes imaginary. This is true as long as 2ϕ remains in the second or third quadrant, that is, while ϕ increases from 45° to 135°. After this point, 2ϕ comes into the fourth quadrant, its cosine is positive, and r is real. From this point on we get the following values for r, which are the same as those obtained above taken in the reverse order:

$$\phi = 135°, \quad r = 0, \qquad \phi = 160°, \quad r = \pm 10.5,$$
$$\phi = 140°, \quad r = \pm 5.0, \qquad \phi = 170°, \quad r = \pm 11.6,$$
$$\phi = 150°, \quad r = \pm 8.5, \qquad \phi = 180°, \quad r = \pm 12.0.$$

If we were to go farther, we should get exactly the same points over again. For instance, when $\phi = 190°$, $r = \pm 11.6$, and these are the same two points which we found by letting $\phi = 10°$. If we were to take negative values for ϕ, we should get no new points of the curve.

Plotting the points whose coördinates we have now computed, we can draw in the curve of Figure 31. This curve is called a *Lemniscate*. It crosses itself at the origin. Such a point is called a *double point* of a curve.

One of the chief difficulties the beginner finds in plotting curves in polar coördinates is to know how far he must go with the values of ϕ. In the example just given, it was sufficient to consider values from $\phi = 0°$ to $\phi = 180°$. In other cases we shall find that we must go up to 360°, or even farther, if we wish to get the whole curve. No general rule can be given except that in each case we must go so far that the curve repeats itself from this point on.

EXERCISES

Plot the following curves, using polar coördinate paper:

1. $r = 5$. **3.** $r = 10 \sin \phi$. **5.** $r^2 = 100 \sin 2\phi$.

2. $\phi = 10°$. **4.** $r = 10 \cos \phi$. **6.** $r = 10 \cos 3\phi$.

36. Transformation from Rectangular to Polar Coördinates, and *Vice Versa*. Let us consider, by the side of the system of polar coördinates so far used in this chapter, a system of rectangular coördinates having the same origin, and having the initial line as the positive half of the axis of x. If the polar coördinates of a point, P, are (r, ϕ) and its rectangular coördinates (x, y), we shall have (see Figure 32)

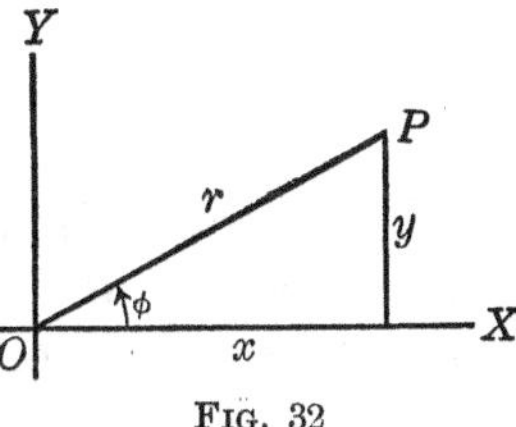

FIG. 32

$$\cos\phi = \frac{x}{r}, \quad \sin\phi = \frac{y}{r}.$$

Moreover, this will be true not merely when ϕ is in the first quadrant, but in all cases, as becomes evident when we recall the definitions of the sine and cosine of an angle in the second, third, or fourth quadrant.

Clearing of fractions, we may write

$$(1) \qquad \boldsymbol{x = r\cos\phi, \quad y = r\sin\phi.}$$

These formulæ enable us, when the polar coördinates of a point are known, to find its rectangular coördinates.

Conversely, either from the figure or by squaring and adding equations (1), we find

$$(2) \qquad r = \pm\sqrt{x^2 + y^2},$$

from which, by means of (1), the angle ϕ may be determined. Thus, knowing (x, y), we can find (r, ϕ).

The most important application of these formulæ is to pass from the equation of a curve in one system of coördinates to its equation in the other system.

Suppose, for instance, that we have the straight line

$$7x - 3y + 2 = 0,$$

and wish to find its equation in polar coördinates. Substituting for x and y their values from (1), we find as the desired equation

$$(7\cos\phi - 3\sin\phi)r + 2 = 0.$$

The transformation of the equation of any curve from rectangular to polar coördinates is performed with the same ease.

The converse problem is hardly less simple.

Suppose, first, that we wish to transform the equation

$$(3) \qquad r = \frac{5}{\sin\phi}$$

to rectangular coördinates. Clearing this equation of fractions, and replacing $r\sin\phi$ by its value from (1), we find $y = 5$. Hence (3) represents a straight line parallel to the initial line and at a distance of 5 units from it.

As a second example, we consider the curve (1) of § 35. The equation in polar coördinates of this curve may, by trigonometry, be written

$$r^2 = 144(\cos^2\phi - \sin^2\phi).$$

Replacing $\cos\phi$ and $\sin\phi$ by their values from (1), and clearing of fractions, gives

$$r^4 = 144(x^2 - y^2).$$

Here the value of r from (2) must be substituted, giving

$$x^4 + 2x^2y^2 + y^4 = 144(x^2 - y^2)$$

as the equation of the lemniscate in rectangular coördinates.

EXERCISES

1. Find the rectangular coördinates of the points of the exercises at the end of § 34.

2. Find the polar coördinates of the points of the exercises at the end of § 3.

3. Transform to polar coördinates the curves of the exercises at the end of § 12.

4. Transform to rectangular coördinates the curves of the exercises at the end of § 35.

PROBLEMS TO CHAPTER V

Plot the following curves, assuming that a stands for a positive constant:

1. $r = a \sin 3\phi$.

2. $r = a(1 - \cos\phi)$.

3. $r = a \cos 2\phi$.

4. $r^2 = a^2 \cos 3\phi$.

5. $r = a \cos \frac{\phi}{2}$.

6. $r = a \cos \frac{\phi}{3}$.

7. $r = a \cos \frac{\phi}{5}$.

8. $r \cos\phi = a \cos 2\phi$.

9. $r^2 \sin^2 2\phi = a^2 \cos 2\phi$.

10. $r^2 = a^2 \operatorname{ctn} \phi$.

11. What changes will be produced in the curves of Problems 1–10 if a is a negative constant?

12. Find the equations in rectangular coördinates of the curves of Problems 1–5.

13. Find the equations in rectangular coördinates of the curves of Problems 8–10, and get, in this way, what additional information you can concerning the shape of the distant parts of these curves.

CHAPTER VI

SOME GENERAL METHODS

37. The Tangent as the Limit of the Secant. We were able to find the equation of the tangent to the circle in § 31 on account of a particular property of the tangent with which we were familiar from elementary geometry, namely, that it is perpendicular to the radius drawn to the point of contact. This method, however, will not be open to us when we come to other curves which have not been studied in elementary geometry. In such cases we shall be obliged to fall back directly on the definition of the tangent.

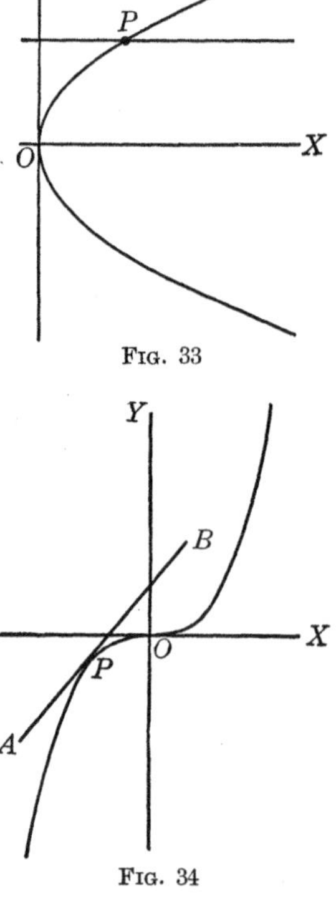

FIG. 33

FIG. 34

In elementary geometry, where we are dealing with the circle alone, we define a tangent as a line which meets the curve in one and only one point. Simple examples show that this definition is not a satisfactory one in many other cases. For instance, in the case of the curve $y^2 = 4x$, plotted in § 12, a line through a point, P, of the curve and parallel to the axis of x will meet the curve at no other point, and yet we shall surely not wish to call such a line a tangent (see Figure 33). On the other hand, the curve $y = x^3$ is shaped as indicated in Figure 34, and the line AB, which we should naturally wish to speak of as tangent to the curve at P, will, if extended, meet it again in another point.

We might be tempted, in view of these examples, to define a tangent to a curve at P as a line through P which *in the immediate neighborhood of this point* lies wholly on one side of the curve. Apart from the fact that even this definition will not give us exactly what we want in all cases, there is the very serious practical objection to it that it would not be an easy definition upon which to base mathematical reasoning. It has therefore been found desirable in all the higher parts of mathematics to approach the subject of tangency in quite a different manner.

If we think of a curve as traced out by a moving point, we shall say that at any moment the point is moving in a definite direction, which we can speak of as the direction of the curve at this point. By the tangent to the curve at P we shall understand the straight line through P whose direction is the direction of the curve at P.

This, however, does not really advance us much, for it simply throws us back on the question of how the direction of the curve at P is to be determined. If P' is a point a little farther along the curve, the direction PP' is obviously not quite the direction of the curve at P. If instead of P' we take P'', a point on the curve between P and P', the direction PP'', while still not the direction of the curve at P, is a better approximation to it than was PP', and if we take P''' on the curve still nearer to P, PP''' is a still closer approximation to the direction of the curve at P. We thus determine the direction of the curve at P as the *limit* of the direction from P to a neighboring point on the curve, as this neighboring point moves down the curve towards P.

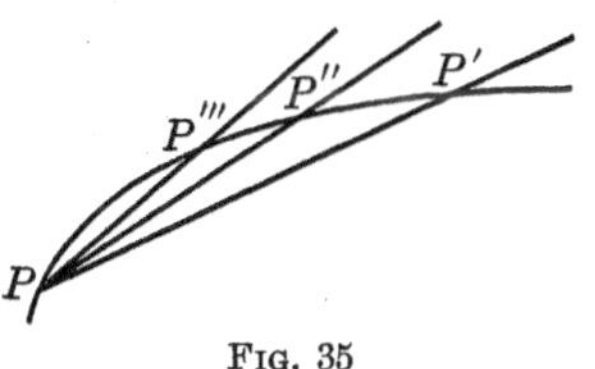

FIG. 35

It is now easy to state our definition of a tangent in the

following form, which is practically the most convenient one:

By the tangent to a curve at a point P is meant the limiting position approached by a secant which connects P with a neighboring point, Q, on the curve as Q moves along the curve and approaches P as its limit.

38. Method of Finding Equation of Tangent and Normal. If we have a curve given by its equation and a point, P_1, with coördinates (x_1, y_1), on the curve, the problem of finding the equation of the tangent at P_1 is clearly solved as soon as we have found the slope, λ, of the tangent, for the equation of the tangent will then, by (2), § 17, be

$$(1) \qquad y - y_1 = \lambda(x - x_1).$$

To find the slope of the tangent, we take a point P_2, with coördinates (x_2, y_2), on the curve near P_1. The slope of the secant connecting these points is, by (1), § 6,

$$\frac{y_2 - y_1}{x_2 - x_1}.$$

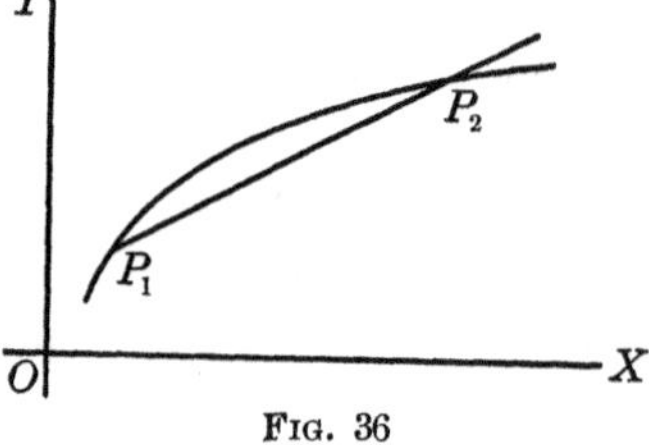

FIG. 36

If, now, we take the limit as P_2 moves along the curve and approaches P_1, we see from the definition at the close of § 37 that

$$(2) \qquad \lambda = \lim \frac{y_2 - y_1}{x_2 - x_1}.$$

It is in determining this limit that the difficulty of the problem lies; for as P_2 approaches P_1, both $y_2 - y_1$ and $x_2 - x_1$ approach zero. Now when the numerator of a fraction approaches zero, the value of the fraction approaches zero; while when the denominator approaches zero, the fraction becomes infinite. When, however, both of these things happen at once, it is impossible to see, without further examination, how these two opposite tendencies balance up.

A moment's consideration will show whence this difficulty comes. We have *said* that the point P_2 is to remain on the curve as it moves towards P_1. We cannot, however, hope to carry through the algebraic work unless in some way we make use algebraically of this fact, and also of the fact that P_1 lies on the curve. We will show in a moment by concrete examples how this is to be done. First, however, we will make a change in notation which, while not necessary, is very convenient. Let us denote the numerator and denominator of the fraction in (2) by k and h, respectively:

$$x_2 - x_1 = h, \quad y_2 - y_1 = k.$$

The point (x_2, y_2) can then be written

$$P_2 \qquad (x_1 + h, y_1 + k),$$

and we have to determine

$$(3) \qquad \lambda = \lim \left(\frac{k}{h}\right).$$

In this notation we can dispense entirely with the letters x_2, y_2.

Let us begin by finding the tangent to the circle

$$(4) \qquad x^2 + y^2 = \rho^2$$

at the point (x_1, y_1).

Since both this point and the point $(x_1 + h, y_1 + k)$ lie on (4), we have

$$(5) \qquad x_1^2 + y_1^2 = \rho^2,$$

$$(6) \qquad (x_1 + h)^2 + (y_1 + k)^2 = \rho^2.$$

By making use of these two equations, we wish to find an alternative expression for the fraction $\frac{k}{h}$ which will enable us to evaluate its limit. On expanding (6) we find

$$x_1^2 + 2hx_1 + h^2 + y_1^2 + 2ky_1 + k^2 = \rho^2.$$

From this we subtract (5) and get

$$2\,hx_1 + h^2 + 2\,ky_1 + k^2 = 0,$$

which, after division by h, becomes

$$2\,x_1 + h + \frac{k}{h}(2\,y_1 + k) = 0.$$

Hence

$$\frac{k}{h} = -\frac{2\,x_1 + h}{2\,y_1 + k}.$$

This is the alternative expression for $\frac{k}{h}$, which, though more complicated than the original one, has the great advantage that its limit, as k and h both approach zero, can be at once determined:

(7) $$\lambda = \lim\left(-\frac{2\,x_1 + h}{2\,y_1 + k}\right) = -\frac{x_1}{y_1}.$$

This being the slope of the tangent, the equation of the tangent is

$$y - y_1 = -\frac{x_1}{y_1}(x - x_1),$$

and the further reduction and simplification is precisely as in § 31.

As a second example, let us find the tangent at (x_1, y_1) to the curve

(8) $$y = x^3.$$

The points (x_1, y_1) and $(x_1 + h, y_1 + k)$ both lying on (8), we have

(9) $$y_1 = x_1^3,$$

(10) $$y_1 + k = (x_1 + h)^3.$$

Expanding (10) and subtracting (9) from it gives

$$k = 3\,x_1^2 h + 3\,x_1 h^2 + h^3$$

or

$$\frac{k}{h} = 3\,x_1^2 + 3\,x_1 h + h^2.$$

Hence

$$\lambda = \lim\left(\frac{k}{h}\right) = 3\,x_1^2.$$

Consequently, the equation of the tangent is

$$y - y_1 = 3\,x_1^2(x - x_1),$$

which reduces, when we make use of (9), to

$$3\,x_1^2 x - y - 2\,x_1^3 = 0. \tag{11}$$

This is the general formula for the tangent to this special curve. In particular, we see that the tangent at the origin is the line $y = 0$, that is, the axis of x. This line, as we see from Figure 34, crosses the curve at the origin. A point like this at which the tangent crosses the curve is called a *point of inflection.**

DEFINITION. *By the normal to a curve at a point P on the curve is meant the line through P perpendicular to the tangent to the curve at P.*

We can obviously write down at once the equation of the normal to a curve at a point (x_1, y_1) as soon as we have found the slope of the tangent at this point. For instance, in the case of the circle (4), the slope of the tangent is given by (7). Consequently, the slope of the normal is $\frac{y_1}{x_1}$, and the equation of the normal is

$$y - y_1 = \frac{y_1}{x_1}(x - x_1)$$

or

$$x_1 y = y_1 x.$$

This is a line through the origin, as we know from elementary geometry should be the case.

* The tangent at a cusp (see Problem 2 at the end of this chapter) will also, in general, cross the curve at this point.

EXERCISES

Find the equations of the tangents to the following curves at the point (x_1, y_1):

1. $y^2 = 4x$. *Ans.* $y_1 y = 2(x + x_1)$.
2. $x^2 + y^2 = 2ax$.
3. $xy = 1$. *Ans.* $y_1 x + x_1 y = 2$.
4. $2x^2 + 3y^2 = 6$.
5. Find the equations of the normals at the point (x_1, y_1) to the curves of Exercises 1–4.

39. Tangents to Curves of the Second Degree. The most general equation of the second degree in (x, y) is

$$(1) \qquad Ax^2 + Bxy + Cy^2 + Dx + Ey + F = 0.$$

Although we do not as yet know what kind of curve is represented by this equation, this does not prevent us from finding the equation of its tangent.

Let (x_1, y_1) be a point on (1), and let $(x_1 + h, y_1 + k)$ be a neighboring point on this curve. Then

$$(2) \qquad Ax_1^2 + Bx_1y_1 + Cy_1^2 + Dx_1 + Ey_1 + F = 0,$$

(3)

$$A(x_1+h)^2 + B(x_1+h)(y_1+k) + C(y_1+k)^2 + D(x_1+h) + E(y_1+k) + F = 0.$$

By expanding (3) and subtracting (2) from it, we find

$$2Ax_1h + Ah^2 + By_1h + Bx_1k + Bhk + 2Cy_1k + Ck^2 + Dh + Ek = 0,$$

which, after division by h, becomes

$$2Ax_1 + Ah + By_1 + Bk + D + \frac{k}{h}(Bx_1 + 2Cy_1 + Ck + E) = 0.$$

Hence

$$\frac{k}{h} = -\frac{2Ax_1 + Ah + By_1 + Bk + D}{Bx_1 + 2Cy_1 + Ck + E}.$$

We thus find as the slope of the tangent

$$\lambda = \lim\left(\frac{k}{h}\right) = -\frac{2Ax_1 + By_1 + D}{Bx_1 + 2Cy_1 + E}.$$

The equation of the tangent is, therefore,

$$(y - y_1) = -\frac{2Ax_1 + By_1 + D}{Bx_1 + 2Cy_1 + E}(x - x_1),$$

or, cleared of fractions,

(4) $$2\,Ax_1x + B(x_1y + y_1x) + 2\,Cy_1y + D(x - x_1) + E(y - y_1) = 2\,Ax_1^2 + 2\,Bx_1y_1 + 2\,Cy_1^2.$$

By means of (2), we see that the second member of (4) is equal to

$$-\,2\,Dx_1 - 2\,Ey_1 - 2\,F.$$

If we make use of this value, transpose, and divide by 2, (4) becomes

(5) $$Ax_1x + \frac{B}{2}(x_1y + y_1x) + Cy_1y + \frac{D}{2}(x + x_1) + \frac{E}{2}(y + y_1) + F = 0.$$

This is the final form for the equation of the tangent to the curve (1) at the point (x_1, y_1). It may be easily remembered as follows:

Write equation (1) in the form

$$Axx + \frac{B}{2}(xy + xy) + Cyy + \frac{D}{2}(x + x) + \frac{E}{2}(y + y) + F = 0,$$

where x^2 and y^2 are split up into two equal factors, while every other term (except the constant term) is split up into the sum of two equal halves. If, in the equation thus written, we put a subscript 1 to *one* of the two variables in each term (but not to the same one in the two xy-terms), we get precisely the equation of the tangent.

EXERCISES

Write down, by the rule just given, the equations of the tangents to the curves in the Exercises to § 38.

40. Addition or Subtraction of the Equations of Two Curves. Suppose that

(1) $$A_1x + B_1y + C_1 = 0,$$

(2) $$A_2x + B_2y + C_2 = 0$$

are two straight lines which intersect in the point (x_1, y_1). Let us inquire what curve is represented by the equation

(3) $$(A_1 + A_2)x + (B_1 + B_2)y + (C_1 + C_2) = 0$$

obtained by adding together equations (1) and (2). Since this is an equation of the first degree,* it represents a

* The only way in which it could possibly not be of the first degree would be if $A_1 = -A_2$, $B_1 = -B_2$. But this would make (1) and (2) parallel (or coincident), whereas we have assumed that they intersect.

straight line. To get further information, let us write (3) in the form

(4) $$(A_1x + B_1y + C_1) + (A_2x + B_2y + C_2) = 0.$$

To find out whether (x_1, y_1) lies on (4), we substitute its coördinates in (4) in place of (x, y) and see whether the resulting equation is fulfilled. In this substitution, the first parenthesis in (4) reduces to zero since it is the first member of (1), and (x_1, y_1) lies on (1) by hypothesis. For a similar reason, the second parenthesis in (4), which is the first member of (2), reduces to zero. Consequently, the line (4) does pass through (x_1, y_1). Hence

If the equations of two lines which intersect in P_1 are added together, the resulting equation represents a straight line which also passes through P_1.

It would seem, at first sight, that we ought to be able to state just what one of the infinitely many lines through P_1 is represented by (3). This, however, is impossible for a reason which will be apparent later. We can, however, make one additional statement; namely, that (3) will not represent either of the lines (1) or (2). For suppose (x_2, y_2) is any point on (1) other than the intersection of (1) and (2). Then, since (x_2, y_2) lies on (1),

$$A_1x_2 + B_1y_2 + C_1 = 0,$$

and since it does not lie on (2),

$$A_2x_2 + B_2y_2 + C_2 \neq 0.$$

If we test (x_2, y_2) to see whether it lies on (4), we see that it does not, since the first parenthesis reduces to zero but not the second. Hence (3) cannot coincide with (1). By similar reasoning, we see that it cannot coincide with (2).

As a second illustration of the principle here involved, let us now consider two circles,

(5) $$A_1x^2 + A_1y^2 + D_1x + E_1y + F_1 = 0,$$

(6) $$A_2x^2 + A_2y^2 + D_2x + E_2y + F_2 = 0.$$

By adding these equations together, we get

$$(7) \quad (A_1 + A_2)x^2 + (A_1 + A_2)y^2 + (D_1 + D_2)x + (E_1 + E_2)y + (F_1 + F_2) = 0.$$

This is a circle, real, null, or imaginary, except when $A_1 = -A_2$, when it is, in general, a straight line. If (5) and (6) intersect in two points, (7) passes through these points. For if (x_1, y_1) is either one of these points, we have

$$(8) \quad A_1x_1^2 + A_1y_1^2 + D_1x_1 + E_1y_1 + F_1 = 0,$$

$$(9) \quad A_2x_1^2 + A_2y_1^2 + D_2x_1 + E_2y_1 + F_2 = 0.$$

Now equation (7) may be written

$$(10) \quad (A_1x^2 + A_1y^2 + D_1x + E_1y + F_1) + (A_2x^2 + A_2y^2 + D_2x + E_2y + F_2) = 0.$$

If we test the point (x_1, y_1) to see whether it lies on (10), we see that it does do so since, by (8) and (9), both parentheses reduce to zero.

On the other hand, if (x_2, y_2) is a point lying on (5) but not on (6), we see, by testing it in (10), that it does not lie on (7). Similarly, (7) does not pass through any point of (6) which does not lie on (5).

The reasoning we have here used in the case of straight lines and circles applies in the same way to other curves, and we thus get the result:

If the equations of two curves which meet in one or more points are added together, the locus of the resulting equation passes through all the points of meeting of the two given curves and meets neither of them in any other point.

If the two given curves do not meet, the sum of their equations either has no locus, or its locus does not meet either of the curves.

Before applying this principle, we may, of course, multiply one or both of the given equations by any constants other than zero. The curve which we then get by adding the two equations will have all the properties we have just stated, but it will, in general, be a different curve from the one we should have obtained by simply adding the equations as they stood. For instance, if we add the equations

$$x - 2y + 3 = 0,$$
$$x + 2y - 1 = 0,$$

we get the line parallel to the axis of y through their point of intersection $(-1, 1)$, while if we first multiply the second equation by 3 and then add, we get the line connecting this point with the origin. We see now why it was that we were unable to state which line through the point of intersection of two given lines we get by adding their equations,—it will all depend on which particular forms of equation we use.

We may, if we please, multiply one of the equations by -1 before adding. In other words, the results stated above remain true if we subtract the equations instead of adding.

In conclusion, we make an application of this principle to the problem of finding the equation of the common chord of two intersecting circles.

Let us write the equations of these circles in the forms

$$x^2 + y^2 + a_1x + b_1y + c_1 = 0, \tag{11}$$

$$x^2 + y^2 + a_2x + b_2y + c_2 = 0. \tag{12}$$

If we subtract these equations, we evidently get an equation which is of the first degree and therefore represents a straight line. By our general principle, this line must pass through both points of intersection of the given circles. *The equation obtained by subtracting one of the equations* (11), (12) *from the other is therefore the equation of their common chord.* This is by far the simplest way of finding the equation of this line since it avoids the necessity of finding the coördinates of the points of intersection of the circles.

EXERCISES

Find the equations of the common chords of the following pairs of circles:

1. $x^2 + y^2 - 2x - 2y = 0$, $x^2 + y^2 - 4x + 3 = 0$.

2. $x^2 + y^2 = 25$, $x^2 + y^2 = 6x$.

3. $x^2 + y^2 + 4x - 2y - 4 = 0$, $x^2 + y^2 - 2x - y + 1 = 0$.

4. $x^2 + y^2 + 4x - 2y - 4 = 0$,
$36x^2 + 36y^2 - 72x - 24y + 31 = 0$.

5. $(x-3)^2 + (y-2)^2 = 4$, $(x-2)^2 + (y+1)^2 = 9$.

6. Find the equation of the straight line which connects the origin with the point of intersection of the lines

$$15x + 7y - 7 = 0,\ 3x + 7y - 3 = 0.$$

[SUGGESTION. Multiply the equations by constants in such a way that, when they are added, the constant term is eliminated.]

7. Find the equation of the straight line parallel to the axis of y and passing through the point of intersection of the lines of Problem 6.

8. Find the equation of the circle which passes through the origin and also through the points of intersection of the circles of Problem 3.

41. Multiplication of the Equations of Two or More Curves. If we start from the two lines

$$A_1x + B_1y + C_1 = 0, \tag{1}$$

$$A_2x + B_2y + C_2 - 0, \tag{2}$$

and multiply their equations together, we get the equation of the second degree

$$(A_1x + B_1y + C_1)(A_2x + B_2y + C_2) = 0. \tag{3}$$

This equation has as its locus the two lines (1) and (2). For, if (x_1, y_1) is any point on (1), we have

$$A_1x_1 + B_1y_1 + C_1 = 0.$$

Consequently, if we substitute (x_1, y_1) in (3), the first factor of (3) becomes zero, and we see that (x_1, y_1) lies on (3). Similarly, any point (x_2, y_2) of (2) also lies on (3). On the other hand, if (x_3, y_3) is a point which lies on neither (2) nor (3),

$$A_1x_3 + B_1y_3 + C_1 \neq 0.$$

$$A_2x_3 + B_2y_3 + C_2 \neq 0.$$

Hence, when (x_3, y_3) is substituted in (3), neither factor is zero, and (3) is not satisfied. Thus we have shown that all the points of (1) and (2), but no other points, lie on (3); that is, that the locus of (3) consists of the whole lines (1) and (2) and of nothing else.

The same reasoning applies without change if instead of starting from straight lines we start from any other curves, the general result being:

If the equations of two curves are written so that their right-hand members are zero, the equation formed by multiplying them together represents the two given curves and nothing else.*

This same principle may be looked at from the point of view of factoring rather than that of multiplication. If we have an equation in the variables (x, y) written in a form where its second member is zero, and if its first member can be resolved into the product of two factors, the locus of the original equation will consist of two parts; namely, the loci of the two equations obtained by equating each factor to zero. In this way we can sometimes determine the locus of a complicated equation.

* This restriction is essential. If, for instance, we take the lines $x = y$ and $x = -y$ (the bisectors of the angles between the coördinate axes) and multiply them together as they stand, we get the equation $x^2 = -y^2$, a null circle at the origin.

EXERCISES

Determine by factoring the loci of the following equations:

1. $xy = 0.$

2. $x^2 - y^2 = 0.$

3. $xy + 2y^2 = 0.$

4. $2x^2 - xy - 3y^2 = 0.$

5. $2x^2 - 3xy + x = 0.$

6. $x^3 + xy^2 - x = 0.$

7. $x^4 - y^4 - 4x^2 + 4y^2 = 0.$

8. $x^2y = xy^2.$

42. Oblique Coördinates. If in § 38 we replace the word *slope* by *direction ratio,* everything in this chapter applies to oblique coördinates except the application in § 40 to the problem of finding the common chord of two circles, — the equations there used no longer representing circles in oblique coördinates.

PROBLEMS TO CHAPTER VI

1. Find the equation of the tangent to the curve $y = x^3$ at the point $(-1, -1)$, and determine the other point at which this tangent meets the curve.

2. Prove that the slope of the tangent to the curve $y^2 = x^3$ at the point (x_1, y_1) is $\frac{3}{2}\sqrt[3]{y_1}$. Hence show that, near the origin, the curve is shaped as in Figure 37. The origin is called a *cusp* of the curve.

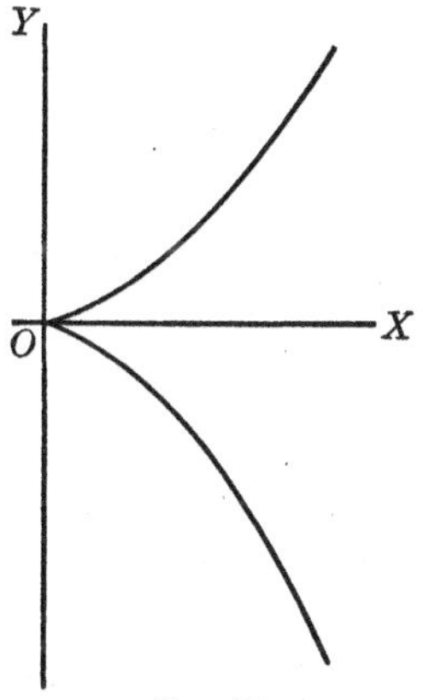

3. Find the equation of the tangent to the curve

$$y^2 = x^3 + x^2 - 6x$$

at the point (x_1, y_1).

4. Plot the curve of Problem 3, making the diagram more accurate by drawing the tangent at each point you plot.

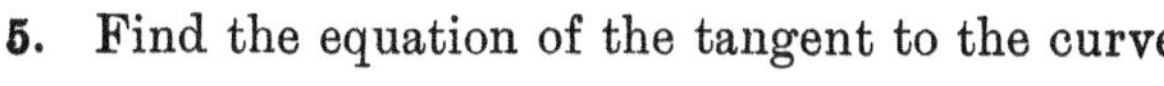

Fig. 37

5. Find the equation of the tangent to the curve

$$y^2 = x^3 + 3x^2$$

at the point (x_1, y_1), and use these tangents in plotting the curve.

6. Prove that the three lines

$$3x - y + 5 = 0,$$
$$2x + 3y + 2 = 0,$$
$$x - 4y + 3 = 0,$$

meet in a point.

[SUGGESTION. Show that the third equation may be obtained by multiplying the first two equations by suitable constants and adding them together.]

7. Prove that the three lines of Example 1, § 28 meet in a point by the method of Problem 6.

8. Prove Problems 1 and 2 at the end of Chapter III by the method of Problem 6.

9. Prove that the common chords of any three intersecting circles meet in a point.

10. If the equations

$$x^2 + y^2 + a_1x + b_1y + c_1 = 0,$$
$$x^2 + y^2 + a_2x + b_2y + c_2 = 0$$

represent two circles which are tangent to each other, prove that their difference represents the tangent at their point of contact.

11. If the second equation of Problem 10 represents a null circle which lies on the circle represented by the first equation, prove that their difference represents a tangent to the first circle. Show that this gives us a new method for establishing the formula for the tangent to a given circle at a given point.

12. Prove that the equation

$$ax^2 + bx + c = 0$$

either has no locus, or represents one straight line parallel to the y-axis, or represents two straight lines parallel to the y-axis.

13. Prove that the equation

$$ax^2 + bxy + cy^2 = 0$$

either represents a single point, or a single straight line, or two intersecting straight lines.

CHAPTER VII

TRANSFORMATION OF COÖRDINATES

43. Shifting Axes Without Change of Direction. It sometimes happens that we wish to change from one system of coördinate axes to another. We consider in this section the simplest case, in which any point (x_0, y_0) is taken as new origin, O', while the new coördinate axes, $O'X'$ and $O'Y'$, are parallel to the old axes of x and y respectively and have their positive directions in the same directions as the old axes. Let the coördinates of any point, P, be (x, y) when referred to the old axes, (x', y') when referred to the new. The projections of $O'P$ on the new coördinate axes are, by definition, x' and y'. These projections are equal to the projections of $O'P$ on the axes of x and y respectively, and these, by § 4, are $x - x_0$ and $y - y_0$. Consequently

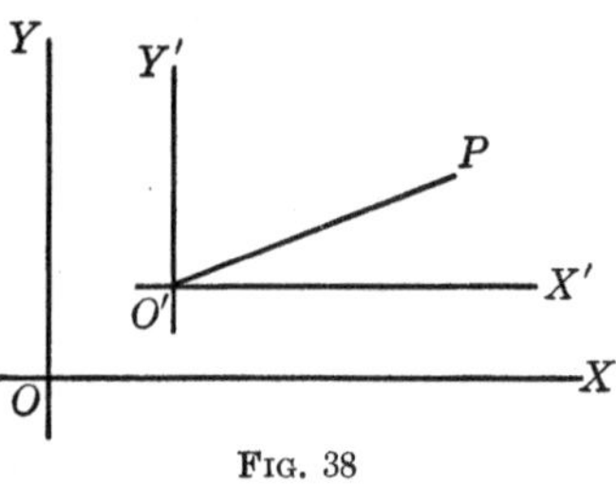

FIG. 38

$$(1)\begin{cases} x' = x - x_0, \\ y' = y - y_0, \end{cases} \quad \text{or} \quad (2)\begin{cases} x = x' + x_0, \\ y = y' + y_0. \end{cases}$$

These are the formulæ for transformation of coördinates. In the form (1) they express the new coördinates in terms of the old; while in the form (2) they express the old in terms of the new. Both forms are useful.

For instance, if the new origin is at (3, 1) and the coördinates of P in the old system were $(-1, 2)$, we find as the coördinates in the new system, by using (1),

$$x' = -1 - 3 = -4, \qquad y' = 2 - 1 = +1.$$

On the other hand, if we have the line whose equation in the old system was

$$2x - y + 7 = 0,$$

we use (2) and find as its equation in the new system

$$2(x' + 3) - (y' + 1) + 7 = 0$$

or, simplified,

$$2x' - y' + 12 = 0.$$

EXERCISES

1. Find the coördinates of the points (2, 3), (– 5, 7), (0, 2) in a system of coördinates whose origin is the point (1, 3).

2. Find the coördinates of the points (1, 0), (0, 0), (0, 1) in a system of coördinates whose origin is the point (2, – 1).

3. Find the equations of the curves

$$3x + 2y - 5 = 0,$$
$$5x - y + 2 = 0,$$
$$x^2 + y^2 - 6x + 4y + 12 = 0,$$
$$x^2 + y^2 = 25$$

in a system of coördinates whose origin is the point (3, – 2).

4. Find the equations of the curves of Exercise 3 in a system of coördinates whose origin is the point (5, 0).

44. Turning the Axes. Let us turn the positive halves, OX and OY, of the coördinate axes about the origin through the angle θ into the positions OX' and OY'. These two lines we use as a new set of coördinate axes.

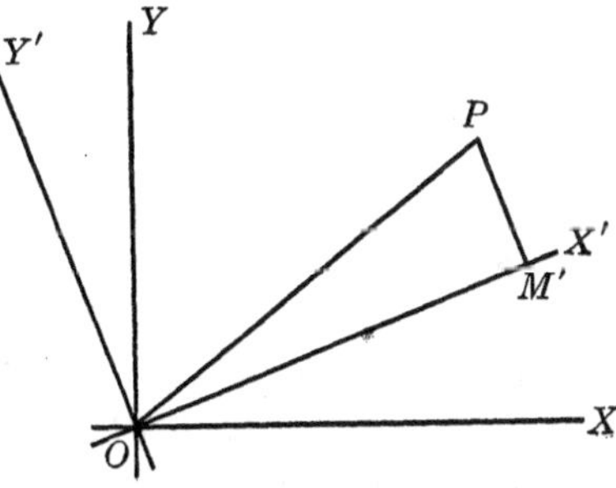

FIG. 39

Let P be any point in

the plane and call its coördinates referred to the old system (x, y), to the new system (x', y'). Let M' be the foot of the perpendicular dropped from P on the new axis of x. Then

$$OM' = x', \quad M'P = y'.$$

Now consider the projections on the old axes of the segments OM', $M'P$, and OP:

Proj. on x-axis of $OP = x$,

Proj. on x-axis of $OM' = OM' \cos\theta = x' \cos\theta$,

Proj. on x-axis of $M'P = M'P \cos(XOY')$
$$= y' \cos(\theta + 90°) = -y' \sin\theta.$$

Similarly,

Proj. on y-axis of $OP = y$,

Proj. on y-axis of $OM' = OM' \sin\theta = x' \sin\theta$,

Proj. on y-axis of $M'P = M'P \sin(XOY')$
$$= y' \sin(\theta + 90°) = y' \cos\theta.$$

Hence, applying to the broken line $OM'P$ the principle of § 2, we find

$$(1) \qquad \begin{cases} x = x' \cos\theta - y' \sin\theta, \\ y = x' \sin\theta + y' \cos\theta, \end{cases}$$

and these are the formulæ for expressing the old coördinates in terms of the new. The formulæ for expressing the new coördinates in terms of the old can be found either by solving the equations (1) for x', y', or directly from the figure. They are

$$(2) \qquad \begin{cases} x' = x \cos\theta + y \sin\theta, \\ y' = -x \sin\theta + y \cos\theta. \end{cases}$$

The general transformation from one system of rectangular coördinates to another will be one in which we have both a new origin and new directions for the coördinate axes. It would be easy to write down the formulæ for such a transformation, but it is hardly worth while to do so, since the transformation can easily be performed in two steps: we can first shift the coördinate axes without turning them until the origin comes to the desired position, using for this purpose the formulæ of § 43; and then turn the axes about the new origin until they have the desired directions,* using for this purpose the formulæ (1) and (2) above.

EXERCISES

1. Find the coördinates of the points (1, 0), (2, 2), (– 3, 4) referred to a system of rectangular coördinates obtained by turning the coördinate axes through an angle of 45°; of 30°.

2. Find the equation of the curve $xy = 1$ after the coördinate axes have been turned through an angle of 45°.

3. Find the equation of the curve $2x^2 = xy$ after the coördinate axes have been turned through the angle $\tan^{-1} 2$.

4. Show, by actually performing the transformation of coördinates, that the equation of a circle whose center is at the origin will not be changed by turning the coördinate axes through any angle.

5. Transform the equation of the curve

$$x^2 - 2xy + y^2 - 2x - 2y + 1 = 0$$

to a new pair of coördinate axes whose origin is the point $(\frac{1}{4}, \frac{1}{4})$ and which make angles of 45° with the old axes.

45. Order of Curves. It is clear that the degree of the equation of a curve cannot be raised by a transformation from one system of rectangular coördinates to another; for, whether we are using formula (2), § 43 or formula (1), § 44, the values we have to substitute for x and y in the given equation are of only the first degree in x' and y', and, consequently, no terms of higher degree will appear than those that were already present.

* This is possible since we consider only right-handed systems of rectangular coördinates (see § 3).

It is not so clear that the degree of the equation might not sometimes be lowered, since it would be conceivable that after the transformation all the terms of highest degree might destroy one another. Further consideration, however, shows that this is impossible. For suppose it did happen that an equation of the nth degree in (x, y) were reduced after the transformation to one of the mth degree in (x', y'). Then start afresh with the last-mentioned equation, — that in (x', y'), — and make the transformation which takes us back to the original (x, y) system. This transformation, of course, takes the equation back to its original form, that is, it raises its degree again to n. We have just seen, however, that no transformation can ever raise the degree of an equation. Consequently, the assumption that a transformation could lower the degree of an equation has led to a contradiction, and we see that every transformation leaves the degree unchanged.

We thus see that the degree of the equation which represents a given curve does not depend at all on the particular system of rectangular coördinates selected, but merely on the curve itself.* We may therefore use the degree of the equation as a means of classifying curves. The degree of the equation is called the *order* of the curve (or sometimes the *degree* of the curve), and thus we speak of curves of order one, of order two, etc. We know that straight lines constitute the class of curves of order one. Circles, we have seen, are curves of order two, but, as we shall see later, there are many other curves of order two which are not circles.

The classification just explained applies only to what are called *algebraic* curves, that is, curves whose equations,

* It is true that the same curve may be represented by equations of various degrees. For instance, the axis of y may be represented not merely by the equation $x = 0$ but also by the equation $x^2 = 0$; the pair of coördinate axes not merely by $xy = 0$ but also by $x^2y = 0$ and also by $xy^2 = 0$; etc. We usually represent the curve by the equation of lowest possible degree, and it is this degree we call the order of the curve.

when simplified as far as possible (cleared of fractions and of radicals), consist only of terms each of which is of the form $Cx^{\alpha}y^{\beta}$, where α and β are zero or positive integers. Other curves, of which $y = \log x$ and $y = 2^x$ are simple examples, are called *transcendental* curves, and have no orders.

EXERCISES

What are the orders of the following curves?

1. $x^3 + y^2 = x + 3$.
2. $xy = 1$.
3. $y = \dfrac{1}{x-1}$.
4. $x = \sqrt{y}$.
5. $\sqrt{x+1} + \sqrt{x-1} = y$.
6. $2^x + 2^{-x} = 2$.
7. $x^{\frac{2}{3}} + y^{\frac{2}{3}} = a^{\frac{2}{3}}$.
8. $y = \dfrac{1}{x+1} + \dfrac{1}{x-2}$.

46. Transformations of Oblique Coördinates. The formulæ of § 43 for changing from a first system of coördinates to a second system whose axes have the same directions as the old apply to the case of oblique coördinates precisely as they do to the case where the coördinates are rectangular.

Let us, then, consider the other case, in which the origin is not changed but the directions of the axes are altered. The formulæ in the general case here would be a little complicated and not very useful. We will therefore deduce the formulæ first in a special case, that in which the (x', y') system is rectangular and the x'-axis coincides both in position and direction with the x-axis. In Figure 40, let $OM = x$, $MP = y$, angle $XOY = \omega$, and consider the following orthogonal projections:

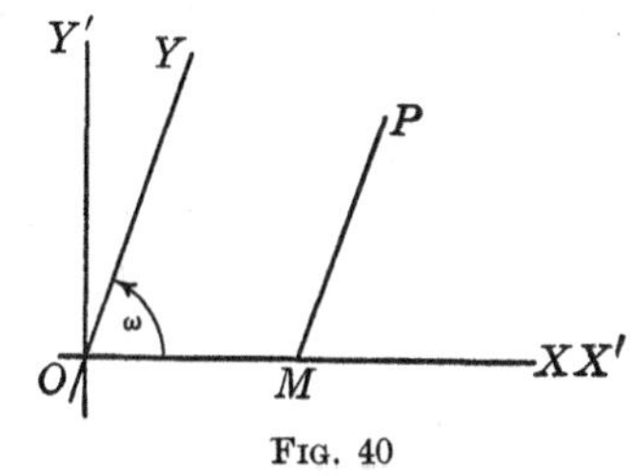

Fig. 40

Proj. of OM on x'-axis $= OM = x$,
Proj. of MP on x'-axis $= y \cos \omega$,
Proj. of OP on x'-axis $= x'$,
Proj. of OM on y'-axis $= 0$,
Proj. of MP on y'-axis $= y \sin \omega$,
Proj. of OP on y'-axis $= y'$.

Consequently, by the principle of § 2,

$$(1)\ \begin{cases} x' = x + y \cos \omega, \\ y' = y \sin \omega, \end{cases} \quad \text{or } (2)\ \begin{cases} x = x' - y' \operatorname{ctn} \omega, \\ y = y' \csc \omega. \end{cases}$$

By combining these formulæ with those of §§ 43, 44, we can pass from any system of Cartesian coördinates to any other such system. For this purpose we can first use formulæ (1) or (2) to pass to a rectangular system having the same origin and the same axis of x as the first given system. Then, by the formulæ of §§ 43, 44, we can pass to a new rectangular system having the same origin and the same axis of x as the second given system. Then, by means of (1) or (2), we pass to this system itself.

Since, in (1) and (2), one set of variables is replaced by expressions of the first degree in terms of the other set, the reasoning of § 45 is applicable, and we see that the degree of an equation is not changed by a transformation from any system of Cartesian coördinates to any other system.

The transformation (1) or (2) of this section may be used to deduce formulæ of various sorts referring to oblique coördinates when the corresponding formulæ for rectangular coördinates are known. We illustrate this by finding the formula for the area of a triangle whose vertices in oblique coördinates are (x_1, y_1), (x_2, y_2), (x_3, y_3).

By (1), these vertices in rectangular coördinates are

$$(x_1 + y_1 \cos\omega, y_1 \sin\omega),\ (x_2 + y_2 \cos\omega, y_2 \sin\omega),\ (x_3 + y_3 \cos\omega, y_3 \sin\omega).$$

The area of the triangle is, then, by formula (3), § 23,

$$\pm\tfrac{1}{2}[(y_1 - y_2)\sin\omega\,(x_3 + y_3\cos\omega) + (y_2 - y_3)\sin\omega\,(x_1 + y_1\cos\omega) \\ + (y_3 - y_1)\sin\omega\,(x_2 + y_2\cos\omega)],$$

and this reduces to the value given in § 27.

In conclusion we will deduce the formulæ, which are sometimes useful, for transforming from a system of rectangular coördinates to *any* system of oblique coördinates having the same origin. Let (x, y) be the rectangular system and (x', y') the oblique system. The angle from the positive half of the axis of x to the positive half of the axis of x' we call θ, the angle from the positive half of the axis of x' to the positive half of the axis of y', ω. We first turn the (x, y) system through the angle θ, thus getting a new rectangular system (x'', y''):

$$x = x'' \cos\theta - y'' \sin\theta,$$
$$y = x'' \sin\theta + y'' \cos\theta.$$

Since the axis of x'' and the axis of x' coincide, we can now pass to the (x', y') system by means of formulæ (1) of this section, which now become

$$x'' = x' + y' \cos\omega,$$
$$y'' = y' \sin\omega.$$

Combining these formulæ, we readily find, on letting $\theta + \omega = \theta_1$,

$$(3) \qquad \begin{cases} x = x' \cos\theta + y' \cos\theta_1, \\ y = x' \sin\theta + y' \sin\theta_1. \end{cases}$$

These are the formulæ for transforming from a rectangular system (x, y) to an oblique system (x', y') with the same origin, where the angles from the axis of x to the axes of x' and y' are θ and θ_1 respectively.

The general formulæ for transforming from oblique coördinates to oblique coördinates with the same origin will be found in Exercise 4.

EXERCISES

1. By using the method of transformation of coördinates, deduce the formula for the distance between two points in oblique coördinates. (See formula (1), § 9.)

2. Find the slope of the segment which connects the points whose oblique coördinates are (x_1, y_1) and (x_2, y_2).

3. The x and y' axes of a system of oblique coördinates make angles $-\theta$ and $+\theta$, respectively, with the x-axis of a system of rectangular coördinates. Show that the formulæ for transformation of coördinates are

$$x = (x' + y') \cos\theta,$$
$$y = (-x' + y') \sin\theta.$$

4. Show that the formulæ for transforming from any system of oblique coördinates to any other having the same origin are

$$x = x' \frac{\sin(x'y)}{\sin(xy)} + y' \frac{\sin(y'y)}{\sin(xy)},$$

$$y = x' \frac{\sin(xx')}{\sin(xy)} + y' \frac{\sin(xy')}{\sin(xy)}.$$

Here (xy) means the angle from the axis of x to the axis of y; $(x'y)$ the angle from the axis of x' to the axis of y; etc.

CHAPTER VIII

PROBLEMS IN THE DETERMINATION OF LOCI

47. Some Simple Cases. We have already determined the equations of certain simple loci. Thus in § 17 we found the equation of the locus of a point which moves so that the slope of the line connecting it with a fixed point is constant; and, in § 11, the locus of a point which moves so that its distance from a fixed point is constant. In these cases we had simply to express in algebraic language the law according to which the point moves. This same method can be employed in many other cases. We illustrate this by two examples.

Example 1. To find the locus of a point which moves so that the sum of the squares of its distances from two fixed points is a constant, which we will call $2a^2$.

Let us take the line connecting the two fixed points as axis of x and the point halfway between them as origin, so that the coördinates of the fixed points may be called $(c, 0)$ and $(-c, 0)$. Let (x, y) be the moving point. The squares of the distances from this point to the two fixed points are

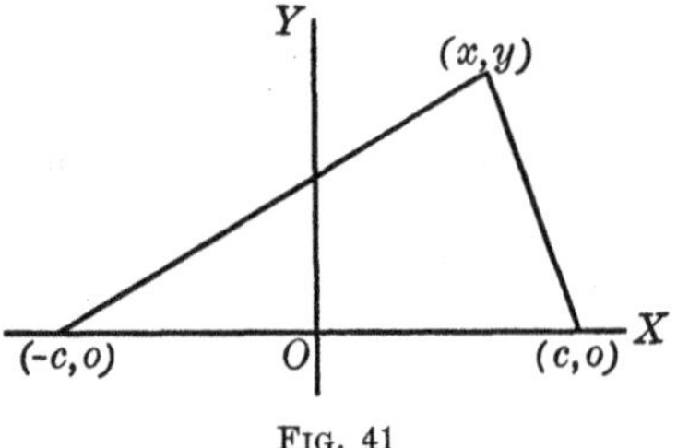

FIG. 41

$$(x-c)^2+y^2 \text{ and } (x+c)^2+y^2.$$

Hence, for any position of the moving point,

(1) $$(x-c)^2+y^2+(x+c)^2+y^2=2a^2,$$

or

(2) $$2x^2+2y^2+2c^2=2a^2,$$

or

(3) $$x^2+y^2=a^2-c^2.$$

Conversely, if (x, y) satisfies (3), it satisfies (2) and hence also (1); and this equation tells us that the sum of the squares of the distances of the moving point from the two fixed points is $2a^2$. Hence, not only does every point of the locus satisfy (3), but, conversely, every point which satisfies (3) is a point of the locus. In other words, (3) is the equation of the locus. Hence, if $a^2 > c^2$, the locus is a circle with center halfway between the two fixed points. If $a^2 = c^2$, the locus is a single point, namely, the point halfway between the two fixed points. If $a^2 < c^2$, there is no locus; that is, it is impossible for a point to be so situated that the sum of the squares of its distances from two fixed points should be less than twice the square of half the segment connecting them.

Example 2. To find the locus of a point which moves so that the sum of its distances from two fixed points is a constant, $2a$, greater than the distance between the points.*

We choose our axes as before and find, precisely as above, that for every point of the locus

$$\sqrt{(x-c)^2+y^2}+\sqrt{(x+c)^2+y^2}=2a, \tag{4}$$

and that, conversely, any point (x, y) which satisfies (4) is a point of our locus.

Let us see if we cannot get an equation for the locus in a form free from radicals. Transposing the second radical in (4) and squaring, we find

$$(x-c)^2+y^2=4a^2-4a\sqrt{(x+c)^2+y^2}+(x+c)^2+y^2, \tag{5}$$

or

$$4a\sqrt{(x+c)^2+y^2}=4a^2+4cx. \tag{6}$$

If we divide this by 4 and square, we get

$$a^2(x+c)^2+a^2y^2=a^4+2a^2cx+c^2x^2,$$

or

$$(a^2-c^2)x^2+a^2y^2=a^2(a^2-c^2). \tag{7}$$

* If $2a$ were less than the distance between the points, there would evidently be no locus, while if it were equal to this distance, the locus would clearly be the segment connecting the points.

This is an equation of the sort we want which is satisfied by the coördinates of every point on the locus. It is not so obvious, however, that every point whose coördinates satisfy (7) is a point of the locus.* For if (x, y) satisfies (7), we cannot infer that it necessarily satisfies (6), but merely that it must satisfy one of the relations

$$\pm 4a\sqrt{(x+c)^2+y^2} = 4a^2 + 4cx,$$

and from this we work back, by means of an equation analogous to (5), not to (4) but to

$$(8) \qquad \pm\sqrt{(x-c)^2+y^2} \pm \sqrt{(x+c)^2+y^2} = 2a,$$

an equation in which there is no necessary connection, so far as we can yet see, between the two ambiguous signs. Since $2a$ is positive, these signs cannot both be minus. On the other hand, one cannot be plus and the other minus for then the difference of the distances from (x, y) to the two fixed points would be $2a$, and this quantity, by hypothesis, is greater than the distance between the points. This, by elementary geometry, is impossible. Hence both signs in (8) are plus, and (x, y) is really a point of the locus. The equation of the locus can therefore be written not only in the irrational form (4) but equally well in the rational form (7). The locus is therefore a curve of the second order. It is the curve which we shall define in § 52 as the ellipse.

EXERCISES

Find the locus of a point which moves in each of the following ways:

1. So that the difference of the squares of its distances from two fixed points is constant.

2. So that the sum of the squares of its distances from the vertices of a square is constant.

* When we clear of radicals, as we have done here, it will frequently happen that the resulting equation gives us not merely the locus we want but also certain extraneous loci, just as, in elementary algebra, when we have a radical equation, the effect of clearing of radicals is often to introduce certain extraneous roots.

3. So that it is twice as far from a first fixed point as from a second.

4. So that the sum of the squares of its distances from the sides, or sides produced, of a square is constant.

48. The Use of Auxiliary Variables. In many cases the method so far used becomes difficult if not impossible to apply. We may then proceed as follows:

Example 1. A variable line is drawn parallel to the base, AB, of a fixed triangle, ABC, and meets the sides in the points D, E. These points are joined crosswise with the ends of the base. To find the locus of the point of intersection of these joining lines.

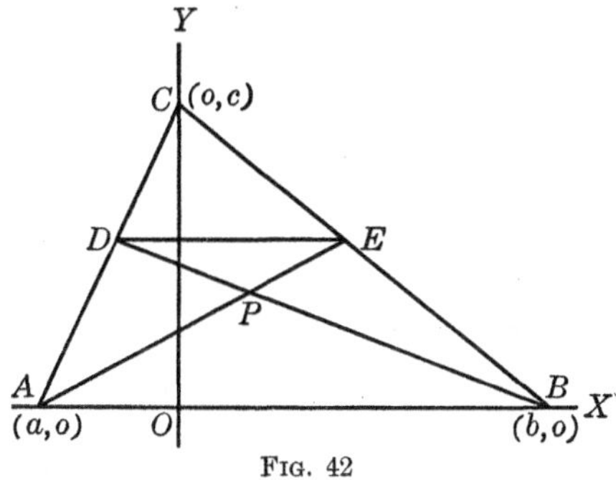

Fig. 42

We choose the coördinates as indicated in Figure 42. Let (X, Y) be the point of intersection, P, of AE and BD. The coördinates X, Y of the point whose locus we want to find we shall call the *principal variables*, and we now introduce as *auxiliary variable*, s, the distance the moving line DE lies above the axis of x. As the line DE moves, all three quantities X, Y, s vary. Let us first regard the line DE as having a fixed but arbitrary position, so that, for the moment, X, Y, s are constants. The equations of the lines AC, BC, DE are

AC $$\frac{x}{a}+\frac{y}{c}=1,$$

BC $$\frac{x}{b}+\frac{y}{c}=1,$$

DE $$y=s.$$

Solving the last of these equations as simultaneous with each of the first two, we find as the coördinates of D and E, respectively,

$$\left(\frac{a}{c}(c-s),\, s\right), \quad \left(\frac{b}{c}(c-s),\, s\right).$$

Hence, we find as the equations of the lines AE and BD

AE $$csx + [bs + (a-b)c]y - acs = 0,$$

BD $$csx + [as + (b-a)c]y - bcs = 0.$$

Since (X, Y) lies on both of these lines, we have

$$csX + [bs + (a-b)c]\,Y - acs = 0,$$

$$csX + [as + (b-a)c]\,Y - bcs = 0.$$

These are relations which are always satisfied by the variables X, Y, s. Let us eliminate s between these equations. This can be done in this case by adding the equations and dividing by s:

$$2\,cX + (a+b)\,Y - (a+b)c = 0,$$

or

$$\frac{2\,X}{a+b} + \frac{Y}{c} = 1.$$

Consequently, the point P always lies on the line

(1) $$\frac{2\,x}{a+b} + \frac{y}{c} = 1,$$

that is, the line through the vertex C of the triangle and the middle point of the base.

It would be a mistake to think that we have proved that this line (1) is the locus required, for we have not proved that P can occupy every position on it, but merely that it can never move off this line. What we have proved, then, is that the desired locus forms the whole *or some part* of this indefinite line. As a matter of fact, it is easy to see from the figure that the locus is not the whole line (1) but merely the segment between the vertex C and the middle point of the base.*

Example 2. A right triangle moves so that the ends of its hypotenuse rest on two fixed lines at right angles to each other. Find the locus of the vertex of the right angle.

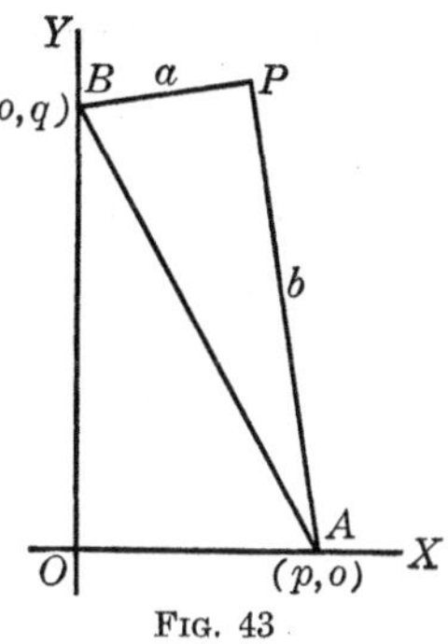

FIG. 43

We take the two fixed lines as coördinate axes and call the intercepts of the hypotenuse p and q. These quantities are therefore auxiliary variables. The coördinates of P are the principal variables (x, y). Let us call the lengths of the two sides of the triangle, as indicated in Figure 43, a and b. These must be regarded as known constants. By expressing the fact that AB, AP, BP have respectively the lengths $\sqrt{a^2+b^2}$, b, a, we find

$$(1) \qquad p^2+q^2=a^2+b^2,$$

$$(2) \qquad (x-p)^2+y^2=b^2,$$

$$(3) \qquad x^2+(y-q)^2=a^2.$$

Between these equations we must eliminate the auxiliary variables p, q. From (2) and (3) we find

$$p=x\pm\sqrt{b^2-y^2},$$
$$q=y\pm\sqrt{a^2-x^2},$$

which, substituted in (1), give

$$\pm x\sqrt{b^2-y^2}=\pm y\sqrt{a^2-x^2}.$$

Squaring this, we find

$$b^2x^2-a^2y^2=0.$$

* If we modify our problem by allowing the moving line to meet the sides of the triangle *or the sides produced* in D, E, the analytic work of our solution will not be in any way affected, but the locus will now be the whole line (1).

By factoring, we see that this equation represents the two straight lines

$$(4) \qquad bx + ay = 0, \qquad bx - ay = 0,$$

which pass through the origin and have slopes $\pm \frac{b}{a}$.

The desired locus therefore consists of these two lines *or some parts of them.* It is easy to see geometrically, or from equations (2) and (3), that in any position of the moving triangle $x^2 \leqq a^2$, $y^2 \leqq b^2$. Consequently, the distance from P to the origin can never exceed $\sqrt{a^2 + b^2}$; that is, the locus cannot extend away from the origin beyond the points $(\pm a, \pm b)$. Since the triangle can evidently be so placed as to bring P into any one of these four positions, and can then be moved gradually, A and B always remaining on the axes of x and y respectively, until P coincides with the origin, we see that the locus consists of that part of the two lines (4) which lies at a distance from the origin not greater than $\sqrt{a^2 + b^2}$.

The general principle involved in the foregoing examples may be formulated as follows: If we introduce a number of auxiliary variables in treating a locus problem, we must deduce from the data of our problem a number of equations connecting these auxiliary variables with each other or with the principal variables (the coördinates of the point which traces the locus). There must be found one more such equation than there are auxiliary variables, and the auxiliary variables must be eliminated between them. The equation thus obtained must involve only the principal variables and constants, and represents a curve which, *or some part of which,* is the desired locus.

If, in the course of the work, we use the equations of certain lines or curves in the figure, which will then involve the variables (x, y), these letters cannot safely be used for the principal variables, which may then conveniently be denoted by (X, Y).

EXERCISES

1. Find the locus of the foot of the perpendicular dropped from a fixed point on a line revolving about another fixed point.

[Suggestion. Take the line connecting the fixed points as axis of x and one of these points as origin. Use the slope of the revolving line as auxiliary variable.]

2. Find the locus of the middle point of a line of constant length which moves so that its ends rest on two indefinite fixed lines at right angles to each other.

49. Use of Formulæ for Sum and Product of Roots of a Quadratic Equation. It is proved in elementary algebra that if x_1, x_2 are the roots of the equation

$$ax^2 + bx + c = 0,$$

then

$$x_1 + x_2 = -\frac{b}{a}, \quad x_1 x_2 = \frac{c}{a}.$$

These formulæ are often useful in analytic geometry, both in solving locus problems and elsewhere. This is illustrated by the following

Example. A chord of a fixed circle swings around a fixed point. Find the locus of its middle point.

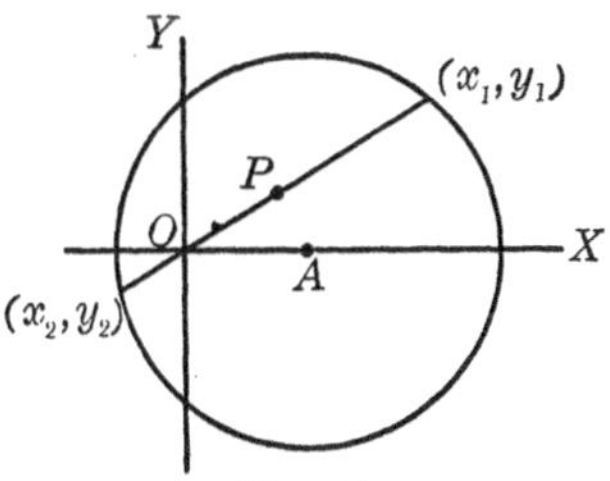

Let us take the fixed point, O, as origin, and the diameter through it as axis of x. Let $(a, 0)$ be the center, A, of the circle. The equation of the circle may, then, be written

Fig. 44

(1) $$(x - a)^2 + y^2 = r^2.$$

We introduce the slope, λ, of the moving chord as auxiliary variable. The equation of this chord in any one of its positions is, then,

(2) $$y = \lambda x.$$

The extremities of this chord we will call (x_1, y_1) and (x_2, y_2). These coördinates will be found by solving (1) and (2) as simultaneous equations. Substituting the value of y from (2) in (1), we find on collecting terms

$$(1+\lambda^2)x^2 - 2\,ax + (a^2 - r^2) = 0, \tag{3}$$

an equation whose roots are x_1 and x_2.

By the property of quadratic equations referred to above, we have

$$x_1 + x_2 = \frac{2\,a}{1+\lambda^2}.$$

If now we denote by (X, Y) the coördinates of the point P whose locus we are seeking, we have

$$X = \frac{x_1 + x_2}{2} = \frac{a}{1+\lambda^2}. \tag{4}$$

A second equation connecting X, Y, λ may be found by using the fact that P lies on (2), so that

$$Y = \lambda X. \tag{5}$$

We now eliminate λ between (4) and (5) by finding its value from (5) and substituting it in (4). This gives

$$X = \frac{a}{1 + \frac{Y^2}{X^2}},$$

or

$$X + \frac{Y^2}{X} = a.$$

Clearing of fractions, and replacing the large letters by small ones, we get, finally,

$$x^2 + y^2 = ax \tag{6}$$

as the equation of the locus. This equation represents the circle described on OA as diameter, and it is easily seen that the whole of this circle is the locus if O lies within the circle (1), while if O lies outside of (1), only so much of (6) as lies inside of (1) is the locus.

EXERCISES

1. Find the locus of the middle point of a chord of the circle $x^2 + y^2 = a^2$ which moves so that it always has slope 2.

[SUGGESTION. Take the equation of the moving chord in the form $y = 2x + b$, where b is an auxiliary variable.]

2. Find the locus of the middle point of a moving chord of the curve $xy = 1$ which has the constant slope λ.

50. Polar Coördinates. Some locus problems admit of particularly simple solution by the use of polar coördinates.

Example. OA is a fixed diameter of a fixed circle. At A a tangent is drawn, while about O a secant revolves which meets the tangent in S and the circle in R. Find the locus of the point, P, so situated on the segment OS that $OP = RS$.

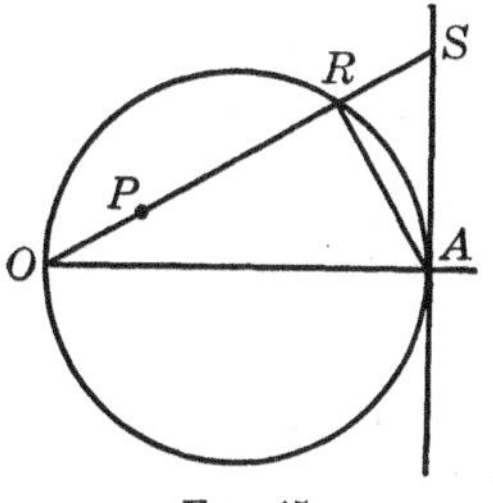

FIG. 45

We take O as origin and OA as initial line of a system of polar coördinates. The length OA we denote by a, and the polar coördinates of P by (r, ϕ). Then, since the angle ORA is a right angle,

$$PS = OR = a \cos \phi.$$

On the other hand,

$$OS = \frac{a}{\cos \phi}.$$

Hence

$$r = OP = OS - PS = \frac{a}{\cos \phi} - a \cos \phi.$$

Thus the equation of the desired locus is

$$r = \frac{a \sin^2 \phi}{\cos \phi},$$

which, when transformed to rectangular coördinates, becomes

$$x(x^2 + y^2) = ay^2.$$

This is a curve of the third order, known as the *Cissoid of Diocles*. It may be plotted from the equation, or directly from the statement of the locus problem given above. It will be found to have a cusp at O, and the line AS as asymptote.

EXERCISES

1. A chord, OA, swings about a fixed point, O, on a circle. A constant length is laid off in both directions along this chord from the point A. Find the locus of the two points thus reached. This locus is known as the *Limaçon of Pascal*.

2. A straight line revolves about a fixed point, O, and meets a fixed straight line in R. From R a fixed length is laid off in both directions along OR. Find the locus of the two points thus reached. This locus is called the *Conchoid of Nicomedes*.

51. Oblique Coördinates. The advantage which may sometimes be gained by the use of oblique coördinates in solving locus problems is that the coördinate axes may frequently be chosen in a more intimate relation to the figure if it is not necessary to take them at right angles to each other. This advantage, however, is usually very dearly bought if, in the course of the work, formulæ have to be used which are less simple for oblique than for rectangular systems. As a rule, therefore, problems involving lengths of lines or magnitudes of angles (including right angles) had better be treated by rectangular coördinates.

Where oblique coördinates are used, the method of work will be exactly the same as that explained in the present chapter for rectangular coördinates.

PROBLEMS TO CHAPTER VIII

In the following problems it must be remembered that the coördinate axes used are merely an instrument for getting a geometric result.* The axes may be chosen at pleasure, but the final result must be stated in a form which has no reference to these axes. In particular, merely giving the

* Except in Problem 8, where a formula is called for.

equation of the locus is not sufficient; this equation must be interpreted.

1. Find the locus of a point the sum of the squares of whose distances from the sides, or sides preduced, of an equilateral triangle is equal to the square of the altitude of the triangle.

Ans. The circle circumscribed about the triangle.

2. Find the locus of the point the ratio of whose distances from two fixed points has a given constant value.

Ans. A circle described on a segment as diameter whose ends divide the segment connecting the given points internally and externally in the given ratio.

3. Find the locus of a point the ratio of the square of whose distance from a fixed point to its distance from a fixed line has a given constant value.

4. Two vertices of a triangle are fixed, and the length of the line joining one of these vertices to the middle of the opposite side is constant. Find the locus of the third vertex.

5. A rectangle is constructed by drawing a variable line parallel to the base of a fixed triangle and dropping perpendiculars on the base from the points where this variable line meets the sides of the triangle. Find the locus of the center of this rectangle.

6. A moving line is drawn parallel to the base of a fixed triangle and is terminated by its sides. Find the locus of the point which divides this line in a given ratio.

7. Two straight lines revolve in a plane about two fixed points, one revolving twice as fast as the other. They start in coincidence. Find the locus of their intersection.

8. Find the equation of the perpendicular bisector of the segment from (x_1, y_1) to (x_2, y_2) by regarding this line as the locus of a point equidistant from the two given points.

9. AB is a fixed diameter of a circle, and R a moving point on the circle. At R a tangent is drawn, and a perpendicular is dropped on this tangent from B. Find the locus of the point of intersection of this last line with the line AR.

10. AB is a fixed chord of a circle, and R a moving point on this circle. Find the locus of the point of intersection of the altitudes of the triangle ABR.

11. A chord revolves about a fixed point, A, of a circle and meets a fixed chord perpendicular to the diameter through A in R. Find the locus of a point on the revolving chord whose distance from A is a mean proportional between the length of the revolving chord and the length AR.

12. Find the locus of the intersection of perpendiculars erected to the sides of a fixed triangle at points equidistant from the ends of the base.

13. A line revolves about a point, A, and meets a fixed circle in P_1 and P_2. Find the locus of a point, P, so situated on this line that the reciprocals of the segments AP_1, AP, AP_2 are in arithmetical progression.

[SUGGESTION. The projections of these segments on the axis of x also have the property that their reciprocals are in arithmetical progression.]

14. A line revolves about a point, A, and meets a fixed circle in P_1 and P_2. Find the locus of a point, P, so situated on this line that AP is a mean proportional between AP_1 and AP_2.

CHAPTER IX

THE CONIC SECTIONS — THEIR SHAPES AND THEIR STANDARD EQUATIONS

52. Definitions. Three curves, the ellipse, the hyperbola, and the parabola, are commonly grouped together under the name *conic section*, since they can all be obtained as plane sections of a right circular cone, and it was from this point of view that they were first studied by the Greek geometers.* In the present chapter we shall study these curves individually, starting from the following definitions:

AN ELLIPSE is the locus of a point which moves in a plane so that the sum of its distances from two fixed points of the plane, called the foci, is a constant greater than the distance between the foci.

A HYPERBOLA is the locus of a point which moves in a plane so that the difference of its distances from two fixed points of the plane, called the foci, is a positive constant less than the distance between the foci.

A PARABOLA is the locus of a point which moves in a plane so that it is always at the same distance from a fixed point of the plane, called the focus, as from a fixed line of the plane, called the directrix, which does not pass through the focus.

Any circle may clearly be regarded as the special case of an ellipse in which the two foci coincide at the center of the circle.

The foci of a hyperbola cannot coincide, since the difference of the distances of a point on the locus would then be

* Apollonius (B.C. 200, approximately) is the greatest of the Greek geometers who made a special study of conic sections.

zero, which is not "a positive constant less than the distance between the foci."

53. Equation and Shape of Ellipse. Center, Axes, Eccentricity, Vertices. In § 47, Example 2, we found the equation of the ellipse taking as axis of x the line connecting the foci, and as origin the point halfway between the foci. Calling the distance between the foci $2c$, and the sum of the distances from any point of the ellipse $2a$, the equation was

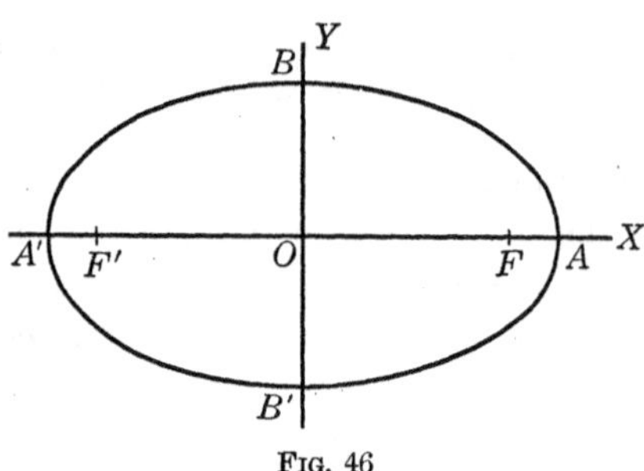

FIG. 46

$$\text{(1)} \qquad \frac{x^2}{a^2} + \frac{y^2}{a^2 - c^2} = 1.$$

The intercepts of this curve on the axis of x are $\pm a$, those on the axis of y, $\pm b$, where

$$\text{(2)} \qquad b = \sqrt{a^2 - c^2}.$$

In terms of a and b, equation (1) becomes

$$\text{(3)} \qquad \boldsymbol{\frac{x^2}{a^2} + \frac{y^2}{b^2} = 1},$$

which is the standard form for the equation of the ellipse.

In the special case when the foci coincide, $c = 0$; so that, by (2), $b = a$. Equation (3) then reduces to the standard form of the equation of the circle with center at the origin and radius a.

Let us, however, assume that $c > 0$. Then the indefinite straight line connecting the foci is called the *transverse axis*, the perpendicular bisector of the segment terminated by the foci is called the *conjugate axis* of the ellipse. The lengths of the portions of these axes included within the curve are called the lengths of the transverse and conjugate axes respectively:

$$A'A = 2\,a, \quad B'B = 2\,b.$$

Since, oy (2), $b < a$, we see that the length of the transverse axis is always greater than the length of the conjugate axis. Consequently the segments $A'A$ and $B'B$ are commonly spoken of as the *major* and *minor* axes respectively; a and b are called the semi-major and the semi-minor axes.

The curve is evidently symmetrical with regard to both of these axes.

The point, O, halfway between the foci is called the *center* of the ellipse. It is clear that any chord through the center is bisected there.

The two points A' and A where the transverse axis meets the ellipse are called the *vertices* of the ellipse.

The curve can readily be described by fastening the ends of a string of length $2\,a$ to pins inserted at the foci and pressing the point of the pencil against this string so as to keep it taut.* The pencil can then slip along the string and describe a curve, which will be the desired ellipse, since the sum of the distances from the pencil-point to the two foci is always equal to the whole length of the string, $2\,a$. The curve is thus seen to have the shape indicated in Figure 46. It is clear that the *shape* of the curve (as distinguished from its size) depends only on the ratio of the length of the string to the distance between the foci. For instance, we shall have an ellipse of the same shape if we take a string three inches long and fasten its ends at points two inches apart as if we take a string three feet long and fasten its ends at points two feet apart. This ratio

$$(4) \qquad e = \frac{c}{a} = \frac{\sqrt{a^2 - b^2}}{a},$$

* Or, better still, by tying together the two ends of a string of length $2\,(a + c)$ and placing the loop thus formed around the pins at the foci.

which determines the shape of the ellipse is called its *eccentricity*. In the case of the circle it is zero; otherwise, it is a positive constant less than one.

EXERCISES

1. Find the values of a, b, c, e for the ellipse $\frac{x^2}{25}+\frac{y^2}{16}=1.$ What are the coördinates of its foci and vertices?

2. Find the equation of the ellipse whose foci are the points $(\pm 2, 0)$, and one of whose vertices is the point $(3, 0)$.

3. The length of the major axis of an ellipse is 6. Find the equation of the ellipse and the coördinates of its foci if

$$(a)\ e=\tfrac{1}{2}, \qquad (b)\ e=\tfrac{1}{3}\sqrt{5}, \qquad (c)\ e=0.$$

Draw the figure of the ellipse in each case.

4. What are the major and the minor axes of the ellipses $4x^2+25y^2-100=0$, $2x^2+5y^2-10=0$, $3x^2+4y^2-5=0$?

[SUGGESTION. Transpose the constant term, and divide by it.]

54. The Equation of the Hyperbola. Let us take the line connecting the foci as axis of x and the point halfway between the foci as origin; and call the distance between the foci $2c$ and the difference of the distances from the moving point to the foci $2a$. The equation

$$(1) \qquad \sqrt{(x+c)^2+y^2}-\sqrt{(x-c)^2+y^2}=2a$$

represents those parts of the curve nearer to $(c, 0)$ than to $(-c, 0)$, while the remainder of the curve is represented by

$$(2) \qquad \sqrt{(x-c)^2+y^2}-\sqrt{(x+c)^2+y^2}=2a.$$

If we clear equation (1) of radicals, as in § 47, Example 2, we find

$$(3) \qquad \frac{x^2}{a^2}+\frac{y^2}{a^2-c^2}=1,$$

and this equation is also found by clearing (2) of radicals. Thus the single equation (3) represents all parts of the curve. It also represents all curves whose equations are obtained from (1) by changing the signs of the radicals in any way; that is, not merely (2), but also

(4) $$\sqrt{(x+c)^2+y^2}+\sqrt{(x-c)^2+y^2}=2\,a,$$

(5) $$-\sqrt{(x+c)^2+y^2}-\sqrt{(x-c)^2+y^2}=2\,a.$$

These equations, however, have no locus; for, since by hypothesis $a < c$ (see the definition of the hyperbola), (4) demands that P move so that the sum of two sides of a triangle be less than the third side, while (5) requires that the sum of two negative quantities be positive. Thus, finally, we see that (3) has as its locus the whole hyperbola and nothing else.

This result seems, at first sight, paradoxical, since (3) is identical with equation (1), § 53, and that equation represented an ellipse. This paradox is resolved by noticing that there we had $a > c$, whereas now $a < c$, so that in (1), § 53, the denominator of the second term was positive, while now it is negative. In view of this fact, we will write (3) in the form

(6) $$\frac{x^2}{a^2}-\frac{y^2}{c^2-a^2}=1.$$

By letting $y=0$, we find as the intercepts on the axis of x the values $\pm a$. By letting $x=0$, we see that the curve does not meet the axis of y at all, as is also obvious from the definition.

If we use the letter b to indicate the value of the real positive quantity

(7) $$b=\sqrt{c^2-a^2},$$

equation (6) takes the form

(8) $$\boldsymbol{\frac{x^2}{a^2}-\frac{y^2}{b^2}=1,}$$

which is the standard form for the equation of the hyperbola.

It should be noticed that, in the case of the hyperbola, b is *not* the intercept on the axis of y, there being no such intercept; and also that the formula (7) for b is different from the corresponding formula in the case of the ellipse; namely, (2), § 53.

55. Shape of Hyperbola. Center, Axes, Eccentricity, Vertices. In order to examine the shape of the hyperbola, we solve equation (8), § 54 for y, getting

$$(1) \qquad y = \pm \frac{b}{a}\sqrt{x^2 - a^2}.$$

The double sign here shows that the curve is symmetrical with regard to the axis of x. From the fact that only the square of x enters, so that the value of y will be the same whether we assign to x a positive or the corresponding negative value, we see that the curve is also symmetrical with respect to the axis of y. Hence it will be sufficient to examine the shape of the curve in the first quadrant. We therefore suppose x positive, and use the upper sign in (1).

When $x < a$, y is imaginary. When $x = a$, $y = 0$. When $x > a$, y is real, and, as x, starting from the value a, increases indefinitely, y, starting from the value zero, also increases indefinitely. We thus see that the hyperbola is shaped as indicated in Figure 47. It consists of two *branches*, one to the right of the axis of y, the other to the left. The points, A and A', where the curve crosses the axis of x are called its *vertices*. Since $c > a$ (see § 54), the foci lie, as indicated in the figure, further from the origin than the vertices.

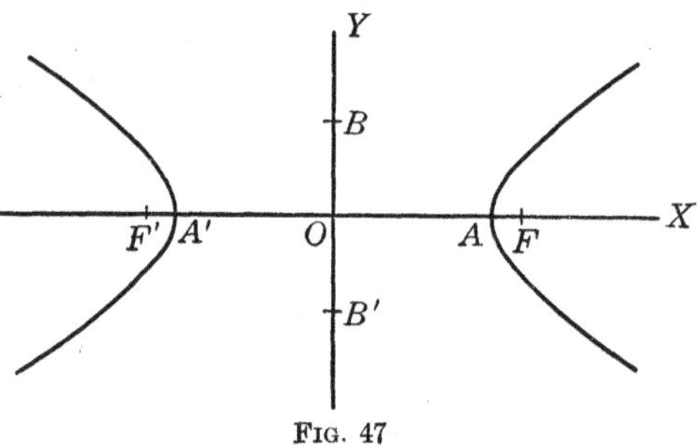

FIG. 47

The indefinite straight line connecting the foci (here the axis of x) is called the *transverse axis* of the hyperbola; a term which is also used for the segment $A'A$, and also for the length, $2a$, of this segment. The point halfway between the foci (the origin, O, in Figure 47) is called the *center* of the hyperbola. The indefinite straight line through the center perpendicular to the transverse axis is called the *conjugate axis*. On this line we lay off the distances OB, OB' equal to b; and the segment $B'B$ is also referred to as the conjugate axis, as is also its length, $2b$.

It is clear that, as in the case of the ellipse, the shape of the hyperbola will not depend on the magnitudes of a and c, but merely on their ratio

$$(2) \qquad e = \frac{c}{a} = \frac{\sqrt{a^2 + b^2}}{a}.$$

This ratio, which in the case of the hyperbola is greater than 1 while for the ellipse it was less than 1, is called the *eccentricity* of the hyperbola.

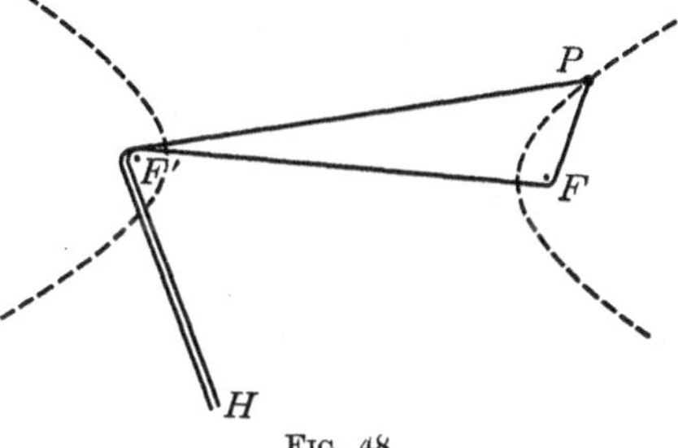

FIG. 48

The following device makes it possible to describe the hyperbola by continuous motion of a pencil-point: tie a pencil, P, firmly at a point near the middle of a string, and pass the two parts of the string around two pegs at F' and F. Holding both parts of the string together at H, pull them downward. The point P then describes an arc of a hyperbola.

EXERCISES

1. The difference of the distances of a point on a hyperbola from the foci is 6, and the foci are the points $(\pm 5, 0)$.

Find the equation of the curve, the lengths of the transverse and conjugate axes, the value of the eccentricity, and the coördinates of the vertices.

2. Solve Exercise 1 if the coördinates of the foci are changed to $(\pm 6, 0)$.

3. What are the foci, vertices, and eccentricities of the hyperbolas

$$\frac{x^2}{25} - \frac{y^2}{16} = 1, \qquad \frac{x^2}{16} - \frac{y^2}{25} = 1?$$

4. Find the axes and foci for the following hyperbolas:

$$x^2 - 4y^2 = 4, \quad 2x^2 - 3y^2 = 6, \quad 5x^2 - 6y^2 = 1.$$

5. Find the equation of the hyperbola whose foci are the points $(\pm 3, 0)$, and whose eccentricity is 2.

6. Find the equation of the hyperbola whose vertices are the points $(\pm 3, 0)$, and whose eccentricity is 2.

7. An ellipse and hyperbola with eccentricities e_1 and e_2 have the same foci, $(\pm c, 0)$. Prove the x coördinates of their points of intersection are $\pm \frac{c}{e_1 e_2}$.

56. The Asymptotes of the Hyperbola. We can get important new information about the shape of the hyperbola by using polar coördinates.

Equation (8), § 54, when transformed to polar coördinates with origin at O and with the positive half of the axis of x as initial line, becomes

$$\frac{r^2 \cos^2 \phi}{a^2} - \frac{r^2 \sin^2 \phi}{b^2} = 1,$$

or, solved for r,

$$r = \pm \frac{ab}{\sqrt{b^2 \cos^2 \phi - a^2 \sin^2 \phi}}.$$

We will consider only points in the first quadrant; that is, we restrict ourselves to values of the angle ϕ in the first quadrant and to positive values of r. After taking out the factor $a^2 \cos^2 \phi$ from under the radical sign, we may then write

$$r = \frac{b}{\cos \phi \sqrt{\frac{b^2}{a^2} - \tan^2 \phi}}.$$

As ϕ increases, starting from the value zero, $\tan \phi$ increases, and consequently the radical in the denominator of r decreases. The other factor in the denominator, $\cos \phi$, also decreases. Consequently r increases. This increase goes on until the radical has decreased to the value zero, that is, until $\tan \phi = \frac{b}{a}$. When ϕ has a greater value than this, the quantity under the radical sign is negative, and r is imaginary. Thus we see that, in the first quadrant, the hyperbola lies wholly below the line through the origin with slope $\frac{b}{a}$, that is, the line

(1) $$bx - ay = 0.$$

We will now show that this line is an asymptote of the hyperbola. For this purpose we must prove that if a point (x_1, y_1) moves out along the hyperbola, its distance, δ, from the line (1) approaches zero. By formula (4), § 22,

$$\delta = \pm \frac{bx_1 - ay_1}{\sqrt{a^2 + b^2}}.$$

Since (x_1, y_1) lies on the hyperbola, we have

$$b^2 x_1^2 - a^2 y_1^2 = a^2 b^2.$$

Hence

$$bx_1 - ay_1 = \frac{a^2 b^2}{bx_1 + ay_1}.$$

Consequently

$$\delta = \pm \frac{a^2 b^2}{\sqrt{a^2 + b^2}} \cdot \frac{1}{bx_1 + ay_1}.$$

Now, as (x_1, y_1) moves out along the curve, both x_1 and y_1 increase indefinitely, and the same is therefore true of

$bx_1 + ay_1$. Consequently, δ approaches zero, as was to be proved.

From the fact that the curve is symmetrical both with regard to the axis of x and with regard to the axis of y, we see that the hyperbola approaches the line (1) as an asymptote not only in the first but also in the third quadrant, while in the second and fourth quadrants it approaches the line through the origin with slope $-\frac{b}{a}$, that is,

$$bx + ay = 0. \tag{2}$$

These two lines are, then, the asymptotes of the hyperbola. The two together may be represented by the single equation

$$b^2x^2 - a^2y^2 = 0,$$

which becomes, after dividing by a^2b^2,

$$\frac{x^2}{a^2} - \frac{y^2}{b^2} = 0. \tag{3}$$

This equation (3) may be easily remembered since it differs from equation (8), § 54 only in having 0 as its second member instead of 1.

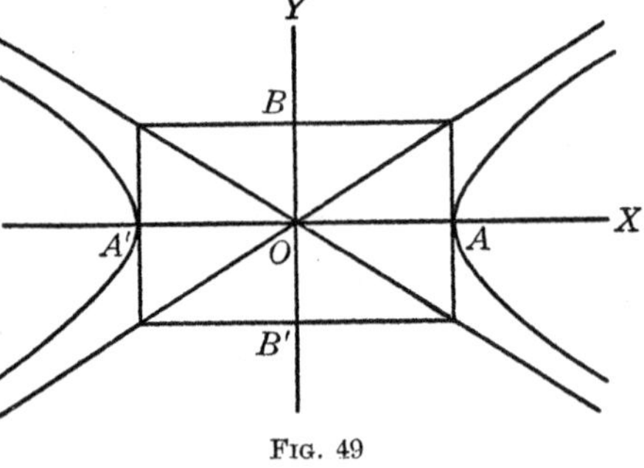

Fig. 49

The conjugate axis $B'B$ (Fig. 47, § 55) can now be brought into closer relation to the hyperbola. If through its extremities, B', B, lines are drawn parallel to the transverse axis, and through the extremities, A', A, of the transverse axis lines are drawn parallel to the conjugate axis, a rectangle is formed whose diagonals are precisely the asymptotes of the hyperbola.

The quantity b was defined in § 54, formula (7), by the equation

$$b = \sqrt{c^2 - a^2}.$$

Since c may be any quantity greater than a, it is clear that b may be either less than, equal to, or greater than a. In the first case, the asymptote in the first quadrant is inclined to the axis of x at an angle less than 45° (since its slope is $\frac{b}{a}$), in the second case at exactly 45°, and in the third case at an angle greater than 45°. If by the angle between the asymptotes we mean the positive angle less than 180° through which the asymptote in the fourth quadrant must be revolved to coincide with the other asymptote, we may, therefore, classify hyperbolas, according as this angle is less than, equal to, or greater than 90°, as follows:

Acute-angled hyperbolas	$a > b$;
Rectangular hyperbolas	$a = b$;
Obtuse-angled hyperbolas	$a < b$.

Since the two axes of a rectangular hyperbola are equal, such a hyperbola is also spoken of as an *equilateral* hyperbola. Its equation may be written

$$x^2 - y^2 = a^2, \tag{4}$$

whence it appears that the rectangular hyperbola is the simplest of hyperbolas just as the circle is the simplest of ellipses.

EXERCISES

1. Find the equations of the asymptotes of the hyperbolas of Exercise 3, § 55. What are the angles between these asymptotes in degrees?

2. Draw the asymptotes of the hyperbolas of Exercise 4, § 55, and by their aid draw in as accurately as possible the curves themselves.

3. Find the equation of the hyperbola which has the points $(\pm 2, 0)$ as foci and the line $y = 2x$ as an asymptote.

4. Find the equation of the hyperbola whose vertices are the points $(\pm 3, 0)$ and the angle between whose asymptotes is 60°.

5. Show that the eccentricity of every rectangular hyperbola is $\sqrt{2}$.

6. Prove that the distance from a focus of a hyperbola to an asymptote is equal to the semi-conjugate axis.

57. Equation and Shape of Parabola. Axis, Latus Rectum. Let AB be the directrix and F the focus of a parabola (see § 52), and call the distance between focus and directrix m. We will take as axis of x the perpendicular dropped from F on AB, and as origin, the point halfway from F to AB. If we take OF as the positive direction of the axis of x, the coördinates of F are $\left(\frac{m}{2}, 0\right)$; and, if the coördinates of a moving point, P, on the curve are (x, y), the length of the perpendicular dropped from P on AB is $x + \frac{m}{2}$. The equation of the curve is, therefore

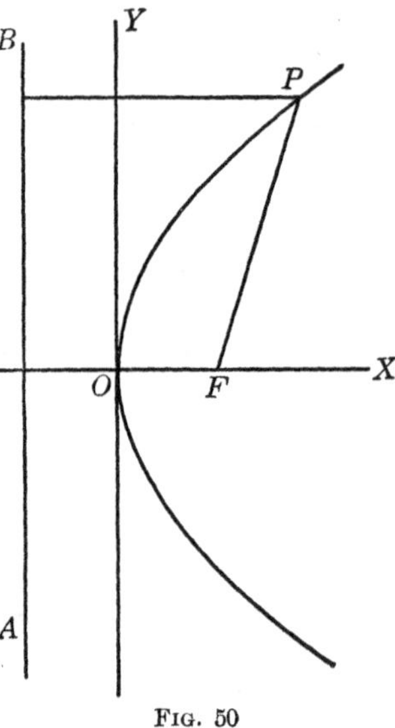

Fig. 50

(1) $$\sqrt{\left(x - \frac{m}{2}\right)^2 + y^2} = x + \frac{m}{2},$$

or, when cleared of radicals and simplified,

(2) $$y^2 = 2mx,$$

which is the standard form for the equation of the parabola.*

In using this form it must be remembered that m represents the distance between focus and directrix, so that the focus is the point $\left(\frac{m}{2}, 0\right)$ and the directrix the line $x = -\frac{m}{2}$.

From (2) we have

$$y = \pm \sqrt{2\,mx}.$$

Consequently, when x is negative y is imaginary. When $x = 0$, $y = 0$. As x increases indefinitely, starting from the value zero, y also increases indefinitely through both positive and negative values, the curve being symmetrical with regard to the axis of x. The parabola, therefore, has the shape indicated in Figure 50, consisting of one open branch which runs out to infinity.

It is clear from the definition that all parabolas are of the same shape, — whether the distance from focus to directrix is one foot or one inch can obviously make a difference only in the scale on which the curve is drawn, not in its shape. The figure plotted in § 12 for the case $m = 2$ will, therefore, serve to represent any parabola.

The indefinite straight line through the focus perpendicular to the directrix is called the *transverse axis* (or simply the axis) of the parabola, the point where it meets the curve, the *vertex*.

By the *latus rectum* of a parabola is understood the chord through the focus perpendicular to the transverse axis. This same term is also applied to the ellipse and hyperbola, each of which curves, therefore, has two *latera recta*, one through each focus.

* From the method of deduction, it is clear that the complete locus of (2) is the parabola (1) and also the curve obtained from (1) by changing the sign of the radical. This last-mentioned equation, however, has no locus, as is easily seen from the fact that no point on the parabola can lie to the left of the directrix.

EXERCISES

1. What are the coördinates of the foci and the equations of the directrices of the parabolas

$$y^2 = 4x, \quad y^2 = x, \quad 3y^2 - 5x = 0?$$

2. What are the lengths of the latera recta of the three parabolas of Exercise 1?

3. Find the equation of the parabola whose focus is at the point (3, 0) and whose vertex is at the origin.

4. Find the equation of the parabola whose transverse axis is the axis of x, whose vertex is the origin, and the length of whose latus rectum is 2.

5. Find the lengths of the latera recta of the ellipses

$$\frac{x^2}{25} + \frac{y^2}{16} = 1, \quad \frac{x^2}{10} + \frac{y^2}{5} = 1.$$

6. Find the lengths of the latera recta of the hyperbolas

$$\frac{x^2}{25} - \frac{y^2}{16} = 1, \quad \frac{x^2}{10} - \frac{y^2}{5} = 1.$$

7. Deduce from the definition of the parabola, without reference to equation (2), the equation of the parabola whose focus is the origin and whose directrix is the line $x + y = 1$.

58. Conics whose Transverse Axis is the Axis of y. When we deduced the equation of the ellipse, we might have taken the line connecting the foci as axis of y instead of as axis of x. The foci would then have been the points $(0, \pm c)$, and the only change necessary in deriving the equation is easily seen to be the interchange of the letters x and y wherever they occur. The equation of the ellipse is, therefore,

$$(1) \qquad \frac{y^2}{a^2} + \frac{x^2}{b^2} = 1.$$

The only difference between this and the form of § 53 is that here the larger denominator occurs in the y^2 instead of in the x^2 term.

Suppose, for instance, that we are given the equation

$$9x^2 + 4y^2 = 16.$$

This may be written

$$\frac{9x^2}{16} + \frac{y^2}{4} = 1,$$

or

$$\frac{x^2}{(\frac{4}{3})^2} + \frac{y^2}{2^2} = 1.$$

This equation, therefore, represents an ellipse whose semi-major axis, $a = 2$, lies along the axis of y, while its semi-minor axis, $b = \frac{4}{3}$, lies along the axis of x. Here $c = \sqrt{a^2 - b^2} = \sqrt{4 - \frac{16}{9}} = \frac{2}{3}\sqrt{5}$. Consequently, the foci are the points $(0, \mp \frac{2}{3}\sqrt{5})$.

Similarly, if the foci of a hyperbola lie on the axis of y while its conjugate axis is the axis of x, its equation is

$$(2) \qquad \frac{y^2}{a^2} - \frac{x^2}{b^2} = 1,$$

obtained from the equation of § 54 by merely interchanging x and y.

The difference between this equation and equation (8), § 54 has nothing to do with the relative magnitudes of the denominators, since either a or b may be the larger; it consists in the fact that here the negative term is the x^2 instead of the y^2 term.

Since the transverse axis, $2a$, now lies on the axis of y, the conjugate axis, $2b$, on the axis of x, it is clear from the rectangle construction explained in § 56 (see Figure 49) that the slopes of the asymptotes are $\pm \frac{a}{b}$. Hence the pair of asymptotes are given by the equation formed from (2) by replacing the 1 in the second member by 0.

We turn, finally, to the parabola. The standard equation,

$$(3) \qquad y^2 = 2mx,$$

was obtained by taking the focus $\left(\frac{m}{2}, 0\right)$ on the positive half of the axis of x. The quantity m was positive. In order to have the focus lie on the negative half of the axis of x, it is clearly sufficient to take m as a negative quantity.

On the other hand, if we wish to get a parabola whose transverse axis is the axis of y and whose vertex is at the origin, we need, obviously, simply to interchange x and y in the work of § 57. We thus find as the desired equation

$$x^2 = 2\,my. \tag{4}$$

The focus is at the point $\left(0, \frac{m}{2}\right)$. This is on the positive or negative half of the axis of y according as m is positive or negative. Hence, if m is positive, the parabola extends upward from the origin, if negative, downward.

In all cases it must be remembered that the origin is the vertex of every parabola represented by an equation of the form (3) or (4).

EXERCISES

So far as the following curves have any, determine the lengths of their axes, the coördinates of their foci, and the position of their asymptotes. Draw a figure to scale for each curve, marking foci and asymptotes.

1. $4\,x^2 + 3\,y^2 - 12 = 0.$

2. $4\,x^2 - 3\,y^2 + 12 = 0.$

3. $x^2 - 4\,y = 0.$

4. $x^2 + 4\,y = 0.$

5. $6\,x^2 = y^2 + 4.$

6. $y^2 + 2\,x = 0.$

7. $3\,x^2 = 12 - y^2.$

8. $y^2 = 1 + x^2.$

9. $2\,x^2 + 9\,y = 0.$

10. $2\,x^2 - 5\,y^2 + 10 = 0.$

11. Find the equation of the ellipse whose foci are at the points $(0, \pm 3)$ and whose eccentricity is $\frac{1}{2}$.

12. Find the equation of the hyperbola whose foci are the points $(0, \pm 3)$ and one of whose vertices is the point $(0, 2)$.

13. Find the equation of the parabola whose vertex is at the origin and whose focus is the point $(0, -2)$.

59. The Parabola as Limit of Ellipse or Hyperbola. About the focus F of an ellipse as center, describe a circle with radius equal to the length of the major axis. Let P be any point on the ellipse, and produce the line FP until it meets the circle in M. The shortest distance from P to the circle is PM, since this distance is measured along the radius. We may speak of it simply as *the* distance from P to the circle. Since

$$FP + PM = 2a$$

and also

$$FP + PF' = 2a,$$

it follows that

$$PM = PF'.$$

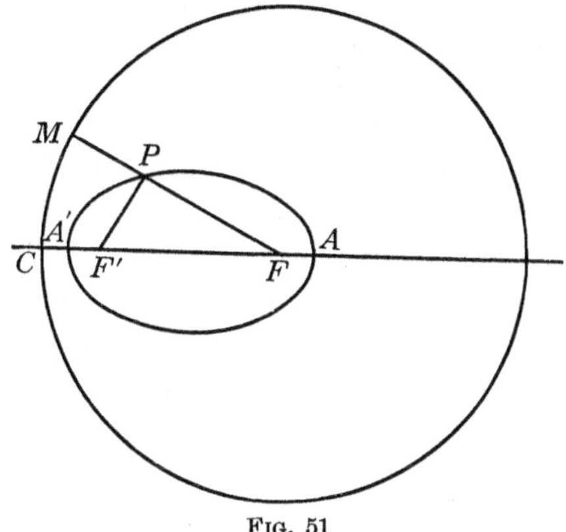

FIG. 51

That is, every point on the ellipse is equally distant from F' and from the circle. Conversely, it is clear that if a point, P, is equally distant from F' and from the circle, the sum of the distances PF and PF' is $2a$. Hence

The locus of a point which moves in a plane so as to be always at the same distance from a given circle and from a given point within the circle is an ellipse having the given point and the center of the circle as foci, and the radius of the circle as the length of its major axis.

On account of the similarity of this result to the definition of the parabola, the circle of Figure 51 is called a *director circle* of the ellipse. There are, of course, two director circles, one with center at F, the other with center at F'.

Of the two points where the transverse axis cuts the

director circle let C be the one which lies nearest to F'. Keeping the points C and F' fixed, let us allow F to move off to the right along the line CF'. At the same time, we suppose the radius of the circle to increase so that it is always equal to CF. As F moves off to infinity, the circle, which always passes through C, approaches as its limit the straight line through C perpendicular to CF'. The ellipse, at the same time, becomes longer and longer; and, since at any stage of this process it is the locus of a point which is equidistant from F' and from the circle, the limit it approaches will be the locus of a point equidistant from F' and from the limit of the director circle; that is, a parabola having F' as focus and the perpendicular to CF' at C as directrix. Thus the parabola may be obtained as the limiting form of an ellipse which becomes infinitely long.

The value of the eccentricity of the ellipse is

$$e = \frac{c}{a} = \frac{2c}{2a} = \frac{F'F}{CF} = \frac{CF - CF'}{CF} = 1 - \frac{CF'}{CF}.$$

Hence, as the ellipse approaches the parabola, e approaches 1 as its limit (since CF' remains constant, and CF becomes infinite). We shall, therefore, say that the parabola has eccentricity 1.

For the minor axis, b, of the ellipse, we may write

$$b^2 = a^2 - c^2 = \tfrac{1}{2}(2a - 2c)(a + c) = \tfrac{1}{2}\, CF'(a + c),$$

and, since, as the ellipse approaches the parabola, both a and c become infinite, we see that the minor axis of the ellipse as well as its major axis becomes infinite. The minor axis, however, becomes infinite much more slowly than the major axis; for we have

$$\frac{b^2}{a^2} = 1 - \frac{c^2}{a^2} = 1 - e^2,$$

and since, as we have seen, e approaches 1, $\frac{b}{a}$ approaches zero. Hence

If one focus and the adjacent vertex of an ellipse are held fast while the other focus and vertex move off to infinity, the ellipse approaches a parabola as its limit, one of the director circles approaches the directrix of the parabola as its limit, and the minor axis of the ellipse also becomes infinite, but so much more slowly than the major axis that b/a approaches zero.

What we have just said concerning the ellipse may be adapted with only slight changes to the hyperbola. The circle described about a focus, F', as center with radius equal to the transverse axis, $2a$, is called a director circle of the hyperbola. If, as in Figure 52, F' is the left-hand focus, the right-hand branch of the hyperbola is clearly the locus of a point, P, equidistant from this circle and from the other focus, F. By the distance from P to the circle is meant the shortest distance, PM; that is, the distance measured along the radius produced.

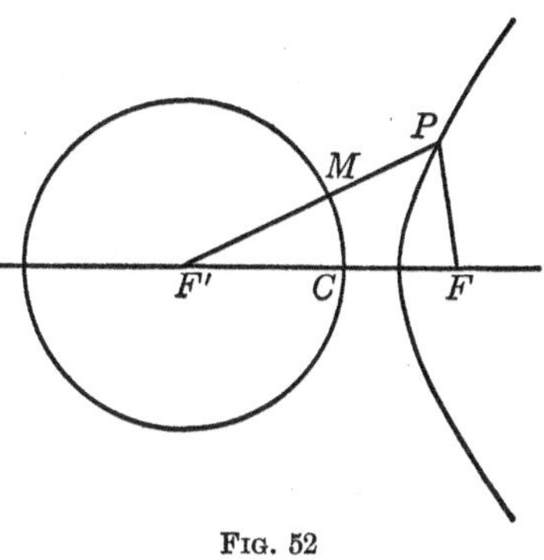

FIG. 52

If, now, holding fast the focus F and the point C where the director circle cuts the segment FF', we allow F' to move off to infinity, it is readily seen that the branch of the hyperbola approaches a parabola as its limit. Since, at the same time, the other branch of the hyperbola is moving off to infinity with F', we may regard the parabola as the limiting form of the hyperbola. We leave the details to the reader; see the following exercises.

EXERCISES

1. Prove that, as F' goes to infinity, the eccentricity of the hyperbola approaches 1 as its limit.

2. Prove that, as F' goes to infinity, the asymptotes of the hyperbola become more and more nearly horizontal, and, at the same time, move off to infinity, one upward and the other downward.

3. What happens to the length, $2b$, of the conjugate axis as F' goes to infinity?

4. Prove that the left-hand branch of the hyperbola (Figure 52) is the locus of a point which moves so that its *greatest* distance from the director circle of the figure is always equal to its distance from the point F.

60. Hyperbola Referred to Asymptotes as Coördinate Axes. Let us start from the equation of the equilateral hyperbola

(1) $x^2 - y^2 = a^2$,

and turn the coördinate axes through the angle $\theta = -45°$. By (1), § 44, we have

$$x = \frac{1}{\sqrt{2}}(x' + y'),$$

$$y = \frac{1}{\sqrt{2}}(-x' + y').$$

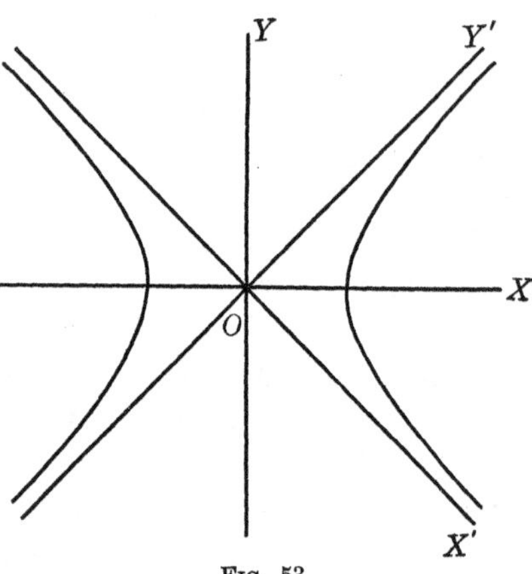

FIG. 53

The equation (1) thus becomes

(2) $$2xy = a^2,$$

which is the standard form of the equation of the rectangular hyperbola referred to its asymptotes as coördinate axes.

On the other hand, if we had turned the axes in (1) through the angle $+45°$, the equation would have taken the form

(3) $$2xy = -a^2.$$

Consequently, an equation of the form

$$xy = k, \tag{4}$$

when k is positive, represents a rectangular hyperbola lying in the first and third quadrants; when k is negative, a rectangular hyperbola in the second and fourth quadrants; the coördinate axes being in both cases the asymptotes.

To get a similar form for hyperbolas which are not rectangular, we must use oblique coördinates. We start from the standard equation of the hyperbola referred to rectangular coördinates

$$b^2x^2 - a^2y^2 = a^2b^2, \tag{5}$$

and use formulæ (3), § 46 in which we let

$$\theta = \tan^{-1}\left(-\frac{b}{a}\right), \ \theta_1 = \tan^{-1}\left(\frac{b}{a}\right).$$

We have, then,

$$x = \frac{a}{\sqrt{a^2+b^2}}(x' + y'), \qquad y = \frac{b}{\sqrt{a^2+b^2}}(-x' + y').$$

Equation (5), therefore, becomes after the transformation

$$4\,xy = a^2 + b^2. \tag{6}$$

If we reverse the positive direction on the axis of x, this equation becomes

$$4\,xy = -(a^2 + b^2). \tag{7}$$

Consequently, equation (4), in the case of oblique coördinates, always represents a hyperbola whose asymptotes are the coördinate axes, except when $k = 0$.

PROBLEMS TO CHAPTER IX

1. A chord of a parabola, perpendicular to the transverse axis, subtends a right angle at the vertex. How many times as long as the latus rectum is the chord, and how many times as far from the vertex is it as the focus?

2. Prove that in any ellipse or hyperbola the conjugate axis is a mean proportional between the transverse axis and the latus rectum.

Apply this to the circle and to the rectangular hyperbola.

3. A point is so situated on a parabola that this point, the foot of the perpendicular dropped from it on the directrix, and the focus form the vertices of an equilateral triangle. Prove that the length of each side of this triangle is equal to the latus rectum.

4. Prove that the line through the vertex of a parabola which makes with the transverse axis the angle $\tan^{-1} 2$ meets the curve at the end of the latus rectum.

5. The latus rectum of a hyperbola is extended by the amount k so that it just reaches the asymptote. Prove that k is equal to the radius of the circle inscribed in the triangle formed by the asymptotes and the tangent at a vertex.

6. The lines joining a point on an ellipse with the ends of the minor axis meet the transverse axis in S and T. Prove that the semi-major axis is a mean proportional between OS and OT, O being the center of the ellipse.

Does this theorem remain true if in the above statement the major and minor axes are interchanged?

7. Through a point, P, on a hyperbola a line is drawn parallel to the transverse axis meeting the asymptotes in S and T. Prove that the semi-transverse axis is a mean proportional between PS and PT.

State and prove a similar theorem if the line through P is parallel to the conjugate axis.

8. Prove that the diameter of the largest circle which can be inscribed in a semi-ellipse bounded by the minor axis is a fourth proportional to the major axis, the minor axis, and the distance between the foci.

9. Find the equation of the parabola whose vertex and focus are at the points $(p, 0)$, $(q, 0)$.

10. The vertex of a parabola is O, and P is any other point on the curve. Through P two lines are drawn, one perpendicular to the transverse axis and the other perpendicular to OP. These lines meet the transverse axis in Q and R. Prove that the distance QR is equal to the latus rectum.

11. Prove that if a point moves along a hyperbola, the product of its distances from the two asymptotes remains constant.

12. Let O be the vertex and F the focus of a parabola. A circle described about O as center and with $3\,\overline{OF}$ as diameter cuts the parabola in S and T. Prove that the line ST bisects OF.

13. Prove that if two ellipses have the same major axis (both in magnitude and in position) perpendiculars erected to this axis at any point and terminated by the curves are to each other as the minor axes.

14. Prove that the areas of two ellipses having the same major axis are to each other as the minor axes.

[Suggestion. Place the ellipses as in Problem 13 and divide them (or the first quadrant of each) into strips by a large number of lines parallel to the minor axis and equally spaced. Each of these strips is approximately a rectangle whose base is the breadth of the strip and whose altitude is the length of the left-hand side of the strip. The desired proportion is established for these rectangles. The proportion for the ellipses is then obtained as a limit.]

15. Prove that the area of an ellipse whose semi-axes are a and b is πab.

[Suggestion. Apply the result of Problem 14 to the ellipse and a circle of radius a.]

16. Prove that a line drawn through a vertex of a hyperbola, and terminated by two lines parallel to the asymptotes and passing through the other vertex, is bisected by the other point where it meets the hyperbola.

17. Prove that if a point, P, moves along an ellipse, starting from a vertex, its distance from the center continually decreases until the point reaches the end of the minor axis.

18. Prove that the quantity

$$\frac{x_1^2}{a^2}+\frac{y_1^2}{b^2}-1$$

is negative if the point (x_1, y_1) lies within the ellipse

$$\frac{x^2}{a^2}+\frac{y^2}{b^2}=1,$$

positive if it lies outside.

19. State and prove a similar proposition for the hyperbola; for the parabola.

20. A chord of an ellipse moves so as always to subtend a right angle at the center. Prove that its distance from the center is constant.

[SUGGESTION. Let λ be the slope of the line connecting one end of the chord with the center, and express in terms of λ the coördinates of the ends of the chord.]

21. Prove that the sum of the squares of the reciprocals of the distances from the center of the ellipse to the ends of the chord of Problem 20 is constant.

22. Prove that the chords of a parabola which subtend a right angle at the vertex all pass through a fixed point.

23. In an ellipse, $a = 2b$, P is a point on the upper half of the ellipse, Q a point on the lower half of the minor axis, and $PQ = a$. Prove that PQ is bisected by the transverse axis.

24. The three vertices of a triangle lie on an equilateral hyperbola. Prove that the point of intersection of perpendiculars dropped from the vertices on the opposite sides also lies on this hyperbola.

25. Let Q be the point on the axis of a parabola so situated that the focus lies half-way between Q and the vertex. Prove that if l_1 and l_2 are the lengths of the segments of a chord through Q, then

$$\frac{1}{l_1^2}+\frac{1}{l_2^2}$$

has the same value for all directions of the chord.

[SUGGESTION. Use polar coördinates with Q as origin.]

26. A chord of a parabola passes through the focus. Prove that the circle described on this chord as diameter is tangent to the directrix.

[SUGGESTION. Show that the equation of the circle is

$$x^2+y^2-\frac{m(2+\lambda^2)}{\lambda^2}x-\frac{2m}{\lambda}y-\frac{3m^2}{4}=0,$$

where λ is the slope of the chord.]

Locus Problems

27. Find the locus of the points of trisection of the chords of a given parabola which are perpendicular to the transverse axis.

28. A line of constant length moves with its ends on two fixed lines at right angles to each other. Prove that the locus of any point on this line (or on the line extended) is an ellipse.

This fact is used in constructing an instrument, known as an elliptic compass, for drawing ellipses of different sizes and shapes.

29. A line moves with its ends on two indefinite straight lines at right angles to each other, and its length varies in such a way that the area of the triangle cut off is constant. Find the locus of the point of the moving line which divides it in a given ratio.

30. Solve Problem 29 if the two indefinite lines are not at right angles to each other.

[Suggestion. Use oblique coördinates.]

31. Two parabolas have the same transverse axis and the same vertex, but different foci. Find the locus of the middle point of a line which moves with one end on each parabola and remains parallel to the transverse axis.

32. Two equal rulers, AB, BC, are connected by a pivot at B. The point A is fixed, while the point C moves along a fixed straight line through A. Find the locus of a fixed point, P, on BC.

33. A point, Q, moves around an ellipse whose foci are F' and F. Find the locus of the center of the circle inscribed in triangle $F'QF$.

[Suggestion. This problem may be much simplified by the use of a little trigonometry. In the triangle $F'QF$, express by the trigonometric formula the tangents of half the base angles in terms of the sides, and thus show that the product of these tangents is constant. From this property, the locus can be found by analytic geometry.]

34. A variable chord, QR, of a fixed ellipse is perpendicular to the major axis. Q is connected by a straight line with one vertex and R with the other. Find the locus of the point of intersection of these lines.

35. A point, Q, moves around an ellipse. Perpendiculars are dropped from each vertex on the line connecting Q with the other vertex. Find the locus of the point of intersection of the two perpendiculars.

36. A variable circle through the vertices of a fixed hyperbola cuts the hyperbola in the points Q, Q'. Find the locus of the points P, P' in which lines through Q, Q' parallel to the conjugate axis meet the circle again.

37. Find the locus of the middle points of chords of a parabola which pass through the vertex.

38. Two fixed points, A and B, lie within a fixed circle at equal distances from its center and on the same diameter. A parabola moves in such a way as always to pass through the points A and B and to have a directrix which is tangent to the given circle. Find the locus of the focus of this parabola.

[SUGGESTION. Since the parabola does not, in most of its positions, have the standard position with regard to any fixed system of coördinates, we must go back to the definition of the parabola in order to get its equation.]

CHAPTER X

PROPERTIES OF CONIC SECTIONS

61. Equations of Tangent at a Point. The equation of the tangent to the ellipse

$$\frac{x^2}{a^2}+\frac{y^2}{b^2}=1$$

at the point (x_1, y_1) is found by the method of § 38, or by an application of the rule of § 39, to be

$$(1)\qquad \frac{x_1x}{a^2}+\frac{y_1y}{b^2}=1.$$

Similarly, the tangent to the hyperbola

$$\frac{x^2}{a^2}-\frac{y^2}{b^2}=1$$

at (x_1, y_1) is

$$(2)\qquad \frac{x_1x}{a^2}-\frac{y_1y}{b^2}=1;$$

and the tangent to the parabola

$$y^2=2\,mx$$

at (x_1, y_1) is

$$(3)\qquad y_1y=m(x+x_1).$$

In case the axis of y is the transverse axis (see § 58), we have, of course, entirely similar formulæ, which need not be explicitly written down.

In the case of the rectangular hyperbola

$$xy=k$$

(see (4), § 60), the formula for the tangent is found, in the same way, to be

$$(4)\qquad x_1y+y_1x=2\,k.$$

This last formula applies also to the case of oblique coördinates, when the hyperbola is not rectangular. See the closing lines of § 60.

EXERCISES

1. Find the equation of the tangent to the ellipse

$$\frac{x^2}{32}+\frac{y^2}{18}=1$$

at the point (4, 3); at the point whose x coördinate is 2.

2. Find the tangent to the parabola $y^2 = 8x$ at the point whose y coördinate is 5.

3. Find the tangents to the parabola $y^2 = 2mx$

(*a*) at the vertex;

(*b*) at the ends of the latus rectum.

4. Find the angle at which the two curves $x^2 + 2y^2 = 9$ and $y^2 = 4x$ intersect, in degrees and fractions of a degree.

5. Find the equations of the tangents at the ends of the right-hand latus rectum of the hyperbola

$$\frac{x^2}{a^2}-\frac{y^2}{b^2}=1.$$

6. Find the equation of the tangent to the hyperbola $xy = 1$ at the point whose x coördinate is 10.

7. Find the equations of the tangents drawn to the hyperbola $x^2 - 2y^2 = 1$ from the point (7, 5).

[SUGGESTION. Use the method of § 32.]

8. Find the equations of the tangents to the parabola $y^2 = 4x$ from the point (0, 3).

9. Two ellipses have the same major axis both in magnitude and in position. A line perpendicular to this axis meets these ellipses in the points $P_1Q_1Q_2P_2$. Prove that the tangents at these points all meet on the transverse axis.

10. State and prove results analogous to that of Problem 9 for the hyperbola and the parabola.

62. Equations of Tangents in Terms of Their Slopes. From the shape of the ellipse

(1) $\frac{x^2}{a^2}+\frac{y^2}{b^2}=1,$

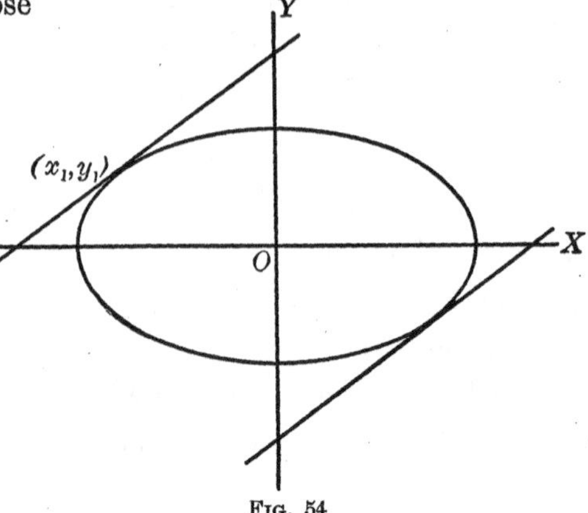

FIG. 54

it is clear that two tangents can be drawn to it having any desired slope, λ. To find the equations of these tangents, let us call the unknown point of contact of one of them (x_1, y_1). In terms of these two unknowns, the tangent may, by § 61, be written

(2) $$\frac{x_1x}{a^2}+\frac{y_1y}{b^2}=1,$$

or, after transposing and dividing by $\frac{y_1}{b^2}$,

(3) $$y=-\frac{b^2x_1}{a^2y_1}x+\frac{b^2}{y_1}.$$

Since the slope of this line is, by hypothesis, λ, we have

(4) $$\lambda=-\frac{b^2x_1}{a^2y_1},$$

so that (3) becomes

(5) $$y=\lambda x+\frac{b^2}{y_1}.$$

This would be the desired equation if it were not for the unknown quantity y_1 which still appears in it. It remains to find the value of this unknown. For this purpose we must use the equation

(6) $$\frac{x_1^2}{a^2}+\frac{y_1^2}{b^2}=1,$$

which expresses the fact that (x_1, y_1) lies on the ellipse. The two unknowns (x_1, y_1) may be determined from the two simultaneous equations (4), (6). Eliminating x_1 between them, we find for y_1 the value

$$y_1 = \pm \frac{b^2}{\sqrt{a^2\lambda^2 + b^2}},$$

which, when substituted in (5), gives

$$(7) \qquad y = \lambda x \pm \sqrt{a^2\lambda^2 + b^2},$$

and this is the final formula for the tangent to (1) with slope λ. The double sign is due to the fact, already noted, that there are two tangents with slope λ. Since (7) is in the form (3), § 17, the radical is the intercept of the tangent on the axis of y. Hence, the plus sign gives the tangent which passes above the ellipse, the minus sign, the tangent which passes below.

By precisely similar reasoning, which we leave to the reader, it will be found that the equation of the tangent with slope λ to the hyperbola

$$(8) \qquad \frac{x^2}{a^2} - \frac{y^2}{b^2} = 1$$

is

$$(9) \qquad y = \lambda x \pm \sqrt{a^2\lambda^2 - b^2}.$$

The expression under the radical sign is positive provided $\lambda^2 > \frac{b^2}{a^2}$, negative in the opposite case. Hence there is no tangent which makes with the transverse axis an acute angle, positive or negative, less than the angle made by the asymptotes with the transverse axis; while there are two tangents, given by (9), making any larger acute angle than this. The reader should corroborate this fact by drawing a figure.

In the case of the parabola,

$$(10) \qquad y^2 = 2\,mx,$$

it turns out that there is always just one tangent with a given slope, λ, not zero, and that this tangent has as its equation

$$(11) \qquad y = \lambda x + \frac{m}{2\lambda}\cdot$$

We leave it to the reader to establish this formula.

EXERCISES

1. Establish formulæ (9) and (11).

2. Find the equations of the tangents to the ellipse $2x^2 + 3y^2 = 6$ whose inclination to the axis of x is 135°.

3. Has the hyperbola $x^2 - y^2 = 1$ any tangents whose inclination to the axis of x is 60°? Whose inclination is 30°? If so, find their equations.

4. Find the equations of the tangents to the parabola $y^2 = 4x$ which are inclined to the axis of x at angles of 30° and 120°. Show that these tangents intersect on the directrix.

5. Prove that the line $x - 20y + 27 = 0$ is tangent to the ellipse $x^2 + 5y^2 = 9$.

[SUGGESTION. Throw the equation of the line into the form $y = \lambda x + \beta$, thus determining the value of λ, and then compare β with the value of the radical in (7).]

6. Is the line $x - 2y + 5 = 0$ tangent to the parabola $y^2 = 4x$?

63. The Optical Property of the Foci. Suppose that P_1, with coördinates $(x_1 y_1)$, is any point on the ellipse

$$(1) \qquad \frac{x^2}{a^2} + \frac{y^2}{b^2} = 1,$$

and that F is the focus $(c, 0)$.

Let us determine the angle from the focal radius FP_1 to the tangent, AB, at P_1:

$$(2) \qquad \frac{x_1 x}{a^2} + \frac{y_1 y}{b^2} = 1,$$

The slope of FP_1 is

$$\lambda_1 = \frac{y_1}{x_1 - c}.$$

The slope of (2) is

$$\lambda_2 = -\frac{b^2 x_1}{a^2 y_1}.$$

Hence, by (3), § 20,

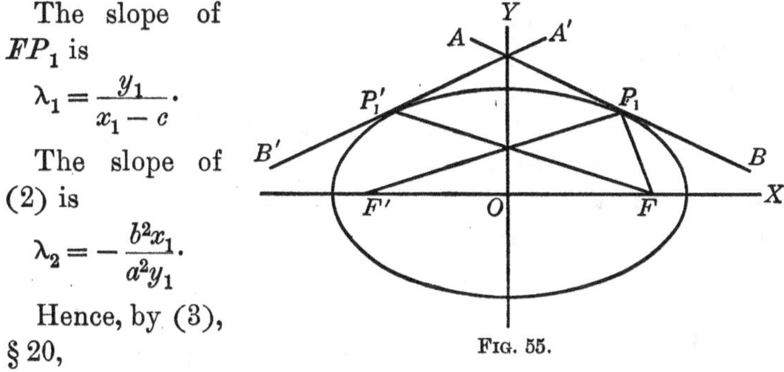

FIG. 55.

$$\tan FP_1B = \frac{-b^2x_1(x_1 - c) - a^2y_1^2}{[a^2(x_1 - c) - b^2x_1]y_1} = \frac{-a^2b^2 + b^2cx_1}{(c^2x_1 - a^2c)y_1},$$

the last reduction being performed by means of the two relations

$$b^2x_1^2 + a^2y_1^2 = a^2b^2,$$
$$a^2 - b^2 = c^2.$$

We get, finally, after canceling the factor $cx_1 - a^2$,

$$(3) \qquad \tan FP_1B = \frac{b^2}{cy_1}.$$

This result depends on the value y_1 but not on the value of x_1. Consequently, if we construct the point P_1' on the ellipse with coördinates $(-x_1, y_1)$, the tangent of the angle $FP_1'A'$ is also given by the second member of (3). Hence

$$\text{angle } FP_1B = \text{angle } FP_1'A'.$$

But, by the symmetry of the figure,

$$\text{angle } FP_1'A' = \text{angle } AP_1F'.$$

Combining these last two results, we see that

The tangent drawn at any point of an ellipse makes equal angles with the focal radii drawn to this point.

The same thing may be put a little differently by saying:

If the focal radii are drawn to any point on an ellipse, the angles between these lines produced are bisected by the tangent and normal drawn at the point.

It is from this important property of the ellipse that the name *focus* is derived, since rays of light starting from F and striking a reflecting surface curved in the form of an arc of an ellipse will be reflected back to F'; so that F' appears as a true optical focus.

Since, as we saw in § 59, the parabola may be regarded as an infinitely long ellipse, that is, as the limit of an ellipse as one focus moves off to infinity, it follows that the focal radii of an ellipse have as their limits the focal radius drawn to a point, P, of the parabola and the line drawn through this point parallel to the transverse axis. These two lines must, therefore, make equal angles with the tangent to the parabola at P. Hence, if rays parallel to the transverse axis fall on a parabolic mirror, they will be concentrated at the focus, F. Conversely, if a light is placed at the focus of a parabolic mirror, the rays, after reflection, will all go off in a direction parallel to the axis of the parabola. It is on this principle that the use of parabolic reflectors for the headlights of locomotives is based.

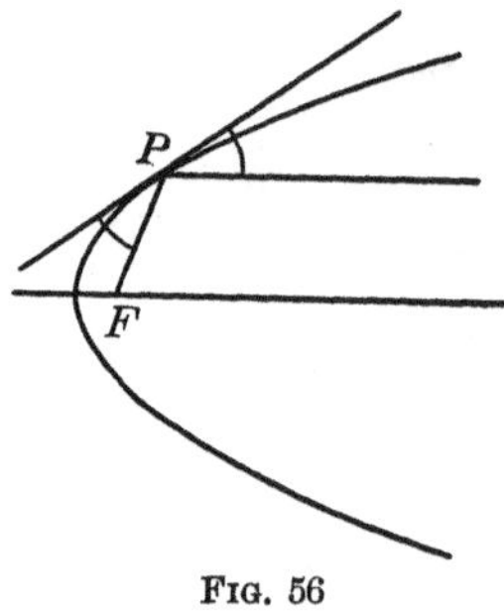

FIG. 56

EXERCISES

1. Prove that the tangent and normal to a hyperbola at any point bisect the angles between the focal radii drawn to this point.

2. Prove directly (that is, without regarding the parabola as an infinitely long ellipse) that the tangent and normal at any point of a parabola bisect the angles between the focal radius to this point and the line through this point parallel to the transverse axis.

64. Lengths of Focal Radii. Since, by the definition of eccentricity, $c = ae$, the coördinates of the foci of an ellipse may be written $(\pm ae, 0)$. The lengths of the focal radii to the point (x_1, y_1) of the ellipse are, therefore,

$$(1) \qquad FP_1 = \sqrt{(x_1 - ae)^2 + y_1^2},$$

$$(2) \qquad F'P_1 = \sqrt{(x_1 + ae)^2 + y_1^2}.$$

These expressions can be considerably simplified by using the fact that P_1 lies on the ellipse.

By combining the two formulæ $c = ae$ and $c^2 = a^2 - b^2$, we find

$$(3) \qquad b^2 = a^2(1 - e^2).$$

Hence, the equation of the ellipse may be written *

$$(4) \qquad \frac{x^2}{a^2} + \frac{y^2}{a^2(1 - e^2)} = 1.$$

Consequently, since (x_1, y_1) lies on (4), we have

$$y_1^2 = (1 - e^2)(a^2 - x_1^2).$$

Substituting this value in (1) and (2), we find

$$(5) \qquad FP_1 = \sqrt{e^2x_1^2 - 2\,aex_1 + a^2} = \pm(ex_1 - a),$$

$$(6) \qquad F'P_1 = \sqrt{e^2x_1^2 + 2\,aex_1 + a^2} = \pm(ex_1 + a),$$

where the sign must be determined in each case so that FP_1 and $F'P_1$ have positive values.

Since, for every position of P_1 on the ellipse, x_1 is numerically less than a, while e is a positive quantity less than 1, it follows that ex_1 is numerically less than a; and consequently, whether x_1 is positive or negative, $ex_1 + a$ is positive, and the upper sign must be used in (6). On the other hand, $ex_1 - a$ is, for the same reason, always negative. Hence, the lower sign must be used in (5). Finally, there-

* This formula is an important one since, as we shall see later in this section, it is applicable both to the ellipse and to the hyberbola.

fore, we have the formulæ *

(7) $$FP_1 = a - ex_1, \qquad F'P_1 = a + ex_1.$$

In the case of the hyperbola, the work is very similar. We find, in place of (3), the formula

(8) $$b^2 = a^2(e^2 - 1),$$

and, consequently, the equation of the hyberbola is precisely (4). Equations (1) and (2), and hence also (5) and (6), require no change. It is merely in the determination of the signs in these last formulæ that a change is necessary, since now $e > 1$ and x_1 is numerically greater than a. It will be seen that the formulæ are different according as P_1 is on one or the other branch of the hyberbola; namely:

If P_1 is on the right-hand branch,

(9) $$FP_1 = ex_1 - a, \qquad F'P_1 = ex_1 + a.$$

If P_1 is on the left-hand branch,

(10) $$FP_1 = a - ex_1; \qquad F'P_1 = -a - ex_1.$$

In the case of the parabola, the formula for the length of the focal radius to a point P_1 on the curve is most readily obtained by noticing that, by the definition of the parabola, it is equal to the distance from P_1 to the directrix, $x = -\frac{m}{2}$. Hence, the formula is

(11) $$FP_1 = \frac{m}{2} + x_1.$$

EXERCISES

1. Establish (11) by using the method used above for the ellipse.

2. What are the lengths of the focal radii of the ellipse

$$9x^2 + 25y^2 = 225$$

at a point whose x coördinate is $2\frac{1}{2}$?

* A simple check on these formulæ is given by the definition of the ellipse: $FP_1 + F'P_1 = 2a$.

3. What are the lengths of the focal radii of the hyberbola $x^2 - y^2 = 1$ at the point $(\frac{5}{3}, -\frac{4}{3})$? At the point $(-\frac{5}{3}, \frac{4}{3})$?

4. Prove that the distance of any point on an equilateral hyberbola from the center is a mean proportional between the focal radii drawn to this point.

65. Directrices. Definition and Equations. One end of the latus rectum of the parabola $y^2 = 2\,mx$ is the point $(\frac{m}{2}, m)$. The tangent at this point, by (3), § 61, is

$$my = m(x + \frac{m}{2}).$$

This tangent meets the transverse axis in the point $(-\frac{m}{2}, 0)$, that is, precisely where the transverse axis is crossed by the directrix. This property of the directrix of the parabola suggests that we use a similar construction for *defining* the directrices of the other conics.

DEFINITION. *If F is a focus of any conic, and we draw the tangent at one end of the latus rectum through this focus, a line perpendicular to the transverse axis at the point where this tangent meets the transverse axis is called a directrix of the conic.*

Since the transverse axis is an axis of symmetry, it clearly makes no difference which end of the latus rectum we use in applying this definition. It does, however, make a difference which focus we use; so that an ellipse or hyperbola has two directrices, one corresponding to each focus, while a parabola has only one.

The tangent

$$\frac{x_1x}{a^2} \pm \frac{y_1y}{b^2} = 1$$

to the ellipse or hyperbola meets the transverse axis at the point $(a^2/x_1, 0)$. If the point of contact, (x_1, y_1), is the end of the latus rectum through the focus $(ae, 0)$, we have $x_1 = ae$, and the point where the tangent meets the transverse axis becomes $(a/e, 0)$. From symmetry, it is clear that the point where the tangent at the end of the other latus rectum meets the transverse axis is $(-a/e, 0)$. Consequently, the equations of the two directrices of the ellipse or hyperbola are

$$x = \pm \frac{a}{e}. \tag{1}$$

It will be seen that the more nearly circular the ellipse, that is, the smaller e, the farther off do the directrices lie. The circle itself clearly has no directrices, since the tangents at the ends of the latus rectum then become parallel to the transverse axis.

EXERCISES

Find the equations of the directrices of the following conics, and draw a figure of the conic to scale in each case, marking foci and directrices:

1. $16x^2 + 25y^2 = 400$.

2. $2x^2 + 3y^2 = 6$.

3. $25x^2 + 9y^2 = 225$.

4. $16x^2 - 9y^2 = 225$.

5. $16x^2 - 9y^2 + 225 = 0$.

Find the equations of the conics which have as their foci and directrices the following points and lines:

6. $(\pm 3, 0)$, $x = \pm 6$.

7. $(\pm 3, 0)$, $x = \pm 2$.

8. $(0, \pm 4)$, $y = \pm 5$.

9. $(0, \pm 4)$, $y = \pm 3$.

10. Prove that the foot of a perpendicular dropped from a focus of a hyperbola on an asymptote lies on the directrix corresponding to that focus, and also on the circle described on the transverse axis of the hyperbola as diameter.

66. A Fundamental Property of Directrices. In the case of the parabola, the fundamental property of the directrix is that every point on the curve is equidistant from the directrix and from the focus.

Let us, then, compare the distance of a point (x_1, y_1) on the ellipse from a focus with its distance from the corresponding directrix.

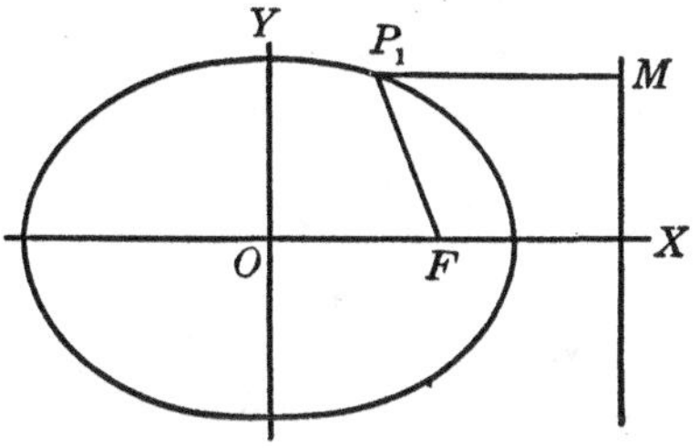

FIG. 57

The distance, FP_1, from the focus $(ae, 0)$ is, by (7), § 64,

$$FP_1 = a - ex_1.$$

The distance to the directrix $x = \frac{a}{e}$ is

$$P_1M = \frac{a}{e} - x_1 = \frac{a - ex_1}{e}.$$

Consequently,

$$\frac{FP_1}{P_1M} = e. \qquad (1)$$

This same formula will, of course, hold on account of the symmetry of the figure, if we use the other focus and directrix. We leave it for the reader to show that it holds without change in the case of the hyperbola.

If we regard the parabola as having eccentricity 1, as we have already done in § 59, formula (1) holds also in the case of the parabola.

Hence, we may say generally :

The distance from a point on any conic to a focus of the conic divided by its distance from the corresponding directrix is equal to the eccentricity of the conic.

67. Boscovich's Definition of Conics. Resulting Equations. The property of conics just obtained is often used as a basis for the following new definition of conics known as

BOSCOVICH'S DEFINITION. A conic is either a circle or the locus of a point which moves so that the ratio of its distance from a fixed point, called the focus, to its distance from a fixed line not passing through the focus, called the directrix, is a constant, called the eccentricity. The conic is called an ellipse, a parabola, or a hyperbola according as the eccentricity is less than, equal to, or greater than 1.

It is clear that this definition is equivalent to the definitions we originally adopted. It has the advantage of including all the conics, except the circle, under a single point of view, whereas for us they appeared as three distinct kinds of curves between which only gradually there appeared certain analogies. All the properties of conics which we have found might, of course, be developed by starting from this definition. Instead of this, we will derive from it two new formulæ.

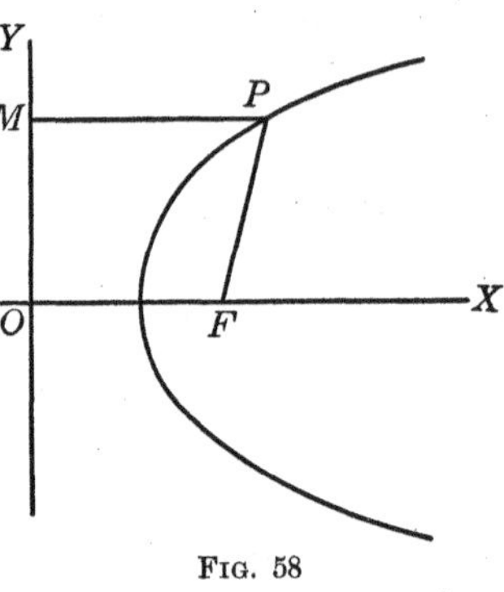

FIG. 58

Let us find the equation of a conic referred to a directrix as axis of y and to the transverse axis as axis of x. Let F be the focus corresponding to the directrix OY, and call its distance from this directrix m. Then, if P is the point (x, y) which traces out the curve, and we use the notation of Figure 58,

$$MP = x, \quad FP = \sqrt{(x-m)^2 + y^2}.$$

Hence, the equation of the curve is

$$\frac{\sqrt{(x-m)^2 + y^2}}{x} = e,$$

or

(1) $$(1 - e^2)x^2 + y^2 - 2\,mx + m^2 = 0.$$

This is the equation sought.

As a second application, let us find the equation of a conic in polar coördinates referred to a focus as origin and to that part of the transverse axis which runs from this focus away from the nearest vertex * as initial line. Then, using the notation of Figure 58,

$$FP = r, \quad \text{angle } XFP = \phi,$$
$$MP = m + r \cos \phi.$$

Hence, the desired equation is

$$\frac{r}{m + r \cos \phi} = e,$$

or

(2) $$r = \frac{em}{1 - e \cos \phi}.$$

It should be understood that every conic except a circle may be represented by equations (1) and (2).

EXERCISES

1. Obtain equation (1) by starting from the standard form of

(*a*) the ellipse,
(*b*) the parabola,
(*c*) the hyperbola,

and making a suitable transformation of coördinates.

2. Obtain equation (2) in the case of the parabola by a transformation of coördinates.

3. Starting from Boscovich's definition, find the equation of the conic of eccentricity 2 which has the line $2x + 3y = 6$ as directrix and the point (5, 2) as the corresponding focus.

68. Diameters. Any line through the center of an ellipse or hyperbola is called a diameter of the curve. Every diameter of an ellipse and some diameters of a hyperbola meet the curve in two points, called the *extremities* of this

* Or, what amounts to the same thing, away from the nearest directrix.

diameter, and the distance between these points is called the *length* of the diameter.

Since the parabola may be regarded as an infinitely long ellipse, whose center has receded to infinity along the transverse axis, the lines parallel to the transverse axis of the parabola are the limiting positions of diameters of the ellipse. We shall, therefore, define the term diameter in the case of a parabola to mean the transverse axis or any line parallel to it.

The diameters of conic sections are intimately associated, as we shall see, with the problem of finding the locus of the middle points of a set of parallel chords of the conic.

We first suppose that the conic is an ellipse or hyperbola. Its equation can, by (4), § 64, be written in the form

$$(1) \qquad \frac{x^2}{a^2} + \frac{y^2}{a^2(1-e^2)} = 1.$$

If λ is the slope of the parallel chords, the equation of any one of them may be written

$$(2) \qquad y = \lambda x + \beta,$$

and, as β is allowed to vary, this line takes on in succession the positions of all the parallel chords.

To find the coördinates of the ends, (x_1, y_1) and (x_2, y_2), of the chord, we solve (1) and (2) as simultaneous equations. Eliminating y between them, we have *

$$(3) \qquad (\lambda^2 + 1 - e^2)x^2 + 2\lambda\beta x + \beta^2 - a^2(1-e^2) = 0.$$

Consequently, if we denote the middle point of the chord by (X, Y), we have, by the principle used in § 49,

$$X = \frac{-\lambda\beta}{\lambda^2 + 1 - e^2}.$$

* The coefficient of x^2 in this equation can never be zero if (1) is an ellipse. If (1) is a hyperbola, it is zero when $\lambda = \pm\sqrt{e^2-1} = \pm b/a$, that is, if the chords are parallel to one of the asymptotes. Such lines, therefore, meet the curve in only one point, since (1) is then of the first degree. We have assumed, however, that we had to deal with chords, that is, with lines meeting the hyperbola in two points.

On the other hand, since (X, Y) lies on the line (2),

$$Y = \lambda X + \beta.$$

Eliminating the auxiliary variable β between these two equations, we find

$$(1 - e^2)x + \lambda y = 0, \tag{4}$$

as the equation of the locus. This equation represents a straight line through the origin, that is, a diameter of the conic (1). Hence:

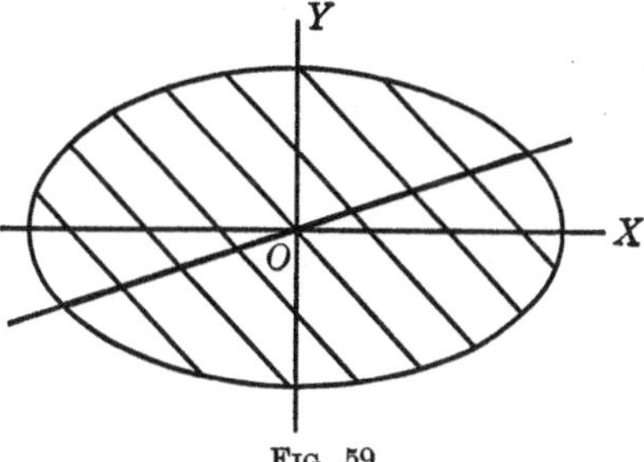

FIG. 59

The locus of the middle points of a set of parallel chords of an ellipse or hyperbola is a diameter of the curve, or a part of a diameter.

It is clear from Figures 59–61 that the locus consists, in the case of the ellipse, of so much of the diameter as is included within the curve; in the

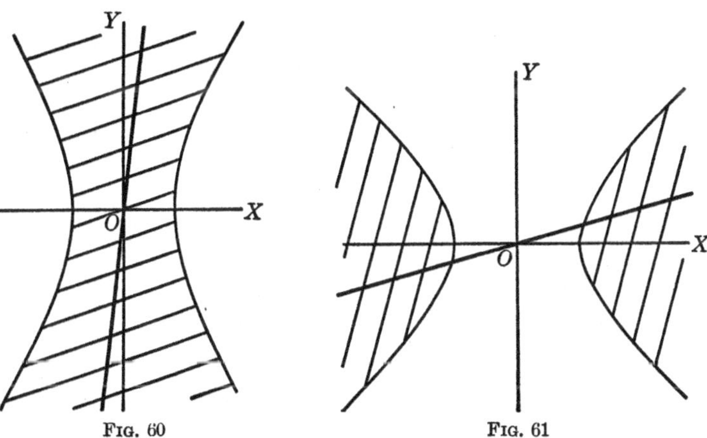

FIG. 60 FIG. 61

case of the hyperbola, of the whole diameter, if the chords to be bisected run across from one branch to the other, and of so much of the diameter as is not included between the branches, if the chords connect points on the same branch.

Since the parabola is the limiting form of an ellipse, it is clear that the locus of the middle points of a set of its parallel chords is that part of a diameter which lies on the concave side of the curve. The equation, if λ is the slope of the chords, will be found to be

$$(5) \qquad y = \frac{m}{\lambda}.$$

EXERCISES

1. Establish formula (5).

2. Find the equation of the diameter of the ellipse

$$2x^2 + 3y^2 = 5$$

which bisects the chords which are inclined at an angle of 45° to the axis of x.

3. Find the equation of the diameter of the parabola $y^2 = 4x$ which bisects the chords whose slope is 2.

69. Conjugate Diameters. Let λ_1 be the slope of a diameter of the conic (ellipse or hyperbola) represented by equation (1), § 68. The middle points of chords having this same slope, λ_1, determine, as we saw in § 68, a second diameter, whose slope, as we see from (4), § 68, is

$$(1) \qquad \lambda_2 = \frac{e^2 - 1}{\lambda_1}.$$

This second diameter is called the conjugate of the first. If, now, we determine the slope, λ_3, of the diameter conjugate to the one with slope λ_2, we have, by (1),

$$\lambda_3 = \frac{e^2 - 1}{\lambda_2} = \frac{e^2 - 1}{e^2 - 1}\lambda_1 = \lambda_1,$$

so that we come back to the original diameter. The relation between the two diameters is therefore a reciprocal one — each is the conjugate of the other.

The relation between the slopes of two conjugate diameters, as we see from (1), is

(2) $$\lambda_1\lambda_2 = e^2 - 1.$$

This formula applies equally to the ellipse and hyperbola. If the curve is an ellipse, $e^2 = \frac{a^2 - b^2}{a^2}$, while for a hyperbola, $e^2 = \frac{a^2 + b^2}{a^2}$. Hence, for the ellipse,

(3) $$\lambda_1\lambda_2 = -\frac{b^2}{a^2};$$

for the hyperbola,

(4) $$\lambda_1\lambda_2 = \frac{b^2}{a^2}.$$

Either from (2) or from (3) and (4) we see that two conjugate diameters always lie in different quadrants if the curve is an ellipse, in the same quadrant if it is a hyperbola. Moreover, in this latter case the slope $\pm\frac{b}{a}$ is seen to be a mean proportional between the slopes of any two conjugate diameters. Consequently, two conjugate diameters of a hyperbola are always separated by an asymptote which lies in the same quadrants with them, and the nearer one diameter lies to the asymptote on one side, the nearer will the other diameter lie to it on the other. An asymptote, there-

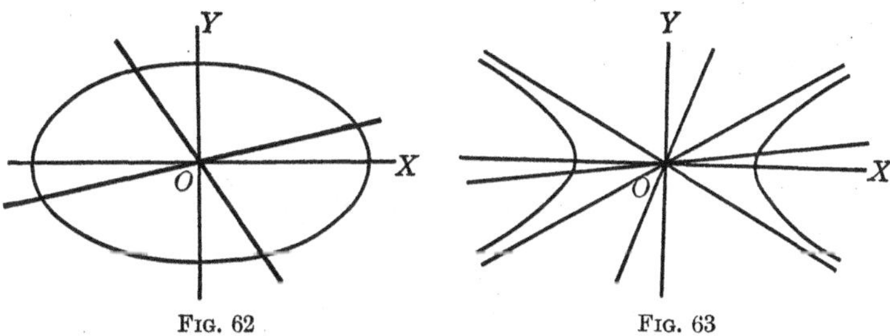

FIG. 62 FIG. 63

fore, regarded as a diameter, is often spoken of as being its own conjugate, although, strictly speaking, it has no conjugate, since, as we have seen, lines parallel to an asymptote meet the curve in only one point. The figures for conjugate diameters are given on the preceding page.

In what has been said it has been assumed that neither of the conjugate diameters is parallel to either coördinate axis, since in that case the slope of one of them would be infinite. It is clear, however, without any formula, that the transverse and conjugate axes of an ellipse or hyperbola form a pair of conjugate diameters.

EXERCISES

1. Why are there no such things as conjugate diameters in the case of a parabola?

2. Prove that every pair of conjugate diameters of a circle are perpendicular to each other; and that no other conic has more than one pair of perpendicular conjugate diameters, namely, the conjugate and transverse axes.

3. Prove that in the case of an equilateral hyperbola the angle between every pair of conjugate diameters is bisected by an asymptote.

70. Conjugate Hyperbolas. Two hyperbolas so related to each other that the transverse axis of each is the conjugate axis of the other, both in magnitude and in position, are called conjugate hyperbolas.*

If one hyperbola is given by the equation

$$\frac{x^2}{a^2} - \frac{y^2}{b^2} = 1, \tag{1}$$

the other will, by § 58, be given by the equation

$$\frac{y^2}{b^2} - \frac{x^2}{a^2} = 1,$$

* There is no such thing as a "conjugate hyperbola." A hyperbola is simply a hyperbola, no matter how it is situated with reference to the coördinate axes. The curve (2) is no more a "conjugate hyperbola" than the curve (1). Each is the conjugate of the other.

or, if we prefer, after changing signs,

$$(2) \qquad \frac{x^2}{a^2} - \frac{y^2}{b^2} = -1.$$

From the construction for the asymptotes indicated in Figure 49, it is clear that two conjugate hyperbolas have the same asymptotes, one hyperbola being acute-angled, the other obtuse-angled, unless they are both rectangular. This is indicated in Figure 64.

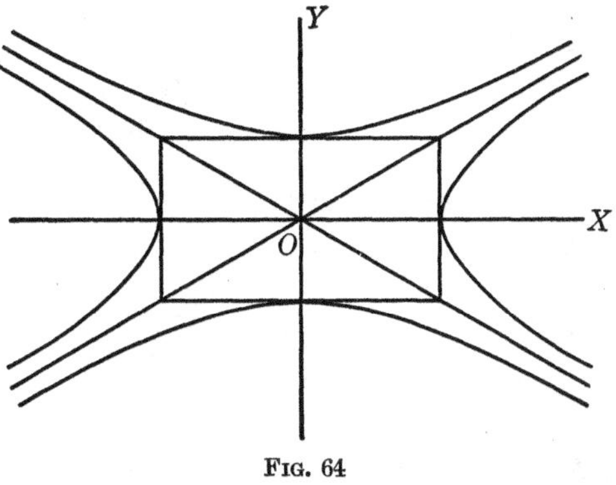

Fig. 64

Except the asymptotes, every diameter meets one or the other of the two hyperbolas in two points. No matter whether the line is regarded as a diameter of one hyperbola or of the other, these points where it meets one of the hyperbolas are called the extremities of the diameter, and the distance between them is called its length. Thus we have extended the conception of the length of a diameter so that it is applicable to every diameter of a hyperbola except the asymptotes.

A property of conjugate hyperbolas, and one on which much of the importance of the conception depends, is that two lines which are conjugate diameters of one hyperbola are also conjugate diameters of the conjugate hyperbola. (See Exercise 1.)

EXERCISES

1. Prove the theorem stated in the last paragraph of this section.

2. Prove that $xy = k$ and $xy = -k$ are conjugate hyperbolas, both when the coördinate axes are rectangular and when they are oblique.

3. Prove that the distance between the foci is the same for a hyperbola as for its conjugate.

4. Compare the ratio of the eccentricities of two conjugate hyperbolas to the ratio of their transverse axes.

71. Harmonic Division. Any point, Q_1, on the segment P_1P_2 extended divides this segment externally in a certain ratio. Let us construct the point Q_2 which divides P_1P_2 internally in the same ratio. The points Q_1Q_2 are said to divide the segment P_1P_2 *harmonically*, and we have the proportion

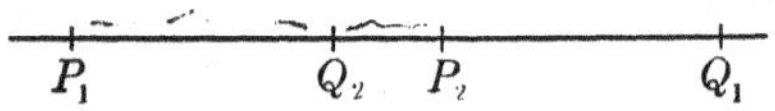

Fig. 65

$$(1)\qquad \frac{P_1Q_2}{Q_2P_2} = \frac{P_1Q_1}{P_2Q_1},$$

This proportion may also be written in the form

$$(2)\qquad \frac{P_2Q_1}{Q_2P_2} = \frac{P_1Q_1}{P_1Q_2},$$

and consequently, P_1, P_2 divide the segment Q_1Q_2 harmonically. Hence

If two points, Q_1, Q_2, divide a segment, P_1P_2, harmonically, then conversely, the two points, P_1, P_2, divide the segment Q_1Q_2 harmonically.

Let us now suppose that the coördinates of P_1 and P_2 are (x_1, y_1) and (x_2, y_2), respectively. The coördinates of Q_1, Q_2 will be given by formulæ (3) and (1)-(2), respectively, of § 8. Dividing numerators and denominators of the fractions in these formulæ by m_2, we find as the coördinates of Q_1 and Q_2, if we let $\mu = \frac{m_1}{m_2}$,

$$Q_1 \qquad \left(\frac{x_1 - \mu x_2}{1 - \mu}, \ \frac{y_1 - \mu y_2}{1 - \mu}\right),$$

$$Q_2 \qquad \left(\frac{x_1 + \mu x_2}{1 + \mu}, \ \frac{y_1 + \mu y_2}{1 + \mu}\right).$$

Whatever the value of μ, positive or negative,* these formulæ give two points dividing the segment P_1P_2 harmonically.

EXERCISES

Answer the following questions on the supposition that P_1, P_2 are the points $(-1, 2)$, $(3, 4)$:

1. Find two points, both in the first quadrant, which divide P_1P_2 harmonically.

2. Find two points, both in the second quadrant, which divide P_1P_2 harmonically.

3. Prove that the points $(-13, -4)$, $(\frac{5}{7}, \frac{20}{7})$ divide P_1P_2 harmonically.

4. Find the point which, together with the point $(0, 2\frac{1}{2})$, divides P_1P_2 harmonically.

72. Poles and Polars. Let a secant revolve about a point P_1, with coördinates (x_1, y_1), and meet the ellipse

$$(1) \qquad \frac{x^2}{a^2} + \frac{y^2}{b^2} = 1$$

in the points Q_1

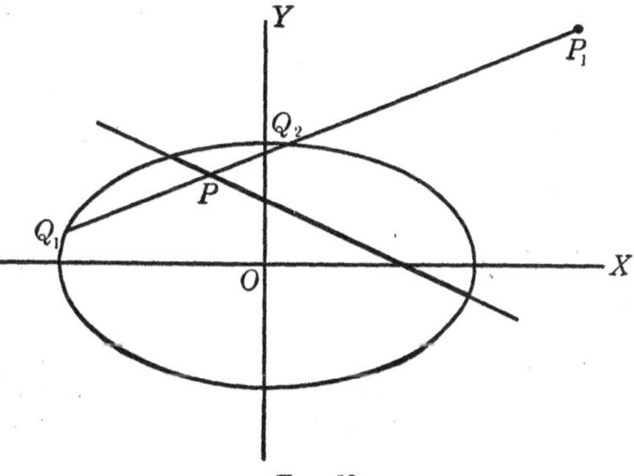

FIG. 66

* Except the values of ± 1, which make the denominators zero.

and Q_2. On this secant we construct the point P, so that P and P_1 divide the segment Q_1Q_2 harmonically.* We will find the locus of P, whose coördinates we call (X, Y).

Since, as we saw in § 71, the points Q_1, Q_2 also divide the segment P_1P harmonically, their coördinates may be written

$$\left(\frac{x_1+\mu X}{1+\mu}, \frac{y_1+\mu Y}{1+\mu}\right), \left(\frac{x_1-\mu X}{1-\mu}, \frac{y_1-\mu Y}{1-\mu}\right),$$

where μ is an auxiliary variable. By substituting the coördinates of Q_1 and Q_2 in (1) and clearing of fractions, we get

$$b^2(x_1+\mu X)^2+a^2(y_1+\mu Y)^2=a^2b^2(1+\mu)^2,$$
$$b^2(x_1-\mu X)^2+a^2(y_1-\mu Y)^2=a^2b^2(1-\mu)^2.$$

Now subtract one of these equations from the other, getting

$$4\,\mu b^2x_1X+4\,\mu a^2y_1Y=4\,\mu a^2b^2.$$

Canceling out the factor $4\,\mu$, we have left an equation involving only the principal variables (X, Y), which we now replace by (x, y). This equation, which when divided by a^2b^2 becomes

$$(2) \qquad \frac{x_1x}{a^2}+\frac{y_1y}{b^2}=1,$$

represents a straight line, which, or some part of which, is the desired locus.† This straight line (2) is called the *polar* of the point P_1 with regard to the ellipse (1). The form of the equation (2) is identical with the form of the equation of the tangent to (1) at the point (x_1, y_1) (see (1), § 61). The difference between the present formula and the earlier one is, of course, that (x_1, y_1) is not now a point on the ellipse.

* This is impossible if P is the center of the ellipse, since every chord through P is then bisected by P, and there is, of course, no point on the chord extended which is equally distant from its ends. The center of the ellipse has no polar, as is also evident from formula (2).

† It is readily seen from the figure that if P_1 lies outside of the ellipse, the locus consists of so much of (2) as lies within the ellipse, while if P_1 lies within the ellipse, the whole line (2), which will then not meet the ellipse, is the locus.

On account of the identity of the form of the equation, we shall define the polar of a point on the ellipse as the tangent at this point. Formula (2) then gives the polar in all cases.

What has been said in this section concerning the ellipse can be applied with slight changes to the hyperbola and the parabola. In this way we find that the polar of the point (x_1, y_1) with regard to the hyperbola

$$\frac{x^2}{a^2} - \frac{y^2}{b^2} = 1 \tag{3}$$

is

$$\frac{x_1x}{a^2} - \frac{y_1y}{b^2} = 1; \tag{4}$$

and that the polar of this point with regard to the parabola

$$y^2 = 2\,mx \tag{5}$$

is

$$y_1y = m(x + x_1); \tag{6}$$

in each case precisely the same formula we found in § 61 for the tangent.

In conclusion, we consider the subject of poles; a point being said to be the pole of a line if the line is its polar.

Suppose, for definiteness, that we are considering poles and polars with regard to the ellipse (1). Formula (2) shows us that the polar of a point never passes through the origin, that is, that a line through the origin has no pole. The equation of any line not through the origin may be written

$$Ax + By = 1. \tag{7}$$

Comparing this with (2), we see that it is the polar of (x_1, y_1) when and only when (see § 24)

$$A = \frac{x_1}{a^2}, \quad B = \frac{y_1}{b^2}.$$

Thus the point (a^2A, b^2B), and no other point, has (7) as its polar; that is, (7) has this point and no other as its pole.

EXERCISES

1. Establish formulæ (4) and (6).

2. Find the pole of the line $7x - y + 2 = 0$ with regard to

(*a*) the ellipse $x^2 + 2y^2 = 3$,
(*b*) the hyperbola $9x^2 - 16y^2 = 144$,
(*c*) the parabola $y^2 = 4x$.

3. Find the equation of the polar of the point (x_1, y_1) with regard to

(*a*) the hyperbola $xy = k$,
(*b*) the conic $(1 - e^2)x^2 + y^2 - 2mx + m^2 = 0$.

4. Prove that in any conic the polar of a focus is the corresponding directrix.

73. Properties of Poles and Polars. The most important property is the following:

If two points, P_1 and P_2, are so situated that P_2 lies on the polar of P_1, then, conversely, P_1 lies on the polar of P_2.

We will prove this theorem merely in the case of the ellipse, the proof for the hyperbola or parabola being precisely similar. The coördinates of P_1 and P_2 we call (x_1, y_1) and (x_2, y_2), respectively. The polars of P_1 and P_2 are

$$\frac{x_1x}{a^2} + \frac{y_1y}{b^2} = 1, \tag{1}$$

$$\frac{x_2x}{a^2} + \frac{y_2y}{b^2} = 1. \tag{2}$$

Since, by hypothesis, P_2 lies on (1),

$$\frac{x_1x_2}{a^2} + \frac{y_1y_2}{b^2} = 1.$$

This, however, is precisely the relation we need in order to prove that P_1 lies on (2). Thus our theorem is proved.

A special case of this theorem is that if the polar of P_1 meets the conic in P_2, the tangent at P_2 passes through P_1.

In other words, the points where the polar of P_1 meets the conic are precisely the points of contact of tangents drawn to the conic from P_1. This gives a convenient way of locating the polar when it meets the conic, namely, by drawing tangents to the conic from P_1 and connecting their points of contact, P_2P_3. Or, on the other hand, if we want the pole of a line which cuts the conic, we get it as the intersection of the tangents drawn at the points where the line meets the conic.

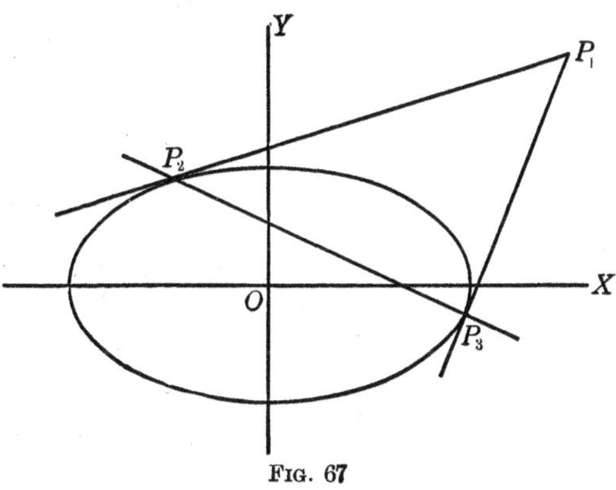

FIG. 67

EXERCISES

1. Establish the results of this section for the hyperbola and the parabola.

2. Prove, by applying the results of this section, that if a secant revolve about a point, R, and tangents are drawn at the points where it meets a conic, the locus of the point of intersection of these tangents is the polar of R or some part of it. Which part will it be?

3. Prove that the polar of any point on a directrix of a conic passes through the corresponding focus. See Exercise 4, § 72.

4. A rectangle is circumscribed about an ellipse by drawing tangents at the ends of the major and minor axes. Find the polars of its vertices.

PROBLEMS TO CHAPTER X*

1. A chord of a parabola, perpendicular to the transverse axis, meets this axis in A, the tangents at its extremities meet the axis in B, and the normals at its extremities meet the axis in C. Prove that the vertex of the parabola lies halfway between A and B; and that AC is equal to the distance between focus and directrix. What is the middle point of BC?

2. Prove that a tangent to a parabola meets the directrix and the latus rectum produced in points which are equidistant from the focus.

3. A triangle is formed by the asymptotes of a hyperbola and a variable tangent. Prove that the area of this triangle is constant.

4. Prove that two equilateral hyperbolas which are so situated that the axes of one are the asymptotes of the other intersect at right angles.

5. A first tangent to a hyperbola meets the asymptotes in the points A and B; a second tangent meets the asymptotes in A' and B'. Prove that the lines AB' and $A'B$ are parallel.

6. Tangents are drawn to the parabola $y^2 = 2\,mx$ at the points (x_1, y_1) and (x_2, y_2). Show that the point of intersection of these tangents is

$$\left(\frac{y_1 y_2}{2\,m}, \frac{y_1 + y_2}{2}\right).$$

7. Prove that the area of the triangle formed by any three tangents to a parabola is one half the area of the triangle whose vertices are the points of contact of these tangents.†

* Problems 1–32 may be taken up after the completion of §§ 61–67. The use of equation (1), § 68 will, however, frequently facilitate the work.

† This last area will be found to have the value $\pm \frac{(y_1 - y_2)(y_2 - y_3)(y_3 - y_1)}{4m}$.

8. Establish the correctness of the following construction for drawing a normal at a point, P, of an equilateral hyperbola:

About P as center, draw a circle passing through the center of the hyperbola. Let R be the point where it cuts the traverse axis again. Then PR is the desired normal.

9. Given a hyperbola, the tangents at its vertices, and any third tangent.' On the part of this last tangent intercepted between the first two, as diameter, a circle is described. Prove that this circle passes through the foci of the hyperbola.

10. Tangents are drawn to an ellipse from a point on the conjugate axis whose distance from the center is equal to the semi-major axis. Determine the points at which these tangents touch the ellipse.

Ans. The ends of the latera recta.

11. Show that the line

$$\frac{x}{\alpha}+\frac{y}{\beta}=1$$

is tangent to the ellipse

$$\frac{x^2}{a^2}+\frac{y^2}{b^2}=1$$

when, and only when,

$$\frac{a^2}{\alpha^2}+\frac{b^2}{\beta^2}=1.$$

12. Obtain results similar to those of Problem 11 for the hyperbola and the parabola.

13. A rectangle is inscribed in an ellipse with sides parallel to the axes of the ellipse. A second ellipse is inscribed in this rectangle with axes along the axes of the first ellipse. Prove that a line connecting ends of the major and minor axes of the first ellipse is tangent to the second.

14. Deduce the results of § 62 by expressing the fact that the line $y = \lambda x + \beta$ is to meet the conic at two coincident points.

15. Prove that an ellipse and a hyperbola having the same foci (confocal conics) intersect at right angles.

[SUGGESTION. Use the result of § 63.]

16. By allowing one of the two foci to recede to infinity, obtain, as a limiting case of Problem 15, a theorem concerning parabolas.

17. Prove the theorem of Problem 16 directly, without the use of limits.

18. A perpendicular is dropped from a focus, F, of an ellipse or hyperbola on a tangent. Prove that this line, the directrix corresponding to the focus F, and the line connecting the center with the point of contact of the tangent meet in a point.

19. What is the theorem for the parabola corresponding to Problem 18? Prove this theorem without regarding the parabola as the limit of an ellipse or hyperbola.

20. Through a point, P, on an ellipse a line is drawn parallel to the minor axis, meeting the major axis in D and the tangent at the end of the latus rectum in E. Prove that DE is equal to the focal radius to P.

In order that this theorem be correct, from which focus must the radius be drawn, and which end of which latus rectum must be used?

21. At a point, D, on the major axis of an ellipse a perpendicular is erected, meeting the ellipse in P and the circle described on the major axis of the ellipse as diameter in Q. Prove that the distance from the focus to P is equal to the distance from the focus to the tangent to the circle at Q.

Which focus must be used here?

22. Find the equation of a parabola referred to the tangents at the ends of the latus rectum as coördinate axes.

23. Show that the equation of a parabola referred to any point on the curve as origin, the tangent at this point as axis of y, and the line parallel to the transverse axis as axis of x is

$$y^2 = 2\,m_1 x,$$

where m_1 is twice the distance of the focus from the origin.

24. At what points of the ellipse, hyperbola, and parabola is the tangent equally inclined to the axes?

25. Find the equations of the common tangents of the ellipses

$$\frac{x^2}{25} + \frac{y^2}{9} = 1, \qquad \frac{x^2}{16} + \frac{y^2}{25} = 1,$$

and check your results by drawing a figure.

[SUGGESTION. Use the formula of § 62.]

26. Find the equation of the common tangents of the curves

$$3\,x^2 + 4\,y^2 = 12, \qquad y^2 = 4\,x.$$

27. Prove that the circle described on a focal radius of an ellipse or hyperbola as diameter is tangent to the circle described on the transverse axis as diameter.

28. State and prove the theorem for the parabola which corresponds to Problem 27.

29. A number of ellipses or hyperbolas have the same transverse axis both in magnitude and in position. At the upper end of the right-hand latus rectum of each a tangent is drawn. Prove that these tangents all pass through a point.

How must this statement be modified if the curves are partly ellipses and partly hyperbolas?

30. Show that from some points on the axis of a parabola three normals can be drawn to the parabola, and from some only one. Describe accurately the positions of the points of the first kind and of those of the second.

31. If $2c$ is the distance between the foci of an ellipse and e the eccentricity, prove that from a point on the transverse axis at a distance from the center greater than ce only one normal can be drawn to the ellipse. How many normals can be drawn from other points on the transverse axis? From points on the conjugate axis?

32. Two parabolas of the same size have the same transverse axis and face in the same direction. From a point, P, on one of them tangents are drawn to the other touching it in P_1 and P_2. Prove that as P moves along the first parabola, the area of the triangle PP_1P_2 does not change.

[SUGGESTION. Use the formula of Problem 6.]

Conjugate Diameters

33. Prove that if (x_1, y_1) is an extremity of a diameter of the ellipse

$$\frac{x^2}{a^2}+\frac{y^2}{b^2}=1,$$

the equation of the conjugate diameter is

$$\frac{x_1x}{a^2}+\frac{y_1y}{b^2}=0,$$

and one of its ends is

$$\left(-\frac{ay_1}{b},\ \frac{bx_1}{a}\right).$$

34. Prove that if (x_1, y_1) is an extremity of a diameter of the hyperbola,

$$\frac{x^2}{a^2}-\frac{y^2}{b^2}=1,$$

the equation of the conjugate diameter is

$$\frac{x_1x}{a^2}-\frac{y_1y}{b^2}=0,$$

and one of its ends is

$$\left(\frac{ay_1}{b}, \frac{bx_1}{a}\right).$$

The proof should be made to cover both the case in which (x_1, y_1) lies on the hyperbola itself, and that in which it lies on the conjugate hyperbola.

35. What interpretation can you give to the similarity between the equations for the conjugate diameter found in Problems 33, 34 and the ordinary formulæ for the tangents?

36. If $2a_1$ is the length of the diameter through the point (x_1, y_1) on the ellipse of eccentricity e, and $2b_1$ the length of the conjugate diameter, prove that

$$a_1^2 = b^2 + e^2x_1^2, \qquad b_1^2 = a^2 - e^2x_1^2.$$

37. Hence, prove that in an ellipse, the sum of the squares of any two conjugate diameters is equal to the sum of the squares of the major and minor axes; and that the product of the focal radii drawn to any point on the ellipse is equal to the square of the semi-diameter conjugate to the diameter through that point.

38. State and prove properties of the hyperbola analogous to those stated in Problems 36, 37 for the ellipse.

39. Prove that if two lines are conjugate diameters of a hyperbola, they are also conjugate diameters of every hyperbola which has the same asymptotes as the first.

40. How must two ellipses be related in order that every pair of conjugate diameters of one should also be conjugate diameters of the other?

41. Two lines connecting a point on a conic with the ends of a diameter are called *supplemental chords*. Prove that such chords are always parallel to a pair of conjugate diameters.

42. In an ellipse which is not a circle, prove that the only pair of equal conjugate diameters are the diagonals of the rectangle formed by tangents at the ends of the major and minor axes.

43. Prove that, in an equilateral hyperbola, focal chords parallel to conjugate diameters are equal.

44. Parallelograms are circumscribed about an ellipse by drawing tangents at the ends of pairs of conjugate diameters. Prove that all these parallelograms have the same area.

45. Prove that the diagonals of any parallelogram formed as in Problem 44 are themselves conjugate diameters.

46. If a parallelogram is formed by drawing tangents to a hyperbola and its conjugate, respectively, at the ends of two conjugate diameters, prove that the diagonals of this parallelogram are the asymptotes of the hyperbola.

47. Prove that, for a given hyperbola, all parallelograms formed as in Problem 46 have the same area.

48. If $2a_1$ and $2b_1$ are the lengths of a pair of conjugate diameters of an ellipse or hyperbola, show that the equation of the curve, referred to these lines as coördinate axes, is

$$\frac{x^2}{a_1^2} \pm \frac{y^2}{b_1^2} = 1.$$

49. If θ is the acute angle between a focal radius of an ellipse or hyperbola and the tangent at its extremity, P_1, prove that $\sin\theta = \frac{b}{b_1}$, where $2b$ is the conjugate axis of the conic, and $2b_1$ the length of the diameter conjugate to the diameter through P_1.

50. From the result of Problem 49, deduce formulæ for the distances from the foci to the tangent to an ellipse or hyberbola at the point (x_1, y_1).

Hence, prove that the semi-conjugate axis is a mean proportional between these distances.

51. Prove that if a parallelogram is inscribed in an ellipse, its sides are parallel to conjugate diameters.

Is the same thing true for parallelograms circumscribed about an ellipse?

52. Two focal chords revolve about a focus, always remaining parallel to conjugate diameters. Prove that the sum of their lengths is constant.

[SUGGESTION. Use the polar equation of the conic referred to the focus as pole.]

53. An ellipse is drawn on paper. Devise a method for constructing by means of ruler and compass (*a*) the center, (*b*) the axes, (*c*) the foci, (*d*) the directrices.

54. Solve the same problem for the hyperbola and the parabola, constructing, in the case of the hyperbola, the asymptotes in addition to what is asked for in Problem 53.

55. An arc of a conic is drawn on paper. Devise a construction for determining whether the arc belongs to an ellipse, to a hyperbola, or to a parabola.

Poles and Polars

56. Prove that the tangent to a parabola parallel to a line AB lies halfway between this line and its pole with regard to the parabola.

57. From a point, P, a perpendicular is dropped on its polar with regard to an ellipse or hyperbola. This perpendicular meets the transverse axis in A and the conjugate axis in B. Prove that $PA : PB = b^2 : a^2$.

State the special case in which P lies on the curve.

58. Prove that the polars of all points on a diameter of an ellipse or hyperbola are parallel to the conjugate diameter.

What can you say about the polars of points on a diameter of a parabola?

59. Prove that the polar of a point, P, with regard to a circle with center O is perpendicular to the line OP, and cuts it in the point, Q, situated on the same side of O as P and so that the radius of the circle is the mean proportional between OP and OQ.

60. Show that the equation of the polar of the point (x_1, y_1) with regard to the curve represented by equation (1), § 39 is given by equation (5) of that section.

61. Prove that the polars of a point with regard to two conjugate hyperbolas are parallel, and that the center of the hyperbolas lies halfway between them.

62. Two rectangular hyperbolas are so situated that the axes of one are the asymptotes of the other. Prove that the polars of a point with regard to these hyperbolas are perpendicular to each other.

Obtain, as a special case, the result in Problem 4.

63. Prove that a focal chord of a conic is perpendicular to the line joining its pole to the focus.

64. Prove that the polar of a point on a hyperbola with regard to the conjugate hyperbola is tangent to the first curve. What is the point of contact of this tangent?

65. Show that the result stated in Problem 64 remains correct if the polar is taken, not with regard to the conjugate hyperbola, but with regard to an ellipse which has the same transverse and conjugate axes as the original hyperbola, both in magnitude and position.

Locus Problems

66. Two tangents to a fixed ellipse move in such a way that they always remain at right angles to each other. Find the locus of their point of intersection.

[SUGGESTION. Use as auxiliary variable the slope, λ, of one of the tangents. It will be found that λ may be eliminated by simply adding the two equations which express the fact that the point lies on the two tangents, after they have been cleared of fractions and of radicals.]

67. Solve Problem 66 if the ellipse is replaced by a parabola.

68. Find the locus of the foot of a perpendicular dropped from a focus of an ellipse or hyperbola on a moving tangent.

69. Solve Problem 68 if the curve is a parabola.

70. Find the locus of the point of intersection of two perpendicular lines, one tangent to one ellipse and the other to a confocal ellipse.

71. Solve Problem 70 if one or both of the curves are hyperbolas, the two curves being still confocal.

72. State and solve a locus problem similar to Problems 70, 71 in which the curves are parabolas.

73. Find the locus of the middle points of chords which connect the ends of pairs of conjugate diameters of a fixed ellipse or hyperbola.

74. To a set of confocal ellipses and hyperbolas, tangents are drawn from a point on the transverse axis. Find the locus of their points of contact. *Ans.* A circle.

75. Two fixed ellipses have axes lying along the same lines. A moving line is tangent to one of them. Find the locus of its pole with regard to the other.

76. A parabola starts from a certain initial position and moves, without changing its size or the direction of its transverse axis, so that its vertex describes the original curve. Tangents are drawn to the moving parabola from the vertex of the initial parabola. Find the locus of their points of contact. *Ans.* Two parabolas.

77. A parallelogram circumscribed about a fixed ellipse moves so that one of its vertices traces out a directrix. Find the locus of each of the other vertices.

Ans. The other directrix, and the circle on the major axis of the ellipse as diameter.

CHAPTER XI

THE GENERAL EQUATION OF THE SECOND DEGREE

74. Certain Simple Cases. We begin with the equation

$$(1) \qquad Ax^2 + Cy^2 + F = 0,$$

and, first, assume that none of its coefficients are zero. It may, then, be written

$$\frac{x^2}{-\frac{F}{A}} + \frac{y^2}{-\frac{F}{C}} = 1.$$

If the two denominators here are positive, we have an ellipse whose transverse axis lies along the axis of x or the axis of y according to the relative magnitudes of the denominators. If one denominator is positive, the other negative, we have a hyperbola whose transverse axis lies along the axis of x or the axis of y according as the first or the second denominator is positive. If both denominators are negative, there is no locus, since the left-hand side of the equation is negative or zero, the right-hand side positive.

Turning, now, to the case in which $F = 0$ while neither A nor C is zero, it is clear that equation (1) has a single point (the origin) as its locus if A and C have the same sign, while, if A and C have opposite signs, the equation breaks up into two of the form

$$ax + by = 0, \quad ax - by = 0,$$

and, therefore, represents two straight lines intersecting at the origin and so situated that the coördinate axes bisect the angles between them.

If $A = 0$ but C is not zero, (1) may be written

$$y^2 = -\frac{F}{C},$$

and, hence, has no locus if F and C have the same sign; while, if F and C have opposite signs, it represents the two lines parallel to the axis of x: $y = \pm\sqrt{-\frac{F}{C}}$. If $F = 0$, it represents a single line, namely, the axis of x.

Similar statements evidently apply if $C = 0$ while A is not zero.

The case $A = C = 0$ need not be considered, since we are concerned with equations of the second degree only.

Summarizing, we may say

$AC > 0,\ AF < 0,$	Ellipse.
$AC > 0,\ AF > 0,$	No Locus (imaginary ellipse).
$AC < 0,\ F \gtrless 0,$	Hyperbola.
$AC > 0,\ F = 0,$	Point (null ellipse).
$AC < 0,\ F = 0,$	Intersecting Lines.
$AC = 0,\ (A + C)F > 0,$	No Locus (imaginary parallel lines).
$AC = 0,\ (A + C)F < 0,$	Parallel Lines.
$AC = 0,\ F = 0,$	One Line.

Besides the equation (1), we mention also equations of the forms

$$(2) \qquad Cy^2 + Dx = 0,$$

$$(3) \qquad Ax^2 + Ey = 0,$$

where we may assume that D and E are not zero, as otherwise the equation would come under the form (1), and also that neither A nor C is zero, as otherwise the equation would not be of the second degree. Under these circumstances, it is clear that (3) and (4) represent parabolas.

75. The Equation Without the xy-Term. In the equation

$$(1) \qquad Ax^2 + Cy^2 + Dx + Ey + F = 0$$

we assume, first, that neither A nor C is zero. The equation may, then, be written

$$A\left(x^2+\frac{D}{A}x \qquad\right)+C\left(y^2+\frac{E}{C}y \qquad\right)=-F.$$

We now complete the squares in each of these parentheses, and get

$$A\left(x+\frac{D}{2A}\right)^2+C\left(y+\frac{E}{2C}\right)^2=\frac{D^2}{4A}+\frac{E^2}{4C}-F.$$

Let us make the transformation of coördinates

$$x'=x+\frac{D}{2A},\quad y'=y+\frac{E}{2C},$$

that is, shift the axes without turning until the origin comes to the point

$$\left(-\frac{D}{2A},\ -\frac{E}{2C}\right). \tag{2}$$

Equation (1) then becomes

$$Ax'^2+Cy'^2+\frac{4ACF-CD^2-AE^2}{4AC}=0.$$

This equation is of the form (1), § 74. Hence we see that if neither A nor C is zero, equation (1), if it has any locus, represents either an ellipse, a hyperbola, a single point, or two intersecting straight lines; the center of the ellipse or hyperbola, the position of the single point, or the point of intersection of the lines being the point (2).

This method of completing the square applies also to the case in which the x^2-term is wanting ($A=0$) provided the x-term is also wanting ($D=0$), since then we need merely to complete the square for the y-terms. Similarly, if $C=E=0$, we need merely to complete the square for the x-terms. In both of these cases, by a mere shifting of the coördinate axes, we reduce equation (1) to the form of equation (1), § 74, where, however, either A or C is zero.

There remain, then, only two cases of equation (1) to be considered, namely, that in which $A=0$, $D\neq 0$, and that in which $C=0$, $E\neq 0$. In the first case, by completing the square for the y-terms, we reduce equation (1) to the form

$$C\left(y+\frac{E}{2C}\right)^2+D\left(x+\frac{4CF-E^2}{4CD}\right)=0.$$

If we now make the transformation of coördinates

$$x'=x+\frac{4CF-E^2}{4CD},\quad y'=y+\frac{E}{2C},$$

that is, if without turning the axes, we take as new origin

$$(3)\qquad \left(-\frac{4CF-E^2}{4CD},\ -\frac{E}{2C}\right),$$

the equation becomes

$$Cy'^2+Dx'=0,$$

which is of the form (2), § 74. Consequently, (1), in this case, represents a parabola whose vertex is at the point (3) and whose transverse axis is parallel to the axis of x.

Similarly, if $C=0$, $E\neq 0$, we reduce (1) to

$$Ax'^2+Ey'=0,$$

which, again, represents a parabola.

Thus, we can easily, in every case, determine not merely what kind of a locus (1) has, but exactly how it is situated.

EXERCISES

Determine what curves are represented by the following equations, drawing a figure to scale in each case which shows not only the size and shape of the curve but also its position with reference to the *original* coördinate axes:

1. $4x^2+9y^2-16x+18y-11=0.$

2. $x^2-4y^2-6x+8y+9=0.$

3. $2x^2+4x+3y-4=0.$

4. $2x^2+5y^2+3x+y+2=0.$

5. $12x^2-18y^2-12x-24y-5=0.$

6. $2x^2+5y^2+3x-3y=0.$

7. $3x^2-x-2=0.$

76. The General Equation. We come, now, to the general equation of the second degree

$$(1) \qquad Ax^2 + Bxy + Cy^2 + Dx + Ey + F = 0.$$

We assume that $B \neq 0$, as otherwise we should have the equation of § 75, and we wish to prove that by turning the axes through a suitable angle we can get rid of the xy-term.

If we turn the axes through an angle θ by means of formulæ (1), § 44, equation (1) becomes

$$\begin{aligned} & A(x' \cos \theta - y' \sin \theta)^2 \\ & + B(x' \cos \theta - y' \sin \theta)(x' \sin \theta + y' \cos \theta) \\ & + C(x' \sin \theta + y' \cos \theta)^2 \\ & + D(x' \cos \theta - y' \sin \theta) + E(x' \sin \theta + y' \cos \theta) + F = 0, \end{aligned}$$

or, expanded,

$$\left.\begin{array}{r} A \cos^2 \theta \\ + B \sin \theta \cos \theta \\ + C \sin^2 \theta \end{array}\right| x'^2 \left.\begin{array}{r} - 2A \sin \theta \cos \theta \\ + B \cos^2 \theta \\ - B \sin^2 \theta \\ + 2C \sin \theta \cos \theta \end{array}\right| x'y' \left.\begin{array}{r} + A \sin^2 \theta \\ - B \sin \theta \cos \theta \\ + C \cos^2 \theta \end{array}\right| y'^2$$

$$(2) \qquad \left.\begin{array}{r} + D \cos \theta \\ + E \sin \theta \end{array}\right| x' \left.\begin{array}{r} - D \sin \theta \\ + E \cos \theta \end{array}\right| y' + F = 0.$$

We wish to choose θ so that the coefficient of $x'y'$ in this equation shall be zero. This coefficient may be more simply expressed in terms of 2θ, and we thus get for determining the angle θ the equation

$$(C - A) \sin 2\theta + B \cos 2\theta = 0,$$

or

$$(3) \qquad \text{ctn } 2\theta = \frac{A - C}{B}.$$

There are an infinite number of values of θ which satisfy this equation, but a single one of them is all we require. There is evidently just one value of 2θ between 0° and 180° which satisfies (3), and, hence, just one value of θ between 0° and 90°. This positive acute angle we call θ_0.

If we turn the axes through this angle θ_0, equation (1) reduces to the equation of § 75, and we can determine its locus by the method of that section. Referring to the results of §§ 74, 75, we see that

An equation of the second degree either has no locus, or it represents an ellipse, a hyperbola, a parabola, two straight lines, one straight line, or a single point.

This same result holds true if the coördinate axes are oblique, since the degree of the equation is not changed if we transform to a system of rectangular coördinates.

EXERCISES

Determine the curves represented by the following equations, and draw a figure in each case, as in the Exercises to § 75.

1. $5x^2 + 2xy + 5y^2 - 12x - 12y = 0.$
2. $x^2 - 2xy + y^2 - 8x + 16 = 0.$
3. $5x^2 - 4xy + y^2 - 4x + 2y + 2 = 0.$
4. $x^2 + 4xy + y^2 - x - y + 4 = 0.$

77. The Invariants. If we turn the coördinate axes through an angle θ, the equation (1), § 76, takes the form

$$(1) \qquad A'x^2 + B'xy + C'y^2 + D'x + E'y + F' = 0,$$

where, as we see from (2), § 76,

$$(2) \qquad \begin{cases} A' = A\cos^2\theta + B\sin\theta\cos\theta + C\sin^2\theta, \\ B' = (C - A)\sin 2\theta + B\cos 2\theta, \\ C' = A\sin^2\theta - B\sin\theta\cos\theta + C\cos^2\theta, \\ D' = D\cos\theta + E\sin\theta, \\ E' = -D\sin\theta + E\cos\theta, \\ F' = F. \end{cases}$$

On the other hand, if we shift the coördinate axes to the new origin (x_0, y_0) without turning, the equation takes the form (1) where

$$(3) \qquad \begin{cases} A' = A, \quad B' = B, \quad C' = C, \\ D' = 2Ax_0 + By_0 + D, \\ E' = Bx_0 + 2Cy_0 + E, \\ F' = Ax_0^2 + Bx_0y_0 + Cy_0^2 + Dx_0 + Ey_0 + F. \end{cases}$$

Thus, while shifting the axes does not change A, B, or C, and turning them does not change F, a *general* transformation of coördinates will change all the coefficients of the equation. There are, however, certain combinations of the coefficients whose values are not changed by any transformation of coördinates. Such combinations of coefficients are called *invariants*.

The simplest of these is

$$\Theta = A + C. \tag{4}$$

That this is not changed when we shift the axes without turning is evident, since, from (3), neither A nor C is then changed. On the other hand, when we turn the axes, we have, by (2),

$$A' + C' = A + C.$$

Consequently, since the value of Θ is not changed either by a shifting or by a turning of the axes, it is not changed by the most general transformation to a new system of rectangular coördinates.

A second important invariant is

$$\Phi = B^2 - 4\,AC. \tag{5}$$

The value of Φ is obviously unchanged by a shifting of the axes, since this leaves the values of A, B, and C unchanged. It remains to show that Φ is unchanged when we turn the axes through any angle θ. For this purpose, we write, from (2),

$$A' - C' = (A - C)\cos 2\,\theta + B \sin 2\,\theta. \tag{6}$$

Squaring this and adding it to the value of B'^2 from (2), we find

$$(A' - C')^2 + B'^2 = (A - C)^2 + B^2.$$

Finally, subtracting from this the equation

$$(A' + C')^2 = (A + C)^2,$$

which we know is true since Θ is an invariant, we find

$$B'^2 - 4\,A'C' = B^2 - 4\,AC.$$

A third invariant is *

(7) $\Delta = 4\,ACF + BDE - A \cdot E^2 - C \cdot D^2 - F \cdot B^2.$

We first prove that the value of Δ is not changed by turning the axes about the origin through any angle θ. For this purpose, we rearrange the terms of Δ as follows:

$$\Delta = -(B^2 - 4\,AC)F - \tfrac{1}{2}(A + C)(E^2 + D^2)$$
$$+ BDE - \tfrac{1}{2}(A - C)(E^2 - D^2).$$

Since, by (2),

$$F' = F, \quad E'^2 + D'^2 = E^2 + D^2,$$

and since, as we have seen, $B^2 - 4\,AC$ and $A + C$ are invariants, neither of the first two terms in the last written expression for Δ are changed when we turn the coördinate axes. It remains, then, to show that the aggregate of the last two terms is not changed. For this purpose, we first deduce from (2) the relations

$$D'E' = DE \cos 2\,\theta + \tfrac{1}{2}(E^2 - D^2) \sin 2\,\theta,$$
$$\tfrac{1}{2}(E'^2 - D'^2) = \tfrac{1}{2}(E^2 - D^2) \cos 2\,\theta - DE \sin 2\,\theta.$$

Using these values, the value of B' from (2), and the value of $A' - C'$ from (6), we easily obtain the formula

$$B'D'E' - \tfrac{1}{2}(A' - C')(E'^2 - D'^2) = BDE - \tfrac{1}{2}(A - C)(E^2 - D^2).$$

This completes the proof that the value of Δ is not changed by turning the axes.

In shifting the axes, we may suppose $y_0 = 0$ in formulæ (3), since the axes may first be turned so that the shifting we wish to perform is in the direction of the axis of x, and, after the shifting, turned back to the original directions.

* In the notation of determinants we may write

$$\Delta = \tfrac{1}{2} \begin{vmatrix} 2\,A & B & D \\ B & 2\,C & E \\ D & E & 2\,F \end{vmatrix}.$$

Then, using (3), we find

$$\begin{aligned} 4\,A'C'F' + B'D'E' - A'\cdot E'^2 - C'\cdot D'^2 - F'\cdot B'^2 \\ = (4\,AC - B^2)(Ax_0^2 + Dx_0 + F) \\ + B(2\,Ax_0 + D)(Bx_0 + E) - A(Bx_0 + E)^2 \\ - C(2\,Ax_0 + D)^2, \end{aligned}$$

from which all the terms in x_0 and x_0^2 cancel out, leaving precisely the value of Δ. Thus the invariance of Δ is completely established.

78. Use of Invariants to Determine Nature of Curve. In §§ 75, 76, we found that every equation of the second degree can be reduced by a transformation of coördinates to one of the three forms (1), (2), (3), § 74. Moreover, the last of these forms obviously reduces to the next to the last by a rotation of the axes through 90°. Hence, any equation of the second degree,

(1) $$Ax^2 + Bxy + Cy^2 + Dx + Ey + F = 0,$$

can be reduced to one or the other of the two forms

(2) $$A'x^2 + C'y^2 + F' = 0.$$

(3) $$C''y^2 + D''x = 0. \quad (C'' \neq 0,\ D'' \neq 0.)$$

If (1) can be reduced to the form (3), we see, on account of the invariance of Φ and Δ, that

(4) $$\Phi = 0,\ \ \Delta = -\,C''D''^2 \neq 0.$$

On the other hand, if (1) can be reduced to the form (2),

(5) $$\Phi = -\,4\,A'C',\ \ \Delta = 4\,A'C'F' = -\,\Phi F'.$$

Hence, (1) can be reduced to the form (3) when, and only when, Φ is zero but Δ is not. Equation (3) represents a parabola, while (2) never does. Consequently

Equation (1) *represents a parabola when, and only when,*

$$\Phi = 0,\ \ \Delta \neq 0.$$

Consider, next, the case $\Phi > 0$. Since we cannot now reduce to the form (3), it must be possible to reduce to the form (2), and we see by (5) that A' and C' have opposite signs; and also that F' is zero when, and only when, $\Delta = 0$. A reference to the summary in § 74 enables us to infer that

Equation (1) *represents a hyperbola if* $\Phi > 0$, $\Delta \neq 0$; *two intersecting lines if* $\Phi > 0$, $\Delta = 0$.

In both cases we may say that the locus of (1) belongs to the *hyperbolic type*, since two intersecting lines are the limit of a hyperbola as the transverse and conjugate axes both approach zero while retaining a constant ratio; the curve fitting more and more closely into the angle between its asymptotes.

If $\Phi < 0$, A' and C' have the same sign, and we may say that our curve is of the elliptic type, since, by the summary of § 74, it may be described as an ellipse real, null, or imaginary. Here, as before, F' is zero when, and only when, $\Delta = 0$, and this is the case of the null ellipse. If $\Delta \neq 0$, we have an imaginary or a real ellipse according as F' has the same sign as A' and C' or the opposite sign; that is, by (5), according as $\Theta = A' + C'$ and Δ have the same or opposite signs. Hence

If $\Phi < 0$, *we have an ellipse if* $\Theta\Delta < 0$, *a point (null ellipse) if* $\Delta = 0$, *no locus (an imaginary ellipse) if* $\Theta\Delta > 0$.

There remains only the case $\Phi = \Delta = 0$ to consider. Here, too, since we cannot reduce to the form (3), it must be possible to reduce to the form (2), and we see from (5) that either A' or C' is equal to zero. By the summary in § 74, the equation either has no locus or represents two parallel lines, or a single line: we may say, for brevity, two parallel lines real, coincident, or imaginary. We will designate all these cases, along with the parabola, as curves of the *parabolic type.**

* These curves may readily be obtained as the limits of parabolas. Thus, if m approaches zero, the parabola

$$y^2 = 2\,mx + c$$

approaches the two parallel lines $y^2 = c$, which are real or imaginary according as c is positive or negative. The parabola

$$y^2 = 2\,mx + \sqrt{m}$$

approaches the single line $y^2 = 0$. The reader should consider carefully the geometrical figures corresponding to these equations.

We may summarize as follows:

I. $\Phi < 0$, Elliptic Type.
  (*a*) $\Theta\Delta < 0$, Ellipse.
  (*b*) $\Theta\Delta > 0$, No Locus (imaginary ellipse).
  (*c*) $\Delta = 0$, Point (null ellipse).

II. $\Phi > 0$, Hyperbolic Type.
  (*a*) $\Delta \neq 0$, Hyperbola.
  (*b*) $\Delta = 0$, Two Intersecting Lines.

III. $\Phi = 0$, Parabolic Type.
  (*a*) $\Delta \neq 0$, Parabola.
  (*b*) $\Delta = 0$, Two Parallel Lines (real and distinct, real and coincident, or imaginary).

It is not possible to distinguish between the three cases included under the last item, III (*b*), of this summary by the use of the values of Θ, Φ, Δ alone.* Our failure to distinguish between these cases is not of much practical importance, since, in all cases III (*b*), the first member of (1) can be factored into two real or imaginary factors of the first degree, and the actual determination of these factors usually presents no difficulty. See Example 2, § 80.

EXERCISES

Determine, by the use of the invariants, the nature of the curves represented by the following equations. In Case III (*b*) distinguish between the different subcases by factoring:

1. $x^2 + 5xy + 3y^2 + 2x - 3y + 1 = 0.$

2. $4x^2 + 12xy + 9y^2 - x + 2y - 3 = 0.$

3. $5x^2 + 10xy + 10y^2 + 8x + 2y + 5 = 0.$

4. $3x^2 + 14xy + 8y^2 + 10y - 3 = 0.$

5. $25x^2 - 10xy + y^2 + 65x - 13y + 36 = 0.$

6. $3x^2 - 4xy + 5y^2 + 7x - y = 0.$

* See, however, Problem 8 at the end of this chapter.

7. $4x^2 + 4xy + y^2 + 8x + 4y + 13 = 0.$

8. $9x^2 - 17xy - 2y^2 + 37x + 21y - 40 = 0.$

9. $2x^2 - 3xy + 2y^2 + x - y + 1 = 0.$

10. $x^2 - 6xy + 9y^2 + 4x - 12y + 4 = 0.$

79. Improved Method of Transforming Coördinates. If, as is usually the case, we wish to determine the exact position with regard to the coördinate axes of the curve represented by an equation of the second degree, we must actually determine the transformation of coördinates which reduces the equation to one of the standard forms. If the equation contains no xy-term, the method of § 75 is as good as any. If there is such a term, the method of § 76 may be somewhat improved.

Consider, first, the case $\Phi = 0$. After turning the axes through any angle, θ, we have $B'^2 - 4A'C' = 0$. Consequently, if we choose θ so that $A' = 0$, we also have $B' = 0$. The equation for determining θ is, then (see formula (2), § 77),

$$A \cos^2 \theta + B \sin \theta \cos \theta + C \sin^2 \theta = 0,$$

or,* replacing C by its value $\frac{B^2}{4A}$, clearing of fractions, and dividing by $\sin^2 \theta$,

$$4A^2 \operatorname{ctn}^2 \theta + 4AB \operatorname{ctn} \theta + B^2 = 0.$$

Since its first member is a perfect square, this equation reduces to

$$\text{(1)} \qquad \operatorname{ctn} \theta = -\frac{B}{2A}.$$

It is from (1) that the angle θ is to be determined. The equation then becomes

$$C'y'^2 + D'x' + E'y' + F = 0,$$

and the further reduction may be effected as in § 75.

In the case $\Phi \neq 0$ it is better not to turn the axes first and

* We assume that $A \neq 0$, as otherwise B would be zero, and no turning would be necessary.

then shift, as we did in § 76, but to reverse the order of these processes, and first shift without turning so as to get rid of the x and y terms.* We see from formulæ (3), § 77, that the coördinates (x_0, y_0) of the new origin must be determined to satisfy the equations

$$(2)\qquad \begin{aligned} 2Ax_0 + By_0 + D &= 0, \\ Bx_0 + 2Cy_0 + E &= 0. \end{aligned}$$

Solving these equations for (x_0, y_0), we find

$$(3)\qquad x_0 = \frac{2CD - BE}{B^2 - 4AC}, \quad y_0 = \frac{2AE - BD}{B^2 - 4AC},$$

and the assumption, $\Phi \neq 0$, which we have made prevents these denominators from being zero.

This point (x_0, y_0) being taken as origin, our equation becomes

$$(4)\qquad Ax^2 + Bxy + Cy^2 + F' = 0,$$

where, by (3), § 77,

$$F' = Ax_0^2 + Bx_0y_0 + Cy_0^2 + Dx_0 + Ey_0 + F.$$

The further reduction by turning the axes is effected as in § 76. It should be noticed that this reduction will not introduce any x or y terms into equation (4).

If the curve is an ellipse or hyperbola, the point (3) is its center, since equation (4) represents a curve whose center is at the origin, as we see by reducing it to the form (1), § 74, by turning the axes.

80. Further Use of the Invariants. In the case $\Phi = 0$, $\Delta \neq 0$ (Case III (*a*), § 78), the values of the coefficients in the reduced equation (3), § 78, can be found without going through the transformation. The values of Θ and Δ, as computed from this reduced equation, are

$$(1)\qquad \Theta = C'', \quad \Delta = -C''D''^2 = -\Theta D''^2.$$

*The reason is that the coefficients A, B, C which determine the amount of turning are not affected by a preliminary shifting, whereas the coefficients which determine the shifting are affected, and may be much complicated, by a turning.

Hence, in this case, the reduced equation may be written

$$\Theta y^2 \pm \sqrt{-\frac{\Delta}{\Theta}}\, x = 0.$$

Either sign may be used here, since the angle θ determined by equation (1), § 79, may be increased by 180°, thus reversing the positive direction on the new axis of x.

A similar use of the invariants is not possible in the case $\Phi = \Delta = 0$ (Case III (*b*), § 78), but it has already been seen that this case is best treated by the method of factoring.

On the other hand, in the cases $\Phi \neq 0$ the invariants are extremely useful. Here, the reduced equation is (2), § 78, and we have

$$(2) \qquad \Theta = A' + C', \quad \Phi = -4\,A'C', \quad \Delta = 4\,A'C'F' = -\Phi F'.$$

Hence, F' may be computed from the formula

$$(3) \qquad F' = -\frac{\Delta}{\Phi},$$

while A' and C' are to be found from the first two equations (2). It follows that A' and C' are the roots of the quadratic equation

$$(4) \qquad z^2 - \Theta z - \tfrac{1}{4}\,\Phi = 0,$$

since this is an equation the sum of whose roots is Θ and the product of whose roots is $-\frac{1}{4}\,\Phi$.

Which root of (4) is to be taken as A' and which as C' is not at once obvious. To determine this, we refer to formula (6), § 77, which may be written

$$A' - C' = [(A - C)\,\text{ctn}\,2\,\theta + B]\,\sin 2\,\theta.$$

Since θ is to be determined from equation (3), § 76, we may write the last formula

$$(5) \qquad B(A' - C') = [(A - C)^2 + B^2]\,\sin 2\,\theta.$$

We agreed in § 76 to choose for θ the positive acute angle which satisfies equation (3) of that section. Consequently, the second factor in the second member of (5) is positive as well as the first factor. Hence,

*B and $A' - C'$ have the same sign.**

This is just what we need in order to decide which root of (4) shall be taken as A'.

Example 1. Let us determine the nature and position of the curve

$$73x^2 + 72xy + 52y^2 + 74x - 32y - 47 = 0.$$

We first compute the values

$$\Theta = 125, \quad \Phi = -10{,}000, \quad \Delta = -1{,}000{,}000.$$

The equation, therefore, belongs to Case I (a) of § 78, and represents an ellipse. Equation (4) now becomes

$$z^2 - 125z + 2500 = 0,$$

whose roots we find to be 100 and 25. Since B is positive, $A' - C'$ is positive, and hence,

$$A' = 100, \quad C' = 25.$$

By formula (3), we have

$$F' = -\frac{\Delta}{\Phi} = -100,$$

and the reduced equation is

$$100x^2 + 25y^2 - 100 = 0,$$

or $$\frac{x^2}{1} + \frac{y^2}{4} = 1.$$

Thus we have an ellipse whose semi-axes are 1 and 2.

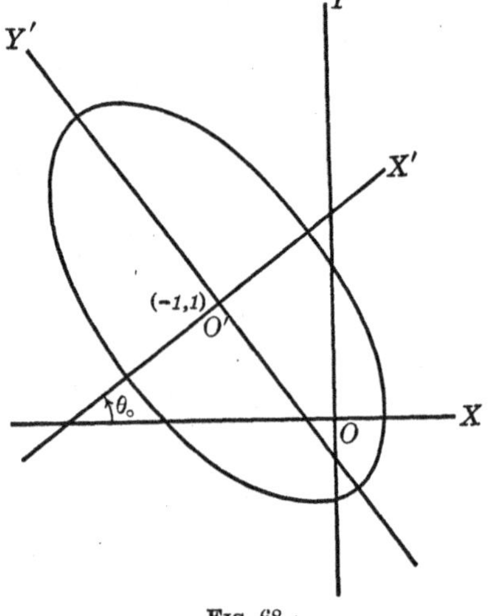

FIG. 68

* If we used a positive obtuse angle θ, just the reverse would be true: B and $A' - C'$ would have opposite signs.

We next locate the center of this ellipse by means of formulæ (3), § 79 (or equations (2) of that section, if we prefer), getting

$$x_0 = -1, \quad y_0 = 1.$$

The angle, θ_0, through which we must turn the axes is given by the equation

$$\text{ctn}\, 2\,\theta = \frac{A - C}{B} = \frac{21}{72} = 0.2917.$$

Whence, we find

$$\theta_0 = 36.87°.$$

We are now able to construct Figure 68.

Example 2. $2\,x^2 + 8\,xy + 8\,y^2 + 3\,x + 6\,y + 1 = 0.$

Here $\Phi = 0$, $\Delta = 0$, and we have Case III (b), that is, two parallel lines real, coincident, or imaginary. It must be possible to factor the first member of the equation into two factors of the first degree, and the coefficients of x and y in these two factors should be the same, since the lines are parallel. This is in accord with the fact that the first three terms form a perfect square:

$$2\,x^2 + 8\,xy + 8\,y^2 = (\sqrt{2}\,x + 2\sqrt{2}\,y)^2.$$

The two factors, therefore, have the form

$$(\sqrt{2}\,x + 2\sqrt{2}\,y + \alpha)(\sqrt{2}\,x + 2\sqrt{2}\,y + \beta).$$

From the constant term, we see that $\beta = \frac{1}{\alpha}$; from the x-term, that

$$\sqrt{2}\left(\alpha + \frac{1}{\alpha}\right) = 3,$$

which, when solved, gives $\alpha = \sqrt{2}$ or $\frac{1}{2}\sqrt{2}$. Hence, the two factors are

$$(\sqrt{2}\,x + 2\sqrt{2}\,y + \sqrt{2})(\sqrt{2}\,x + 2\sqrt{2}\,y + \tfrac{1}{2}\sqrt{2}),$$

and our locus consists of the two lines

$$x + 2\,y + 1 = 0,$$
$$2\,x + 4\,y + 1 = 0,$$

which may be readily located.

In such a simple case as this, the factoring could easily have been done by inspection without the introduction of radicals, but the method just explained may always be used if we are unable to detect the factors by inspection.

EXERCISES

Draw an accurate figure for the following curves, indicating the original coördinate axes in it:

1. $11x^2 + 6xy + 3y^2 + x + 6y = 0.$
2. $x^2 + 2xy - y^2 + 8x + 4y - 8 = 0.$
3. $2x^2 - 5xy + 5y - 1 = 0.$
4. $x^2 + 4xy + 4y^2 - 22x + 6y - 29 = 0.$
5. $2x^2 + xy + y^2 + 7x + 7 = 0.$
6. $2xy + 4x - 6y + 1 = 0.$
7. $x^2 + 3xy + y^2 + x - y - 1 = 0.$

81. Determination of Conics Satisfying Five Conditions. The method of undetermined constants, which we used in § 33 to find the equation of the circle through three given points, applies, with no essential change, to the problem of passing a conic through five points.

Example 1. Suppose the points are (5, 0), (3, 4), (4, 3), (0, 5), (– 5, 0).

After the general equation of the second degree has been divided by the coefficient of x^2, it becomes

$$x^2 + bxy + cy^2 + dx + ey + f = 0. \tag{1}$$

The coördinates of the five given points are to satisfy this equation, and we thus get the relations

$$\begin{aligned} &25 + 5d + f = 0, \\ &9 + 12b + 16c + 3d + 4e + f = 0, \\ &16 + 12b + 9c + 4d + 3e + f = 0, \\ &25c + 5e + f = 0, \\ &25 - 5d + f = 0. \end{aligned}$$

From the first and last of these equations, we find $d = 0$, $f = -25$. Substituting these values in the three middle equations, we easily get $c = 1$, $e = 0$, $b = 0$. Hence, the desired conic is the circle

$$x^2 + y^2 - 25 = 0.$$

Instead of dividing the general equation of the second degree by the coefficient of x^2, we might equally well divide by any of the other coefficients. There is, however, always the danger that we may, without knowing it, divide by a coefficient whose true value is zero, and this is, of course, impossible. This will show itself by our getting a system of equations for determining the coefficients which lead to a contradiction when we try to solve them.* If this occurs, we must go back and divide by some other coefficient.

If three or more of the points lie on a straight line, there will be no conic through them.

The reason we were able to pass the conic through just *five* points is that this gives us five equations, which is just enough to determine the five coefficients. It is possible to determine the conic in many other ways by imposing on it five conditions; for instance, we can attempt to pass a parabola through four points. We have, then, four equations exactly like those we used in Example 1, that is, equations of the first degree for determining the unknown coefficients; while our fifth equation will be

$$(2) \qquad B^2 - 4AC = 0.$$

This last equation being quadratic, we shall expect two answers to our problem. These may, however, be imaginary.

It should be noticed that (2) expresses, not that the curve is to be a parabola, but merely that it is to be of the parabolic

* This will be illustrated if, in Example 1, we first divide by the coefficient of the xy-term, and thus write the equation in the form

$$a'x^2 + xy + c'y^2 + d'x + e'y + f' = 0.$$

The reader should attempt to carry the work through in this way.

type. We shall, then, get among our answers not merely all parabolas that can be passed through the four points, but also all pairs of parallel lines; and these latter must be discarded as not being answers to our problem. We take as an illustration a case which brings out the various difficulties which may arise.

Example 2. Find all parabolas through the points (0, 0) (1, 2), (1, − 2), (4, 4).

Writing the equation of the conic in the form (1), we find as our five equations

$$\begin{aligned}
&f = 0,\\
&1 + 2b + 4c + d + 2e + f = 0,\\
&1 - 2b + 4c + d - 2e + f = 0,\\
&16 + 16b + 16c + 4d + 4e + f = 0,\\
&b^2 - 4c = 0.
\end{aligned}$$

We easily find, as the only solution of these equations,

$$b = -1,\ c = \tfrac{1}{4},\ d = -2,\ e = 1,\ f = 0.$$

Consequently, the only curve of the parabolic type through the four points *whose equation can be written in the form* (1) is

(3) $$x^2 - xy + \tfrac{1}{4}y^2 - 2x + y = 0,$$

and this curve is readily seen to consist of the parallel lines

$$x - \tfrac{1}{2}y = 0,\quad x - \tfrac{1}{2}y - 2 = 0.$$

We infer that there is no parabola of the form (1) which passes through the four points.

There may, however, be a parabola for which $A = 0$, and, hence, also $B = 0$. In this case, C cannot be zero, and we can surely divide by C, getting the equation in the form

$$y^2 + d'x + e'y + f' = 0.$$

The fifth equation is now identically satisfied. The other four can easily be written out and solved; and we find the parabola

(4) $$y^2 - 4x = 0.$$

In this case, then, there is only one parabola through the four given points, though there are two curves of the parabolic type, (3) and (4). We should have found these curves at one stroke if we had divided by C at the start.

EXERCISES

Find the equations of the conics through each of the following sets of five points:

1. $(2, 2)$, $(8, 2)$, $(10, 0)$, $(9, -\frac{3}{2})$, $(5, -\frac{5}{2})$.
2. $(0, 0)$, $(0, 1)$, $(1, 0.5)$, $(0.6, 0.9)$, $(-0.6, 0.1)$.
3. $(0, 3)$, $(1, 6)$, $(-8, 3)$, $(1, 0)$, $(-9, 6)$.
4. $(0, 0)$, $(0, 1)$, $(\frac{2}{3}, 2)$, $(\frac{3}{2}, 3)$, $(-6, -2)$.
5. $(2, 7)$, $(3, 4)$, $(4, 3)$, $(-5, 0)$, $(-1, -2)$.

Find all the parabolas through each of the following sets of four points:

6. $(0, 0)$, $(-2, 2)$, $(-\frac{3}{2}, 1)$, $(0, 4)$.
7. $(0, 0)$, $(2, 0)$, $(2, 4)$, $(8, 4)$.
8. $(0, 0)$, $(0, 1)$, $(1, 0)$, $(2, 3)$.
9. $(0, 0)$, $(1, 1)$, $(1, -1)$, $(-1, 0)$.

PROBLEMS TO CHAPTER XI

1. Prove that $\Theta = 0$ if the locus of an equation of the second degree is a rectangular hyperbola or two perpendicular lines, and that these are the only curves for which $\Theta = 0$.

2. If the equation

$$Ax^2 + Bxy + Cy^2 + F = 0$$

represents a hyperbola, prove that the asymptotes are represented by

$$Ax^2 + Bxy + Cy^2 = 0.$$

What is the equation of the conjugate hyperbola?

3. Find the equation of the rectangular hyperbola through the points

$$(1, 1), (2, 0), (1, -2), (3, -3).$$

[SUGGESTION. Use the result of Problem 1.]

4. Determine all the conics through the points

$$(0, 1), (3, 3), (4, 4), (0, 5)$$

which are tangent to the axis of x.

5. Determine all the conics through the points

$$(1, 3), (4, 4), (3, 1)$$

which are tangent to both coördinate axes.

6. If an equation of the second degree represents a hyperbola, prove that the equation of the asymptotes may be obtained by suitably altering the constant term. Express by means of the invariants the change which must be made in the constant term.

Find the equation of the conjugate hyperbola.

7. Determine all the hyperbolas which have the lines

$$x - y + 1 = 0, \quad y = 3$$

as asymptotes and pass through the point (0, 2).

[SUGGESTION. Use the results of Problem 6.]

8. Assuming that $\Phi = \Delta = 0$, so that the equation of the second degree represents two parallel lines, show that

(*a*) These lines are real and distinct, real and coincident, or imaginary according as the quantity

$$D^2 + E^2 - 4(A + C)F$$

is positive, zero, or negative.

(*b*) Provided $A \neq 0$, the expression in (*a*) may be replaced by $D^2 - 4AF$; and, provided $C \neq 0$, by $E^2 - 4CF$.

[SUGGESTION. It may be found convenient to use the relation $AE^2 = CD^2$. If so, this relation should be established.]

9. If the equation

$$Ax^2 + Bxy + Cy^2 + F = 0$$

represents a hyperbola or an ellipse which is not a circle, show that the transverse and conjugate axes together are represented by the equation

$$Bx^2 + 2(C - A)xy - By^2 = 0.$$

Locus Problems

10. A chord moves so as to remain parallel to the horizontal diameter of a fixed circle. A first line connects the right-hand end of the moving chord with the center of the circle; a second connects the right-hand end of the horizontal diameter with the middle point of the moving chord. Find the locus of the point of intersection of these two lines.

11. A family of ellipses and hyperbolas have the same transverse axis both in magnitude and in position. Find the locus of the extremities of their latera recta.

12. A line swings around a fixed point and meets two fixed perpendicular lines in A and B. Find the locus of the middle point of the segment AB.

13. Solve Problem 12 if the two fixed lines are not assumed to be perpendicular.

14. A moving line, which always retains the same direction, touches in succession a set of confocal ellipses and hyperbolas. Find the locus of the point of contact.

15. Two vertices of a triangle of fixed size and shape move along two perpendicular lines. Show that the locus of the third vertex is, in general, two ellipses. Consider special cases.

CHAPTER XII

ELEMENTS OF THE DIFFERENTIAL CALCULUS. DIFFERENTIATION OF ALGEBRAIC FUNCTIONS

82. Functions. If two quantities are such that when the first is given the value of the second is thereby determined, the second quantity is said to depend on the first, or to be a *function* of the first.

Thus, for instance, at a given spot on the earth's surface, the distance, s, a heavy body falls from rest depends on the time, t, during which it has been falling, and we say: s is a function of t. Or, again, the temperature, u, in a deep mine depends on the depth, s, below the surface of the earth, and we say that u is a function of s.

As a third example, consider the parabola

$$y = 4x^2.$$

If (x, y) is a point which traces out this curve, it is clear that y is a function of x, since when x is given, y is thereby determined.

As the first and third of the above examples show, we frequently have a mathematical formula for expressing the dependence of the second quantity on the first: in the case of the falling body $s = \frac{1}{2} gt^2$. This is, however, not necessary, as the second example shows.

If y is a function of x, we write $y = f(x)$, which is to be read: y equals f of x.

In different problems the symbol $f(x)$ will stand for different functions. If in a single problem several functions occur, we use different symbols for them, such as $f(x)$, $F(x)$, $\phi(x)$, $\psi(x)$, etc.

If $y = f(x)$, then by $f(3)$, $f(-1)$, $f(a)$, etc., are meant the values y takes on when $x = 3, -1, a$, etc. Thus if

$$f(x) = \frac{x^2 - 1}{x^2 + 1},$$

then $f(3) = \frac{8}{10}, f(-1) = 0, f(a) = \frac{a^2 - 1}{a^2 + 1}$, etc.

When we have a function of x, x itself is called the *independent variable.* Other letters can, of course, be used for the independent variable. Thus in the first of the above illustrations, the time, t, is the independent variable; in the second, the distance, s.

In conclusion, we note that if we lay off the value of the independent variable as abscissa, and the corresponding value of the function as ordinate, the function will be represented graphically by a curve, called sometimes the *graph* of the function.

EXERCISES

1. If $f(x) = 2x^2 + 3$, find $f(1), f(0), f(-10)$.

2. If $f(t) = \frac{1}{t}$, find $f(3), f(\frac{1}{3}), f(-\frac{1}{4})$.

3. If $\phi(x) = \sqrt{x^2 + 1}$, find $\phi(0)$, $\phi(1)$, $\phi(-3)$.

4. If $F(x) = 5x^3 - x$, find $F(a)$, $F(-a)$. Prove that $F(a) + F(-a) = 0$.

5. If $f(x) = 2x^2 + 3$, find $f(a + b)$.

6. If* $f(x) = \log x$, find $f(1), f(37.42)$.

7. If $f(x) = \log x$, prove that $f(a) + f(b) = f(ab)$.

8. If $f(x) = 2^x$, prove that $f(x) \cdot f(y) = f(x + y)$.

83. Increments. One frequently has occasion to consider the change produced in the value of a function by a certain change in the independent variable. For instance, if at a depth of 1000 feet in a mine we go down a further distance

* The ordinary, denary, logarithm is meant.

of 10 feet, by what fraction of a degree will the temperature be raised? Such changes are called *increments*, since the change is regarded as positive when it is an increase, as negative when a decrease.

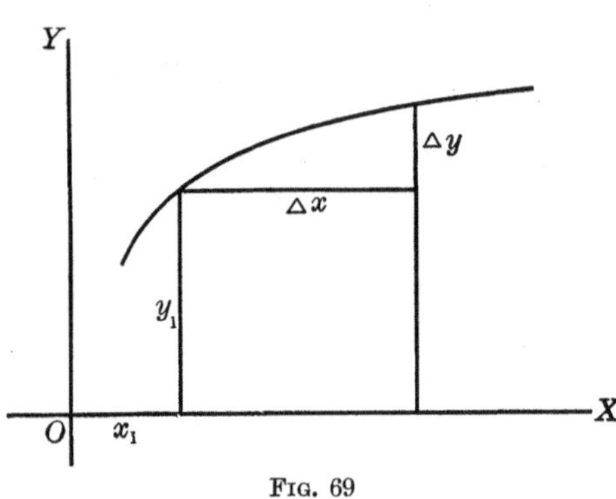

FIG. 69

Let $y = f(x)$, and suppose that to the value x_1 corresponds the value $y_1 = f(x_1)$. Now give to x the increment* Δx. To the value $x_1 + \Delta x$ thus reached corresponds the value $f(x_1 + \Delta x)$ of y. The increment of y, which we denote by Δy, is therefore

$$(1) \qquad \Delta y = f(x_1 + \Delta x) - f(x_1).$$

If, here, we replace $f(x_1)$ by its value y_1 and transpose, we find

$$(2) \qquad y_1 + \Delta y = f(x_1 + \Delta x).$$

These two forms, (1) and (2), are equivalent to each other. Sometimes one and sometimes the other is the more convenient.

It should be noticed that Δy, which may be computed from (1), depends not merely on the magnitude of Δx but also on the value, x_1, from which we start.

EXERCISES

1. If $f(x) = x^2 + 1$ and $x_1 = 1$, find Δy when $\Delta x = 1$; when $\Delta x = 0.1$; when $\Delta x = 0.01$. *Ans.* 3; 0.21; 0.0201.

* Read: delta x. The letter Δ alone has here no meaning. Δx must be regarded as a symbol for a single quantity, just like various other symbols consisting of two characters like x_1.

2. If $s = 16\,t^2$ and $t_1 = 2$, find Δs when $\Delta t = 1$; when $\Delta t = 0.1$; when $\Delta t = 0.01$; and interpret the results for falling bodies.

84. Derivatives. The fundamental conception of the differential calculus * is the *derivative* of a function, defined, if we use the notation of § 83, as the limit approached by the quotient $\frac{\Delta y}{\Delta x}$ as Δx approaches zero. If we represent the function $y = f(x)$ graphically by a curve, see Figure 70, the quantity $\frac{\Delta y}{\Delta x}$ is seen to be the slope of the secant P_1P_2. If, now, Δx approaches zero, the point P_1 remains fixed, while P_2 moves down the curve and approaches P_1 as a limit. Consequently, the secant P_1P_2 approaches as its limit the tangent at P_1 (see † § 37), and the slope of the secant approaches the slope of the tangent. Hence, the slope of the tangent is given by precisely the quantity which we called above the derivative.

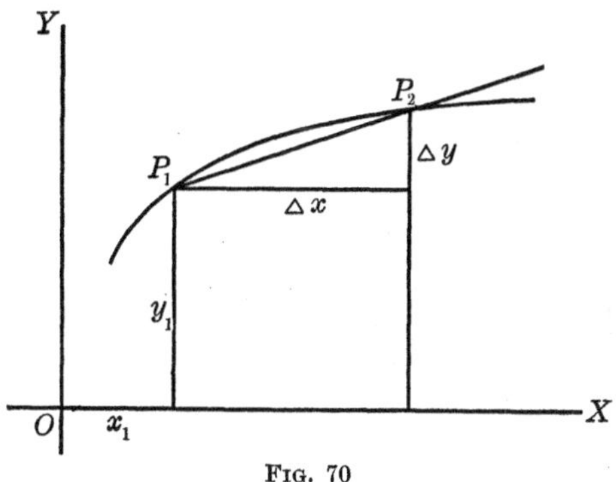

FIG. 70

The notation we shall use for the derivative is one due to Cauchy,‡ D_xy, so that §

$$D_xy = \lim_{\Delta x \doteq 0}\left(\frac{\Delta y}{\Delta x}\right).$$

* The conceptions of the differential calculus were developed gradually throughout the 17th century. They were consolidated into a science and further developed by Newton (1642–1727) in England and Leibniz (1646–1716) in Germany.

† See also § 38, where h and k are precisely the quantities we now call Δx and Δy.

‡ A French mathematician, 1789–1857.

§ The symbol $\lim\limits_{\Delta x \doteq 0}$ is to be read: limit as Δx approaches zero.

This notation must, of course, be suitably modified if other letters are used. Thus, if u is a function of t, we should write

$$D_t u = \lim_{\Delta t \doteq 0}\left(\frac{\Delta u}{\Delta t}\right).$$

85. The Evaluation of Derivatives by the Fundamental Method. In this section we will show how the derivative can be actually found in the case of a few simple functions which we take as illustrations.

Example 1. $y = x^2$. Here

$$f(x_1) = x_1^2,$$

$$f(x_1 + \Delta x) = (x_1 + \Delta x)^2 = x_1^2 + 2\,x_1\Delta x + (\Delta x)^2.$$

Hence,
$$\Delta y = f(x_1 + \Delta x) - f(x_1) = 2\,x_1\Delta x + (\Delta x)^2,$$

$$\frac{\Delta y}{\Delta x} = 2\,x_1 + \Delta x,$$

$$\lim_{\Delta x \doteq 0}\left(\frac{\Delta y}{\Delta x}\right) = \lim_{\Delta x \doteq 0}(2\,x_1 + \Delta x) = 2\,x_1.$$

Hence, the value of the derivative *when x has the value x_1* is $2\,x_1$. Inasmuch as x_1 is any value, we may drop the subscript and write

$$D_x x^2 = 2\,x.$$

Example 2. $y = \dfrac{1}{x}$.

$$f(x_1) = \frac{1}{x_1}, \quad f(x_1 + \Delta x) = \frac{1}{x_1 + \Delta x},$$

$$\Delta y = f(x_1 + \Delta x) - f(x_1) = \frac{1}{x_1 + \Delta x} - \frac{1}{x_1} = \frac{-\Delta x}{x_1(x_1 + \Delta x)},$$

$$\frac{\Delta y}{\Delta x} = \frac{-1}{x_1(x_1 + \Delta x)},$$

$$\lim_{\Delta x \doteq 0}\left(\frac{\Delta y}{\Delta x}\right) = \lim_{\Delta x \doteq 0}\left(\frac{-1}{x_1(x_1 + \Delta x)}\right) = \frac{-1}{x_1^2}.$$

Hence, dropping subscripts,

$$D_x\left(\frac{1}{x}\right) = -\frac{1}{x^2}.$$

To find the derivative of a function is technically called to *differentiate* the function. The method of differentiation explained in this section shall be called the *fundamental method*, and consists simply in a direct application of the definition of the derivative.

EXERCISES

Differentiate by the fundamental method the following functions:

1. x^3. *Ans.* $3x^2$.
2. x^4. *Ans.* $4x^3$.
3. $2x + 3$. *Ans.* 2.
4. $\frac{1-x}{1+x}$. *Ans.* $\frac{-2}{(1+x)^2}$.
5. $3x^2 + 1$.
6. $\frac{1}{x^2}$.
7. $2x^3 - 3x + 5$.
8. $\frac{1}{1-x}$.

86. Derivatives of x and c. The variable x may itself be regarded as a function of x. Since the curve $y = x$ is a straight line with slope 1, we have the formula

$$(1) \qquad D_x x = 1.$$

A constant, c, can also be regarded as a function of x; and, since $y = c$ is a line parallel to the axis of x, its slope is at every point zero. Consequently

$$(2) \qquad D_x c = 0.$$

EXERCISES

1. Deduce formulæ (1) and (2) by the fundamental method.

2. Use the method of this section to establish the result of Exercise 3, § 85.

87. Differentiation of a Constant Times a Function and a Sum of Functions. The process of differentiation is greatly facilitated by a few rules, the two simplest of which we shall obtain in this section.

If we know the value of the derivative of a certain function $u = f(x)$, we can easily find the derivative of $y = cf(x)$. For let

$$y_1 = cf(x_1),$$
$$y_1 + \Delta y = cf(x_1 + \Delta x),$$
$$\Delta y = cf(x_1 + \Delta x) - cf(x_1) = c\Delta u,$$
$$\frac{\Delta y}{\Delta x} = c\frac{\Delta u}{\Delta x},$$
$$\lim_{\Delta x \doteq 0}\left(\frac{\Delta y}{\Delta x}\right) = c\lim_{\Delta x \doteq 0}\left(\frac{\Delta u}{\Delta x}\right) = cD_x u.$$

Thus

(1) $$\boldsymbol{D_x(cu) = cD_x u.}$$

It must be carefully noticed that this formula is correct *only* if c is a constant. It does not, for instance, enable us to differentiate xu or x^2u.

A second important formula is obtained by supposing that we have two functions

$$u = f(x), \quad v = \phi(x)$$

which we know how to differentiate, and wish to differentiate their sum $y = f(x) + \phi(x)$. Let

$$y_1 = f(x_1) + \phi(x_1),$$
$$y_1 + \Delta y = f(x_1 + \Delta x) + \phi(x_1 + \Delta x).$$

Then

$$\Delta y = f(x_1 + \Delta x) - f(x_1) + \phi(x_1 + \Delta x) - \phi(x_1) = \Delta u + \Delta v,$$
$$\frac{\Delta y}{\Delta x} = \frac{\Delta u}{\Delta x} + \frac{\Delta v}{\Delta x},$$
$$\lim_{\Delta x \doteq 0}\left(\frac{\Delta y}{\Delta x}\right) = \lim_{\Delta x \doteq 0}\left(\frac{\Delta u}{\Delta x}\right) + \lim_{\Delta x \doteq 0}\left(\frac{\Delta v}{\Delta x}\right) = D_x u + D_x v.$$

Hence the formula

(2) $$\boldsymbol{D_x(u+v)=D_xu+D_xv.}$$

To get the derivative of the sum of three functions, $u+v+w$, we may first group u and v together, regarding $(u+v)$, for the moment, as a single function:

$$D_x(u+v+w)=D_x[(u+v)+w].$$

This, by (2), equals

$$D_x(u+v)+D_xw=D_xu+D_xv+D_xw.$$

Hence

(3) $$D_x(u+v+w)=D_xu+D_xv+D_xw.$$

In the same way, if we have the sum of four functions, we may write

$$u+v+w+r=(u+v+w)+r.$$

This, being the sum of two functions, can be differentiated by (2), and the result reduced by (3). We can proceed in the same way with any larger number of functions, and thus we see that *to differentiate the sum of any number of functions we need merely to differentiate each function separately and add the results together:*

(4) $$\boldsymbol{D_x(u+v+\cdots)=D_xu+D_xv+\cdots.}$$

EXERCISES

In the following Exercises the results of §§ 85, 86, and of the Exercises in § 85 should be used.

Differentiate, without using the fundamental method:

1. $5x^2, \quad -2x^4.$ *Ans.* $10x, \quad -8x^3.$

2. $3x^3, \quad -x.$

3. $x^2+x^3.$ *Ans.* $2x+3x^2.$

4. $x^4+x+3.$

5. $\dfrac{3}{x}, \quad -\tfrac{1}{2}\cdot\dfrac{1-x}{1+x}.$

6. $5x^4+2x^3-x^2-4x+2.$

88. Differentiation of a Product of Functions. Let

$$u = f(x), \quad v = \phi(x)$$

be two functions. It is required to find the derivative of their product

$$y = f(x) \cdot \phi(x).$$

We write

$$y_1 = f(x_1) \cdot \phi(x_1),$$

$$y_1 + \Delta y = f(x_1 + \Delta x) \cdot \phi(x_1 + \Delta x),$$

$$\Delta y = f(x_1 + \Delta x) \cdot \phi(x_1 + \Delta x) - f(x_1) \cdot \phi(x_1).$$

But

$$u_1 = f(x_1), \qquad v_1 = \phi(x_1),$$

$$u_1 + \Delta u = f(x_1 + \Delta x), \quad v_1 + \Delta v = \phi(x_1 + \Delta x).$$

Hence

$$\Delta y = (u_1 + \Delta u)(v_1 + \Delta v) - u_1 v_1$$

$$= u_1 \Delta v + v_1 \Delta u + \Delta u \Delta v,$$

$$\frac{\Delta y}{\Delta x} = u_1 \frac{\Delta v}{\Delta x} + v_1 \frac{\Delta u}{\Delta x} + \Delta u \frac{\Delta v}{\Delta x}.$$

Now as Δx approaches zero, both Δu and Δv approach zero, while $\frac{\Delta u}{\Delta x}$ and $\frac{\Delta v}{\Delta x}$ approach $D_x u$ and $D_x v$ respectively. Hence

$$\lim_{\Delta x \doteq 0} \left(\frac{\Delta y}{\Delta x}\right) = u_1 D_x v + v_1 D_x u.$$

Consequently, dropping subscripts,

(1) $$\boldsymbol{D_x(uv) = uD_x v + vD_x u.}$$

We next differentiate the product of three factors, $y = uvw$.

$$D_x y = D_x[(uv)w] = (uv)D_x w + D_x(uv)w.$$

Hence

(2) $$D_x(uvw) = uv(D_x w) + u(D_x v)w + (D_x u)vw.$$

Again, if we have four factors, $y = uvwr$,

$$D_x y = D_x[(uvw)r] = (uvw)D_x r + D_x(uvw)r,$$

which, by (2), gives us

(3) $D_x(uvwr)$

$$= uvw(D_x r) + uv(D_x w)r + u(D_x v)wr + (D_x u)vwr.$$

Proceeding in this way, we see that to differentiate the product of any number of factors we must form a sum of the same number of terms, each term being obtained from the original product by differentiating *one* factor and leaving all the others unchanged:

(4) $\boldsymbol{D_x(uvw \cdots)}$
$$\boldsymbol{= (D_x u)vw \cdots + u(D_x v)w \cdots + uv(D_x w) \cdots + \cdots.}$$

EXERCISES

Differentiate the following functions by using the Examples and Exercises in § 85:

1. $x^4(2x+3)$.

2. $\dfrac{1}{x^3} = \dfrac{1}{x} \cdot \dfrac{1}{x} \cdot \dfrac{1}{x}$.

3. $\dfrac{x^2(1-x)}{1+x}$.

4. $\dfrac{1-x}{x(1+x)}$.

89. Differentiation of u^n and x^n. If $u = f(x)$, and we wish to differentiate the function u^2, we may write $y = u \cdot u$, and then, using (1), § 88, we find

$$D_x u^2 = u(D_x u) + (D_x u)u = 2\,uD_x u.$$

Similarly, to differentiate u^3 we write $u^3 = u \cdot u \cdot u$ and use (2), § 88:

$$D_x u^3 = u \cdot u(D_x u) + u(D_x u)u + (D_x u)u \cdot u = 3\,u^2 D_x u.$$

In the same way we may regard u^n, if n is any positive integer, as the product of n factors u, and using (4), § 88, we find

(1) $$\boldsymbol{D_x u^n = nu^{n-1} D_x u,}$$

a formula which, it should be noticed, has been established so far only when n is a positive integer. It is obviously true when $n = 1$, and when $n = 0$ it reduces to (2), § 86.

In particular, this formula may be applied to the differentiation of x^n. Here $u = x$, $D_x u = D_x x = 1$. Hence

(2) $$\boldsymbol{D_x x^n = nx^{n-1},}$$

The difference between (2) and (1) is that (2) merely enables us to differentiate a power of the independent variable, while (1) enables us to differentiate a power of any function of x provided we know how to differentiate the function itself.

We can now differentiate any polynomial in x, that is, the sum of a number of terms each of which is a constant, or the product of a constant by a positive integral power of x. Thus

$$\begin{aligned} D_x(2\,x^5 - 3\,x^2 + 4\,x - 1) &\\ &= D_x(2\,x^5) + D_x(-3\,x^2) + D_x(4\,x) + D_x(-1) \\ &= 2\,D_x x^5 - 3\,D_x x^2 + 4\,D_x x \\ &= 10\,x^4 - 6\,x + 4. \end{aligned}$$

If we have the product of two or more polynomials, as

$$(2\,x^2 - x + 3)(x^4 + x^2 - 1),$$

to differentiate, we may either expand before differentiating, or we may differentiate without expanding, by means of the formulæ of § 88.

EXERCISES

Differentiate the following functions:

1. x^7. *Ans.* $7\,x^6$.
2. x^{10}.
3. $x^{12} + x^5 + 2$.
4. $2\,x^3 + x^2 - 3\,x + 5$.
5. $(3\,x^2 - x)^7$.
6. $(2\,x + 1)(x - 3)$.
7. $(x^2 + 3\,x - 1)(x^3 - x^2 + 3\,x + 2)$.
8. $(3\,x - 2)^3(5\,x^2 + x - 1)^2$.

90. Differentiation of Implicit Algebraic Functions. The great majority of functions of x which occur in analytic geometry and elsewhere are not polynomials. For instance, the equation of the circle $x^2 + y^2 = 25$ determines y as a function of x, or more accurately, the upper half of the circle gives y as one function of x ($y = \sqrt{25 - x^2}$), the lower half as another ($y = -\sqrt{25 - x^2}$). In this case it is possible to solve the equation for y and thus express y *explicitly* as a function of x. In more complicated cases this is not possible, as, for instance, when we have the curve

$$x^4 + y^4 + x + y = 0.$$

Nevertheless, since to each value of x there correspond one or more values of y, the various parts of the curve really determine y as functions of x. Such functions, for which we cannot or do not care to determine explicit expressions, are called *implicit* functions. If the equation which determines the function is an algebraic equation (as distinguished, for instance, from a logarithmic or a trigonometric one) the function is called an implicit algebraic function. Every algebraic equation in (x, y) by clearing of fractions and of radicals, can be so expressed that each member is a sum of terms of the forms

$$c, \quad cx^n, \quad cy^n, \quad cx^n y^m,$$

where n and m are positive integers, and c is a constant. We shall, in this section, suppose the equation reduced to this form.

Every implicit algebraic function may be easily differentiated, as will be clear from the following illustrations:

Example 1. $x^2 + y^2 = 25.$

Since, as we have said, this equation determines y as a function of x, y^2 is also a function of x, and consequently the whole first member is a function of x. The second member, 25, may also be regarded as a function of x. Since these two members are equal for all values of x, that is, since they are the *same* function, their derivatives are equal. The derivative of the first member is $2x + 2yD_xy$, while the derivative of the second is 0. Hence,

$$2x + 2yD_xy = 0.$$

Therefore $$D_xy = -\frac{x}{y}.$$

In this case, since we can express y explicitly as a function of x, $y = \pm\sqrt{25 - x^2}$, we can express $D_x y$ in terms of x alone, namely

$$D_x y = \mp \frac{x}{\sqrt{25 - x^2}},$$

the upper sign referring to the upper half of the circle, the lower sign to the lower half. In general, however, the value of $D_x y$ will have to be left in a form involving both x and y. We shall see, when we come to the applications, that this form is usually entirely satisfactory.

Example 2. $x^4 + y^4 + x + y = 0.$

Here, again, since y is a function of x, the two members can be regarded as different expressions for the same function of x. Their derivatives are, therefore, equal:

$$4\,x^3 + 4\,y^3 D_x y + 1 + D_x y = 0.$$

Hence
$$D_x y = \frac{-4\,x^3 - 1}{4\,y^3 + 1}.$$

EXERCISES

Differentiate the functions y determined by the following equations:

1. $xy = 1.$
2. $xy^2 = 1.$
3. $x^2 - y^2 = 1.$
4. $y^2 = x^3.$
5. $2\,x^3 - 3\,xy^2 + xy - 3 = 0.$
6. $y^3 + 2\,x^2 y + 5 = 0.$
7. $x^3 - 3\,axy + y^3 = 0.$
8. $Ax^2 + Bxy + Cy^2 + F = 0.$
9. Express the values of $D_x y$ in Exercises 1–4 in terms of x alone.

91. Fractional Powers and Radicals. Suppose $u = f(x)$, and we wish to differentiate

$$y = u^{\frac{p}{q}},$$

where p and q are positive integers. Raising both sides of this equation to the power q, we have

$$y^q = u^p.$$

Here, as in § 90, the two sides of this equation are merely two different expressions for the same function of x. Hence their derivatives are equal:

$$qy^{q-1}D_xy = pu^{p-1}D_xu.$$

Consequently, $$D_xy = \frac{pu^{p-1}}{qy^{q-1}}D_xu = \frac{pu^{p-1}}{qu^{\frac{p}{q}(q-1)}}D_xu = \frac{p}{q}u^{\frac{p}{q}-1}D_xu.$$

If we let $n = \frac{p}{q}$, we may write this result in the form

(1) $$D_xu^n = nu^{n-1}D_xu.$$

Hence, this formula, which is identical with formula (1), § 89, is valid not merely when n is a positive integer, but also when it is a positive fraction.*

The special case (2), § 89, is, of course, also valid under these more general conditions.

If $n = \frac{1}{2}$, formula (1) may be written

(2) $$D_x\sqrt{u} = \frac{1}{2\sqrt{u}}D_xu.$$

Here, too, we have the special case

(3) $$D_x\sqrt{x} = \frac{1}{2\sqrt{x}}.$$

EXERCISES

Differentiate the following functions:

1. $x^{\frac{2}{3}}$. *Ans.* $\frac{2}{3}x^{-\frac{1}{3}} = \frac{2}{3\sqrt[3]{x}}$.
2. $\sqrt[3]{x}$.
3. $(2x+1)^{\frac{4}{3}}$.
4. $\sqrt{2x^2+3x+5}$.
5. $\sqrt{1+x}+\sqrt{1-x}$.
6. $\sqrt[3]{2x-3}$.

92. Negative Exponents. Let u be a function of x, and consider the function

$$y = u^{-m},$$

* If n is an irrational number, for instance $\sqrt{2}$, formula (1) is still valid. This is what we should expect, since such a number can be approximated to as closely as we please by a fraction p/q. We shall, however, give no proof of formula (1) in this case.

where m is a positive integer or a positive fraction. Multiplying both sides of this equation by u^m, we find

$$yu^m = 1.$$

Differentiate both sides of this equation:

$$myu^{m-1}D_x u + u^m D_x y = 0.$$

Hence $D_x y = -\dfrac{myu^{m-1}}{u^m} D_x u = -myu^{-1}D_x u = -mu^{-m-1}D_x u.$

If, now, we let $n = -m$, this result may be written

(1) $$D_x u^n = nu^{n-1}D_x u.$$

Hence this formula (identical with (1), § 89 and (1), § 91) is valid not merely when n is a positive integer or a positive fraction but also when it is a negative integer or fraction. The same is, of course, also true of the special case $u = x$, formula (2), § 89.

These formulæ are, in fact, true for *all* real values of n. See the footnote to § 91.

EXERCISES

Differentiate the following functions:

1. $(2x + 3)^{-3}$. *Ans.* $-6(2x + 3)^{-4}$.

2. $(x^2 + 1)^{-2}$.

3. $x^{-\frac{2}{3}}$.

4. $\dfrac{1}{\sqrt{x}}$.

5. $\dfrac{1}{(x^3 - 1)^2}$.

6. $(\sqrt{1 - x})^{-3}$.

93. Differentiation of Fractions. Let u and v be two functions of x, and consider the function

$$y = \frac{u}{v}.$$

Since this fraction may be written $u \cdot v^{-1}$, it may be differentiated by formula 1, § 88:

$$\begin{aligned} D_x y &= uD_x(v^{-1}) + v^{-1}D_x u \\ &= -uv^{-2}D_x v + v^{-1}D_x u. \end{aligned}$$

Hence

(1) $$D_x\left(\frac{u}{v}\right)=\frac{vD_xu-uD_xv}{v^2}.$$

EXERCISES

Differentiate the following functions :

1. $\dfrac{1-x}{1+x}$.
2. $\dfrac{x}{1+x^2}$.
3. $\dfrac{x}{2x-3}$.
4. $\dfrac{2x^4}{1-x^2}$.
5. $\dfrac{x^2}{(1+x^3)^2}$.
6. $\dfrac{x}{\sqrt{1-x}}$.

PROBLEMS TO CHAPTER XII

Differentiate the following functions:

1. $5x^2-2bx+3c^2$.
2. $(a+bx)^n$.
3. $(2t-1)^{20}(3t+2)^7$.
4. $\dfrac{2x^2+3x-1}{3}$.
   Ans. $\dfrac{4x+3}{3}$.
5. $\dfrac{at^2+bt+c}{t}$.
   Ans. $a-\dfrac{c}{t^2}$.
6. $\dfrac{ax^2+bx+c}{x^2}$.
7. $\dfrac{(5x+3)^3}{8}$.
8. $(2-z)\sqrt{z}$.
9. $(3+x)\sqrt{3-x}$.
   Ans. $\dfrac{3-3x}{2\sqrt{3-x}}$.
10. $\dfrac{1}{3x+7}$.
11. $\dfrac{s}{\sqrt{a^2-s^2}}$.
12. $\dfrac{ax+b}{cx+d}$.
    Ans. $\dfrac{ad-bc}{(cx+d)^2}$.
13. $\dfrac{z^3}{\sqrt{(1-z^2)^3}}$.
    Ans. $\dfrac{3z^2}{(1-z^2)^{\frac{5}{2}}}$.
14. $\dfrac{2x^2-3}{\sqrt{x}}$.
15. $(x^{\frac{2}{3}}+a^{\frac{2}{3}})^{\frac{3}{2}}$.
16. $x(a^2+x^2)\sqrt{a^2-x^2}$.
    Ans. $\dfrac{a^4+a^2x^2-4x^4}{\sqrt{a^2-x^2}}$.
17. $\sqrt{x+\sqrt{x}}$.
18. $\left(1+\sqrt{\dfrac{1-x}{1+x}}\right)^7$.

Obtain $D_x y$ in each of the following problems, *first* by using the method of implicit functions, and *secondly* by expressing y as an explicit function of x and differentiating y in that form. Show, in each case, that the two answers are equivalent to each other.

19. $2xy - x + 3y + 1 = 0$.

$$\textit{Ans.}\quad D_x y = \frac{1-2y}{2x+3} = \frac{5}{(2x+3)^2}.$$

20. $2x^2 + 3y^2 = 6$. **21.** $y^2 = 4x$. **22.** $x^2y^2 - x^2 + y^2 = 0$.

CHAPTER XIII

SIMPLE APPLICATIONS OF THE DIFFERENTIAL CALCULUS

94. Slopes and Tangents. We have seen that $D_x y$ is the slope of the curve* $y = f(x)$. Thus if the curve is

(1) $$y = x^3$$

(see § 37, Figure 34), its slope is

(2) $$\lambda = D_x y = 3x^2.$$

This slope is, of course, different at different points of the curve, and if we want the slope at some particular point, we must substitute in (2) the special value of x. Thus the slope of (1) at the point (2, 8) is $\lambda = 12$. The slope at (x_1, y_1) is $\lambda = 3x_1^2$. The *equation* of the tangent at (x_1, y_1) is

$$y - y_1 = 3x_1^2(x - x_1),$$

which can, of course, be reduced as in § 38, formula (11).

What has just been said applies also to the case in which y is given not explicitly but only implicitly as a function of x. Thus the general formula for the slope of the circle

(3) $$x^2 + y^2 = a^2$$

is, by § 90, Example 1,

$$\lambda = D_x y = -\frac{x}{y}.$$

Consequently, the slope at (x_1, y_1) is $-x_1/y_1$, and the equation of the tangent at this point is

$$y - y_1 = -\frac{x_1}{y_1}(x - x_1),$$

which can be reduced, as in § 31, to the ordinary form.

* By the slope of the curve at a point we mean the slope of the tangent to the curve at that point.

The value $\lambda = D_x y$ for the slope of the curve also enables us to find the slope, $-1/\lambda$, of the normal.

If we use oblique coördinates, it is clear that $\frac{\Delta y}{\Delta x}$ is the direction ratio of the secant, and, consequently, that $D_x y$ is the direction ratio of the tangent. The methods of the calculus may be used freely in connection with oblique coördinates provided we remember this fact.

EXERCISES

Find by differentiation the slopes of the following curves at the points indicated:

1. $y = x^4$ at $(1, 1)$; at $(-1, 1)$; at $(2, 16)$.
2. $y = x^2 - 2x$ at $(0, 0)$; at $(1, -1)$; at $(2, 0)$.
3. $y = x(x-1)(x-2)(x-3)$ at the origin; at $(2, 0)$.
4. $y^2 = x^2(x-1)$ at $(2, 2)$; at $(2, -2)$.
5. $x^4 + y^4 + x + y = 0$ at the origin; at the points whose abscissas are -1.

Find, by the use of derivatives, the equations of the tangents to the following curves at the points indicated:

6. $y = x^4$ at (x_1, y_1).
7. $y^2 = x^3$ at (x_1, y_1).
8. $y = x^2 - 2x$ at $(0, 0)$; at $(1, -1)$.
9. $\frac{x^2}{a^2} + \frac{y^2}{b^2} = 1$ at (x_1, y_1).
10. $Ax^2 + Bxy + Cy^2 + Dx + Ey + F = 0$ at (x_1, y_1).
11. $y^2 = x^2(x-1)$ at $(2, -2)$.

95. The Highest and Lowest Points of Curves. Let us consider the curve

$$y = x(x+1)(x-2). \tag{1}$$

It crosses the axis of x at the points $x = -1$, $x = 0$, $x = 2$. Between the first two of these points the first and last factors in (1) are negative, the second positive. Hence, from $x = -1$ to the origin the curve lies above the axis of x. Similarly we find that from $x = 0$ to $x = 2$, y is negative; when $x > 2$, y is positive; and when $x < -1$, y is negative. Consequently, the curve is shaped as indicated in Figure 71.

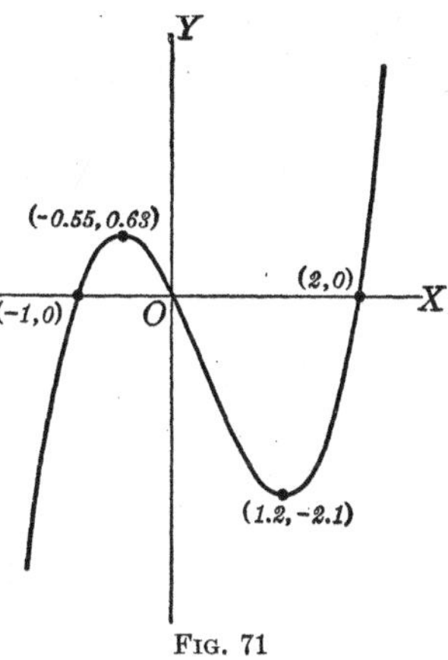

FIG. 71

We now ask ourselves: how high does the curve rise between $x = -1$ and $x = 0$, and how low does it fall between $x = 0$ and $x = 2$? It is clear from the figure that these highest and lowest points are the points where the tangent is horizontal, that is, where $D_x y = 0$. On differentiating, we find

$$D_x y = 3x^2 - 2x - 2.$$

Equating this to zero, we have a quadratic equation, whose roots we find to be

$$x_1 = \frac{1 - \sqrt{7}}{3} = -0.549, \quad x_2 = \frac{1 + \sqrt{7}}{3} = +1.215.$$

These are the x coördinates of the two points we are seeking. Their y coördinates are found, by substituting these values in (1), to be

$$y_1 = +0.63, \quad y_2 = -2.1.$$

These are the maximum and minimum values of the function y.

The method, here used, of finding these maximum and minimum values by equating $D_x y$ to zero is not always applicable, since the curve may reach its highest and lowest points at corners or cusps, as is indicated in Figure 72. These, however, are exceptional points at which the derivative becomes infinite or has no meaning; and the formula for D_xy in any given case will usually, as in the example just given, make it clear that there are no such points.

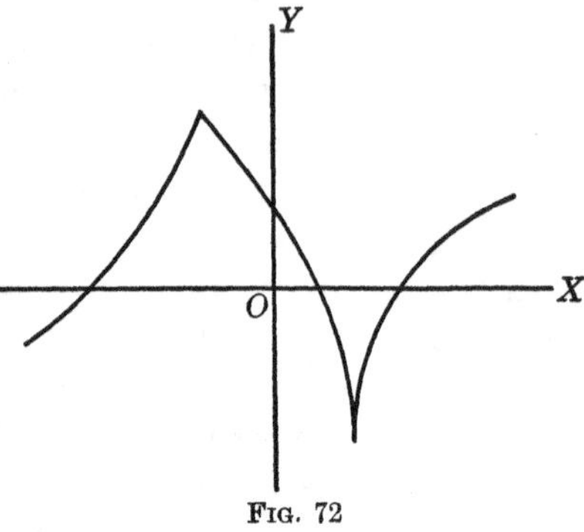

FIG. 72

Another matter to be noticed is that all points at which D_xy is zero are not necessarily maxima or minima, though in the particular example we have just considered, this was the case. For the curve $y = x^3$, for instance, the only point where D_xy is zero is the origin, and this, as we see from Figure 34, § 37, is neither a maximum nor a minimum.

The value $x = -0.55$, in the example above considered, while it gives us what we have called a maximum, does not give us the largest value of the function. For instance, when $x = 3$, the function has a much larger value, 12. In this case, there is no largest value of the function, since y becomes positively infinite when x increases indefinitely. The maxima and minima we have considered in this section are, for this reason, sometimes called *relative* maxima and minima to indicate that they are merely greater (or less) than the values of the function at nearby points.

On the other hand, if we restrict ourselves to negative values of x, we should say that the function has not merely a relative, but an absolute maximum at the point $x = -0.55$. Again, if we consider values of x from $x = -1$ to $x = +3$, we have merely a relative maximum at $x = -0.55$, the absolute maximum being at the point $x = +3$. If, then, for any reason, we restrict ourselves to a limited range of values of x, the absolute maximum of the function is either one of the relative maxima in this interval, or it is situated at one end of the interval, where, of course, $D_x y$ will not usually be zero.

Similar remarks apply to relative and absolute minima.

The method we have used to determine maxima and minima seems, at first sight, rather unsatisfactory since, in the first place, it gives no means of distinguishing between maxima and minima, or even of distinguishing these from certain points which are neither maxima nor minima; and, in the second, the maxima and minima which it gives may be merely relative. Nevertheless, as we shall see in the next section, these objections are, in a great many cases, more apparent than real.

EXERCISES

Sketch roughly the following curves, and locate accurately their highest and lowest points (relative maxima and minima). If any of these points give absolute maxima or minima, state the fact.

1. $16y = 32x - x^4.$
2. $4y = x^3 - 12x.$
3. $9y = x^4 - 4x^3.$
4. $y = \dfrac{x}{1+x^2}.$
5. $y = \dfrac{1}{2x(1-x)}.$
6. $y^2 = \dfrac{1}{x(1-x)}.$

Mark all the points where the slopes of the following curves are 0 or ∞, and use the information thus gained in making the drawing of the curve more accurate:

7. $y^2 = x^4 - x^6.$
8. $y^2 = x^3 - x^4.$
9. $y^4 = x^3 - x^4.$

96. Problems in Maxima and Minima. We illustrate the methods to be used by two typical examples.

Example 1. A piece of cardboard six inches square is to be made into an open box by cutting out equal squares at the four corners and bending up the sides. It is desired that this box have as large a capacity as possible. What should its dimensions be?

Let x inches be the length of a side of each of the small squares cut out at the corners. The length of a side of the bottom of the box is, then, $6 - 2x$, and the height of the box is x. Its contents, measured in cubic inches, is therefore, $u = x(6 - 2x)^2$. It is this function we wish to make as large as possible.

$$u = 4x^3 - 24x^2 + 36x.$$
$$D_x u = 12x^2 - 48x + 36.$$

Equating this to zero, in order to determine relative maxima or minima, gives $x = 3$ or 1. The first of these values is surely not what we want, since then the whole cardboard would be cut away and we should get no box at all.

The true answer to our problem is $x = 1$. In order to see this, let us consider the problem on its merits, apart from any mathematics. If the corners cut out are very small, the contents of the box will also be very small since, though its bottom is almost 6 in. square, its height is very small. If, on the other hand, the corners are very large (nearly 3 in. square) the height of the box will be fairly large (nearly 3 in.), but the bottom will be very small, so that, again, the capacity of the box is very small. Somewhere between these two very unfavorable extremes there must be a most favorable size for the corners, that is, the maximum must be reached for some value of x between 0 and 3. Such a value is a relative maximum, and since the only possible relative maximum is, as we have seen, $x = 1$, it follows that this is the answer to our problem.

The dimensions of the box in inches are, therefore, 4, 4, 1; its contents, 16 cubic inches.

Example 2. Find the rectangle of largest area which can be inscribed in a given circle.

Let a be the radius of the circle and $2x$ and $2y$ the dimensions of an inscribed rectangle. Then

$$x^2 + y^2 = a^2, \tag{1}$$

so that we might express y in terms of x and thus dispense with the letter y altogether. It is, however, here and in many similar cases, more convenient to retain y as an *auxiliary variable.*

The area of the rectangle is

$$u = 4xy,$$

and this to be made a maximum. Differentiation gives

$$D_x u = 4xD_x y + 4y.$$

To find $D_x y$, we differentiate (1):

$$2x + 2yD_x y = 0,$$

or

$$D_x y = -\frac{x}{y}.$$

Hence

$$D_x u = -4\frac{x^2}{y} + 4y.$$

Equating this to zero in order to get relative maxima or minima, we find $x^2 = y^2$, and consequently, since x and y are both essentially positive, $x = y$. Hence we infer that the rectangle of largest area is the inscribed square.

That this is the true answer is seen as in Example 1; if either dimension, $2x$ or $2y$, is very small, the area of the rectangle is very small. Hence there must be a largest rectangle, and the only possible maximum is when $x = y$.

EXERCISES

1. Divide the number 10 into two parts in such a way that the product of the first by the square of the second is as large as possible.

2. Find the largest rectangle whose perimeter is c.

3. Prove that of all circular sectors of given perimeter the greatest is that in which the arc is double the radius.

4. What is the most economical shape for a cylindrical tin cup which is to hold half a pint?

Ans. Height = radius.

5. What is the most economical shape for a cylindrical tin tomato can? *Ans.* Height = diameter.

6. A Norman window consists of a rectangle surmounted by a semicircle. If the perimeter is given, find the shape in order that the amount of light admitted shall be as great as possible. *Ans.* Height = breadth.

7. A man can walk five miles an hour and row four miles an hour. He is in a rowboat three miles off shore and wishes to reach as quickly as possible a point on the beach five miles from the point nearest to him. Towards what point of the beach should he row?

97. Increasing and Decreasing Functions. Concavity. A very useful principle is the following, whose truth is at once evident when we consider the graph of the function and remember that the derivative is equal to the slope of this graph:

If the derivative of a function is positive, the function increases as the independent variable increases; if the derivative is negative, the function decreases.

The slope, λ, of a curve may itself be regarded as a function of x. Hence, by the principle just stated, if $D_x\lambda > 0$, λ increases with x, so that the curve rises more and more steeply (or falls off less and less steeply) as x increases. In other words, the curve is concave upward. Similarly, if $D_x\lambda$ is negative, the curve is concave downward. The derivative of the slope may be written

$$D_x\lambda = D_x(D_x y),$$

and is called the *second derivative* of y and denoted, for brevity, by D_x^2y. Thus we have the

TEST FOR CONCAVITY. If $D_x^2y > 0$, the curve $y = f(x)$ is concave upward. If $D_x^2y < 0$, it is concave downward.

It should be clearly understood that the question as to whether a curve is rising or falling (sign of D_xy) has nothing whatever to do with whether it is concave upward or downward (sign of D_x^2y).

Example. Consider the curve $y = x^3$ (see Figure 34, § 37). Here $D_xy = 3x^2$, which is positive for all values of x (except $x = 0$). Hence this curve is constantly rising. The second derivative is $D_x^2y = 6x$, which has the same sign as x. Hence this curve is concave upward to the right of the axis of y, concave downward to the left.

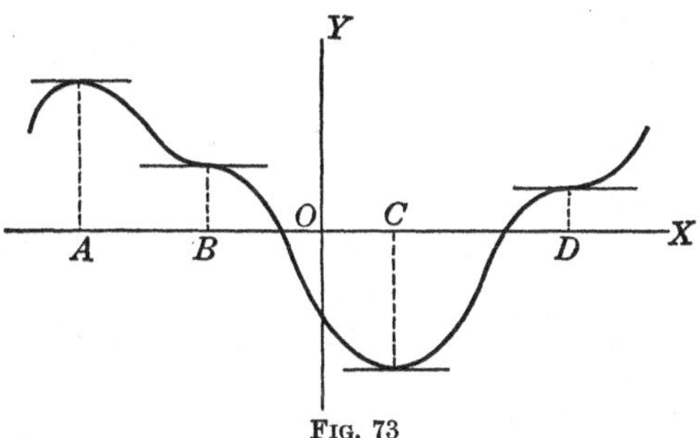

FIG. 73

Since at a maximum (see A, Figure 73) a curve is concave downward, at a minimum (C), concave upward, while at a point where $D_xy = 0$ but which is neither a maximum nor a minimum (see B and D, Figure 73) the curve is concave upward on one side, concave downward on the other, we deduce the following:

TEST FOR DISTINGUISHING MAXIMA FROM MINIMA. At a point where $D_xy = 0$, if $D_x^2y < 0$, we have a maximum; if $D_x^2y > 0$, a minimum.

If $D_x^2y = 0$, this test gives us no information. See, however, the closing lines of § 98.

EXERCISES

Where do the following curves rise and where do they fall; where are they concave upward and where concave downward?

1. $y = x(x+1)(x-2)$. See § 95, Figure 71.

2. $y = \dfrac{x^3}{(x^2-1)^2}$. See § 12, Figure 18.

3. $y = x^{\frac{2}{3}}$. 4. $y = \dfrac{x}{1+x^2}$. 5. $y = \dfrac{1}{1-x^2}$.

98. Points of Inflection. A point of a curve on one side of which the curve is concave upward, on the other concave downward, is called a point of inflection.* It is clear from this definition that the tangent at a point of inflection always crosses the curve at the point of contact; see Figure 34, § 37, where the origin is a point of inflection and the axis of x the tangent there.

Since $D_x^2 y$ is positive on one side of a point of inflection, negative on the other, it follows that at a point of inflection we usually † have $D_x^2 y = 0$. It is not true that every root of this equation is a point of inflection, but we evidently have the following:

FIRST TEST FOR A POINT OF INFLECTION. A point where $D_x^2 y = 0$ is a point of inflection if $D_x^2 y$ is positive on one side of it and negative on the other. If $D_x^2 y$ has the same sign on both sides, it is not a point of inflection.

Example

$$y = 3x^5 - 5x^4 + 2x - 1.$$
$$D_x y = 15x^4 - 20x^3 + 2.$$
$$D_x^2 y = 60x^3 - 60x^2 = 60x^2(x-1).$$

* We assume in this definition, and throughout this section, that the curve has no corner at the point. The maximum in Figure 72, § 95, is not a point of inflection.

† Namely when $D_x^2 y$ varies continuously, as will usually be the case. $D_x^2 y$ may, however, become infinite at a point of inflection, even in very simple cases such as the curve $x = y^3$.

Equating this to zero, we find as the only possible points of inflection, $x = 0$, $x = 1$. For small positive as also for small negative values of x we see that D_x^2y is negative. Consequently, $x = 0$ is not a point of inflection. On the other hand, as x passes from a value a little less than 1 to a value a little greater, D_x^2y changes sign; and 1 is the x coördinate of a point of inflection. The point itself is $(1, -1)$. The slope of the curve at this point of inflection is $\lambda = -3$.

Another test for a point of inflection consists in examining the third derivative of y:

$$D_x(D_x^2y) = D_x^3y.$$

If this derivative is positive at a point, x_1, where $D_x^2y = 0$, we infer, by the principle stated at the beginning of § 97, that D_x^2y is increasing, and consequently, as we pass through x_1, D_x^2y changes sign. Similarly, if D_x^3y is negative at x_1, D_x^2y is decreasing and therefore, since it vanishes at x_1, changes sign there. Thus, whenever $D_x^3y \neq 0$ at x_1, D_x^2y changes sign there. Hence

Second Test for a Point of Inflection. A point where $D_x^2y = 0$ is a point of inflection provided $D_x^3y \neq 0$.

In particular, if, in searching for maxima and minima, we find a point where $D_xy = 0$ and also $D_x^2y = 0$, so that the test at the close of § 97 gives us no information, we may go on and compute D_x^3y, and if this value is different from zero, we have a point of inflection, and hence neither a maximum nor a minimum.

EXERCISES

Find all the points of inflection of the following curves, and the slopes of the curves at these points:

1. $y = x^3 - x$.
2. $y = 2x^6 - 5x^4 + 3x + 1$.
3. $y = x^5$.
4. $y = (x^2 - 1)^3$.
5. $y = (x^2 - 1)^4$.

99. Curve Tracing. It is always well to get such a general idea of a curve as is possible before beginning the work of plotting individual points. For this purpose we should consider first how many real values of y correspond to each value of x, and, in particular, whether there are some values of x to which no real values of y correspond. Then we should locate any values of x for which y becomes infinite (vertical asymptotes) and we should also consider how the curve runs when x has very large positive or negative values. We illustrate this last point by two examples.

Example 1. $y = \dfrac{x+1}{x-1}.$

Here, to each value of x corresponds one real value of y, except when $x = 1$, when we have a vertical asymptote. When x becomes infinite, both numerator and denominator become infinite, and we cannot see directly how the value of the fraction is changing. However, if we divide numerator and denominator by x, we get

$$y = \frac{1 + \frac{1}{x}}{1 - \frac{1}{x}},$$

and the limit as x becomes infinite, either through positive or negative values, is now obviously $+1$. Hence the curve has the line $y = +1$ as an asymptote.

Example 2. $y = \dfrac{x^2+1}{x-1}.$

Here we divide numerator and denominator by x. Then we see that as x becomes positively infinite y becomes positively infinite, and when x becomes negatively infinite y becomes negatively infinite.

After this general investigation of a curve, we begin plotting points. Instead of taking these points at random, as we did in § 12, it is desirable to plot, first, points which are really characteristic of the shape or position of the curve, such as

(1) Points where the curve meets the coördinate axes;
(2) Maximum and minimum points;
(3) Points where the tangent is vertical;
(4) Points of inflection.

It should be noted where the curve is concave upward and where concave downward; and the tangent at each point of inflection should be drawn *before* the curve is drawn. The arc of the curve should then be drawn so as really to touch and cross the tangent at the point of inflection and to be concave on the two sides of it in the right directions.

Example 3. $y = 2x^3 - x^4$.

To each value of x corresponds just one value of y, and this is always real. When x becomes positively infinite, y becomes negatively infinite since the negative term $-x^4$ is then very much larger than the positive term $2x^3$. When x becomes negatively infinite, y also becomes negatively infinite. There are, therefore, neither vertical nor horizontal asymptotes.

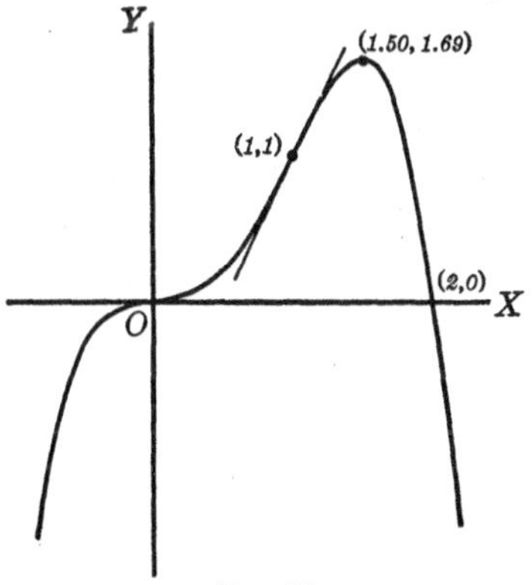

The curve meets the axis of x in the points (0, 0) and (2, 0).

On differentiating we find

$$D_x y = 6x^2 - 4x^3 = 2x^2(3 - 2x).$$
$$D_x^2 y = 12x - 12x^2 = 12x(1 - x).$$
$$D_x^3 y = 12 - 24x.$$

We infer that the curve has a maximum at the point $(\frac{3}{2}, \frac{27}{16})$, no minimum, and two points of inflection, namely, the origin and the point (1, 1). At the origin the axis of x is the tangent, at (1, 1) the slope of the tangent is $\lambda = 2$.

Y
(1.50, 1.69)
(1,1)
(2,0)
X
O

Fig. 74

Between these points of inflection the curve is concave upward, everywhere else concave downward.

We can now draw in the curve as indicated in Figure 74.

EXERCISES

Trace the following curves, plotting only characteristic points, and being careful to make the curves have the right directions at each point of inflection:

1. $y = x^3 + 6x^2 + 9x$.
2. $4y = x^4 - 4x^2 - 5$.
3. $x^3 + y^3 = 1$.
4. $3y = x^{\frac{2}{3}}(x - 5)$.
5. $4y = \dfrac{1}{x} + \dfrac{1}{x-1}$.
6. $y^2 = x^3 + x^2$.

100. Parametric Representation of Curves. If the coördinates of a moving point are expressed in terms of an auxiliary variable, or *parameter*, t,

$$x = f(t), \quad y = \phi(t), \tag{1}$$

then, as t varies, the point (x, y) describes a certain locus whose equation might be obtained by eliminating t between these equations. It is, however, in many cases, better not to perform this elimination, but to take the equations (1) as they stand to represent the curve. We have, then, what is called a *parametric representation* as distinguished from the representation by a single equation. It is easy, in any special case, to plot the curve directly from equations (1) by giving to t in succession different numerical values and computing the corresponding values of x and y.

In order to find the slope of the curve, $D_x y$, we start from a value t_1 and give to t the increment Δt. The increments this produces in x and y we call Δx and Δy; and we write the identity

$$\frac{\Delta y}{\Delta x} = \frac{\dfrac{\Delta y}{\Delta t}}{\dfrac{\Delta x}{\Delta t}}. \tag{2}$$

Now let Δt approach zero. Δx and Δy will also approach zero, and the limiting form approached by (2) is

(3) $$D_x y = \frac{D_t y}{D_t x}.$$

Example.

(4) $$x = t(t+1), \quad y = t(t+2).$$

$$D_t x = 2t+1, \quad D_t y = 2t+2, \quad \lambda = D_x y = \frac{2t+2}{2t+1}.$$

Now give to t the values indicated below, and compute the corresponding values of x, y, λ:

$t = -\frac{5}{2}$,	$x = \frac{15}{4}$,	$y = \frac{5}{4}$,	$\lambda = \frac{3}{4}$,
$t = -2$,	$x = 2$,	$y = 0$,	$\lambda = \frac{2}{3}$,
$t = -\frac{3}{2}$,	$x = \frac{3}{4}$,	$y = -\frac{3}{4}$,	$\lambda = \frac{1}{2}$,
$t = -1$,	$x = 0$,	$y = -1$,	$\lambda = 0$,
$t = -\frac{3}{4}$,	$x = -\frac{3}{16}$,	$y = -\frac{15}{16}$,	$\lambda = -1$,
$t = -\frac{1}{2}$,	$x = -\frac{1}{4}$,	$y = -\frac{3}{4}$,	$\lambda = \infty$,
$t = 0$,	$x = 0$,	$y = 0$,	$\lambda = 2$,
$t = \frac{1}{2}$,	$x = \frac{3}{4}$,	$y = \frac{5}{4}$,	$\lambda = \frac{3}{2}$.

We plot these points, and draw through each a line having the computed slope, λ; see Figure 75. The curve can then readily be drawn.

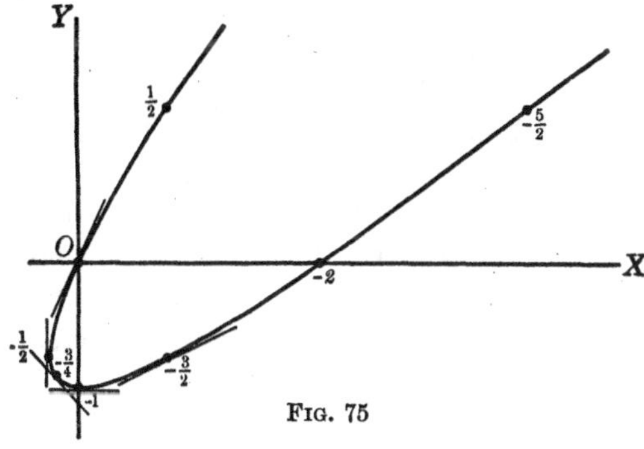

FIG. 75

The curve is a parabola, whose equation we find, by eliminating t between equations (4), to be

$$x^2 - 2xy + y^2 - 2x + y = 0.$$

If we wish to go a step further and find the value of $D_x{}^2y = D_x\lambda$, we may write

$$\frac{\Delta\lambda}{\Delta x} = \frac{\frac{\Delta\lambda}{\Delta t}}{\frac{\Delta x}{\Delta t}},$$

from which, by taking the limit, we find,

$$(5) \qquad D_x\lambda = \frac{D_t\lambda}{D_t x}.$$

EXERCISES

Plot each of the following curves from its parametric representation, drawing the tangent at each point which is plotted; and find the equation of each curve:

1. $x=(t-1)^2,\ y=t(t-1)^2.$
2. $x=\dfrac{1}{t(t-1)},\ y=\dfrac{1}{t-1}.$
3. $x=\dfrac{t}{1+t^3},\ y=\dfrac{t^2}{1+t^3}.$
4. $x=t^3-t,\ y=t^4-t^2.$

101. Velocities. If we note how far a moving body goes during a certain interval of time, the ratio of this distance to the time elapsed is what is known as the average velocity of the body during this interval of time:

$$(1) \qquad \text{Average velocity} = \frac{\text{Distance}}{\text{Time}}.$$

For instance, if a steamer makes a trip of 3000 miles across the ocean in 6 days, its average velocity for the whole trip is 500 miles a day. If during a single hour of one of the days it goes 20 miles, its average velocity during that hour is $\frac{20}{\frac{1}{24}} = 480$ miles a day.

In general, this average velocity will be greater for some intervals of time than for others. The actual velocity at any moment of time is obtained by first finding the average velocity for a short interval of time just following this moment, and then taking the limit of this average velocity as the interval of time becomes shorter and shorter.

This may be expressed in symbols as follows: Let s be the distance the body has moved from some initial position in the time t. Then

$$s = f(t).$$

Let t_1 be the time at which we wish to find the velocity, and let Δt be the length of a short interval of time following the moment t_1. Then, Δs being the distance gone during the time Δt, the average velocity is $\frac{\Delta s}{\Delta t}$. Hence the velocity at the moment t_1 is

$$v = \lim_{\Delta t \doteq 0}\left(\frac{\Delta s}{\Delta t}\right) = D_t s. \tag{2}$$

We illustrate all this by the case of a body falling from rest, in which case, if we measure distance in feet and time in seconds, we have approximately

$$s = 16\,t^2.$$

At the end of 2 seconds, $s = 64$. At the end of 2.1 seconds, $s = 16(2.1)^2 = 70.56$. Hence, if we let $t_1 = 2$, $\Delta t = 0.1$, we have $\Delta s = 6.56$. Hence the average velocity during this tenth of a second is $\frac{6.56}{0.1} = 65.6$ feet per second. We get a better approximation to the actual velocity by taking a smaller value of Δt, say $\Delta t = 0.01$. We readily compute $\Delta s = 0.642$. Hence, for this shorter interval, the average velocity is $\frac{0.642}{0.01} = 64.2$ feet per second. The actual velocity is obtained by differentiation:

$$D_t s = 32\,t.$$

Letting $t = 2$, we find as the velocity at the end of 2 seconds $v = 64$, to which it will be seen that the average velocities computed above are approximations.

It must be understood that the average velocity during a certain interval of time is not, in general, the average of the velocities at the two ends of the interval,* but must be computed by formula (1). The actual velocity (or simply the velocity) must be computed by (2).

EXERCISES

1. Assuming it to be known that a stone thrown downward with a certain velocity goes a distance of

$$s = 16\,t^2 + 40\,t$$

feet in t seconds measured from the moment it is thrown, find

(*a*) its average velocity during the first five seconds;
(*b*) its average velocity during the second five seconds;
(*c*) its average velocity during the tenth of a second following the end of the third second;
(*d*) its velocity at the end of t seconds;
(*e*) its velocity at the end of 3 seconds;
(*f*) its velocity at the moment it is thrown.

2. A man 6 ft. high walks directly away from a lamppost 10 feet high with a uniform velocity of 4 miles an hour. How fast does the end of his shadow move along the pavement?

102. Rates of Change. By the average rate at which a function $u = f(x)$ increases as x varies from x_1 to $x_1 + \Delta x$ is meant the total increase of the function divided by the increase of the variable:

$$\frac{f(x_1 + \Delta x) - f(x_1)}{\Delta x} = \frac{\Delta u}{\Delta x}.$$

By the actual rate of increase when $x = x_1$ is meant the limit, $D_x u$, of this fraction as Δx approaches zero.

* The steamer mentioned at the beginning of this section starts from its dock with velocity zero, and ends up on the other side with the velocity zero. Nevertheless, its average velocity for the trip is not zero.

The derivative of any function may, therefore, be regarded as giving the rate at which the function is increasing per unit increase of the independent variable. If the function is decreasing, this will, of course, be shown by the derivative being negative.

It is merely a special case of this when we say, as in § 101, that if s is the distance a moving body has gone and t the time, $D_t s$ is the velocity, that is, the rate of increase of s per unit time.

Let v be the velocity of a moving body, t the time, and s the distance traversed. Then $D_t v = D_t^2 s$ is the rate at which the velocity is increasing, that is, it is the acceleration of the moving body.

Example 1. In the case of a body falling from rest

$$s = 16\,t^2.$$
$$\text{Velocity} = D_t\,s = 32\,t.$$
$$\text{Acceleration} = D_t^2 s = 32.$$

Thus we see that while the velocity of a falling body increases with the time, its acceleration is constant.

It must not be supposed that rates necessarily refer to the time as independent variable. If, for instance, x denotes the distance measured in feet down from the surface of the earth into a mine, and $u = f(x)$ is the temperature measured in degrees at any point of the mine, then $D_x u$ is the rate in degrees per foot that the temperature increases as we go down the mine.

Again, the slope, $D_x y$, of a curve gives the rate at which the curve is rising per unit of advance along the axis of x; and $D_x^2 y = D_x \lambda$ gives the rate at which the slope is increasing.

Example 2. Two ships start together. One sails due east at the rate of 12 miles an hour and the other due south at the rate of 8 miles an hour. How fast are they separating at the end of two hours?

At the end of t hours the first ship has sailed $12t$, the second $8t$ miles. Their distance apart is, therefore,

$$s = \sqrt{(12t)^2 + (8t)^2} = 4\sqrt{13}\,t.$$

The rate at which they are separating is, therefore, in miles per hour,

$$D_t s = 4\sqrt{13} = 14.4.$$

It happens that this does not contain t, so that this is the rate at which the ships are separating at any time, and, therefore, in particular, at the end of two hours. If the value of $D_t s$ had contained t, we should have substituted $t = 2$ in it to get our answer.

It should be noticed that the special value $t = 2$ is not to be used until we are at the very end of our problem. We must always *first* work out the rate at the time t, even if we are not asked for this.

EXERCISES

1. Two ships start abreast half a mile apart and sail due east at the rates of 10 and 12 miles an hour, respectively. How far apart are they at the end of half an hour, and how fast are they separating at that time?

2. A locomotive running 30 miles an hour over a high bridge dislodges a stone lying near the track. The stone begins to fall just as the locomotive passes the point where it lay. How fast are the stone and the locomotive separating 2 seconds later?

PROBLEMS TO CHAPTER XIII

1. The curves $y^2 = x$ and $y = x^3$ intersect in two points. Find the angles they make with each other at each of these points. *Ans.* 90° and 45°.

2. Find the angle, in degrees and fractions of a degree, which the curve

$$3y = x(x-1)^2(x-3)$$

makes with the axis of x at each point where it meets the axis.

3. Find all the points where the curves

$$y = x^3 - x, \quad 6y = x^3$$

intersect; and find the angles in degrees and fractions of a degree which the curves make with one another at each of these points.

4. A point moves along the curve

$$\sqrt{x} + \sqrt{y} = \sqrt{a}.$$

Prove that the sum of the intercepts of the tangent at this point is constant.

5. A point moves along the curve

$$x^{\frac{2}{3}} + y^{\frac{2}{3}} = a^{\frac{2}{3}}.$$

Prove that the part of the tangent at this point intercepted between the coördinate axes is of constant length.

Trace the following curves:

6. $y = 2x^5 + x^4 + 2x^3.$

7. $4y = x^6 - 6x^4 + 12x^2 - 8.$

8. $x^3 - 2xy - 4y = 0.$

9. $45y + 3x^5 - 55x^3 + 270x = 0.$

10. $12y = 2x^6 - 9x^4 + 18x^2.$

11. $10y^2 = 3x - x^3.$

12. $y^2 = x^3(x + 1)^2.$ Note that the point $(-1, 0)$ lies on this curve.

13. $y^2 = (x^2 + 1)^2(4 - x^2)^3.$

14. Prove that the equation

$$3x^5 - 10x^3 + 15x - 2 = 0$$

has only one real root, and that this root is positive and less than 1.

[SUGGESTION. Consider the shape of the curve

$$y = 3x^5 - 10x^3 + 15x - 2.]$$

15. Prove that the equation

$$3x^4 - 4x^3 + 12x - 3 = 0$$

has just one positive and just one negative root.

16. Prove that the equation

$$x^4 + 4x^3 + 4x^2 + c = 0$$

has no real root if $c > 0$, two real roots if $c < -1$, and four real roots if c has a value between zero and -1.

17. What can you say about the number, sign, and size of the roots of the equation

$$900x^4 - 300x^3 + 1 = 0?$$

Trace the curves which are represented in parametric form as follows:

18. $x = t^2 - 1,\quad y = 2t^3(t^2 - 1).$

19. $x = 16t^2(t - 1),\quad y = 8t^3(t - 1).$

20. $x = 1 - t^2,\quad y = (1 - t)^4(1 + t)^3.$

Maxima and Minima

21. The radius of the base of a cone of revolution is a, its altitude b. Find the volume of the greatest cylinder which can be inscribed in this cone. *Ans.* $\frac{4}{27}\pi a^2 b$.

22. Find the altitude of the cylinder of greatest curved surface which can be inscribed in the cone of Problem 21.

23. Find the altitude of the cylinder of greatest *total* surface which can be inscribed in the cone of Problem 21.

Explain your result when $2a > b$.

24. Find the altitude of the greatest cone of revolution that can be inscribed in a sphere of radius c. *Ans.* $\frac{4}{3}c$.

25. What are the most economical proportions for an open cylindrical water tank if the cost of the sides per square foot is two thirds the cost of the bottom per square foot?

26. What are the most economical proportions for a cylindrical tin tomato can if the round ends are cut out of a sheet of tin in such a way that a regular hexagon circumscribing the required circle is used up for each?

27. If the strength of a rectangular beam is proportional to the product of its breadth by the square of its depth, find the dimensions, in inches, of the strongest beam that can be cut from a log one foot in diameter.

28. From a given circular piece of paper it is desired to remove a sector in such a way that when the rest of the paper is bent into the form of a cone, the volume of this cone shall be as large as possible. Find (*a*) the altitude of this cone; and (*b*) the angle (in degrees) of the sector which should be removed.

29. A physical measurement is made a number of times, with results which differ slightly. It is customary to take the *average* of these results as the most probable value for the quantity measured. Show that of all possible values, this one makes the sum of the squares of the errors of observation smaller than any other.

30. One end of a crow-bar is pushed in horizontally $1\frac{1}{2}$ feet under the lowest part of a rock weighing 100 pounds and finds there a firm support. A man pulls up at the other end, and thus raises the rock. What is the most advantageous length for the crow-bar if it is made of material weighing 2 pounds to the foot? How much force will the man have to exert if he is fortunate enough to have a crow-bar of just the best length?

31. What is the shortest distance from the point (1, 0) to the curve $y^2 = x^3$?

32. A point is at distances a and b from two mutually perpendicular lines. Show how to draw the shortest line through the point terminated by the given lines; and prove that the length of this shortest line is $(a^{\frac{2}{3}} + b^{\frac{2}{3}})^{\frac{3}{2}}$.

33. An ellipse has semi-axes a and b. Determine the shortest line which can be drawn tangent to the ellipse and terminated by the transverse and conjugate axes. Show that this line is of length $a + b$, and find the lengths of the segments into which it is divided by the point of contact.

34. The cost per hour of running a certain steamboat is proportional to the cube of its velocity in still water. At what speed should it be run to make a trip up stream against a four-mile current most economically?

Ans. Six miles an hour.

35. Assuming that the amount of coal burned in running a steamboat is proportional to the cube of the velocity, and that 15 dollars' worth of coal is burned each hour if the boat is run at the rate of 10 miles an hour, find the most economical rate at which to run the boat in still water if all expenses of running the boat besides coal amount to 300 dollars a day.

36. What is the most economical rate at which to run the steamboat of Problem 35 against a four-mile current?

Rates and Velocities

37. Two straight railway tracks intersect at right angles at a point A. A train on one of these tracks passes A at 12 o'clock running 30 miles an hour. A train on the other track passes A at five minutes past twelve, running 40 miles an hour. How fast are the trains separating at ten minutes past twelve?

38. Are the trains of Problem 37 approaching one another or separating at three minutes past twelve, and at what rate?

39. A ladder 25 feet long rests against a house. A man takes hold of the bottom of the ladder and walks off with it at the uniform rate of 2 feet per second. What is the velocity of the top of the ladder when the man is 4 feet from the house? The acceleration?

40. A man fishing in 20 feet of water feels a bite, and at the same moment notices that his cable has come loose and that he is drifting to leeward at the rate of $1\frac{1}{2}$ miles an hour. He drops the fish-line to secure the cable, and the fish begins swimming along the bottom at the rate of 6 miles an hour in a direction at right angles to the wind. How fast is the fish-line going overboard three seconds later?

41. A lamp-post stands on the edge of the sidewalk 10 feet from the end, C, of a street crossing, and 60 feet from the houses across the street. A man walks towards C on the crossing at the rate of 4 miles an hour. How fast is his shadow moving on the houses opposite when he is 40 ft., 20 ft., 5 ft. from C?

42. A June-bug is two feet from a light and his shadow, thrown on the wall of the room, covers two square inches. He is flying directly towards the light in a horizontal direction at right angles to the wall at the rate of 4 feet per second. The light is 6 feet from the wall. How fast is his shadow increasing at this moment?

Ans. 8 sq. in. per second.

www.ingramcontent.com/pod-product-compliance
Lightning Source LLC
LaVergne TN
LVHW010554110826
845149LV00003B/658

* 9 7 8 1 4 1 8 1 8 1 5 1 2 *